Praise for

By Permission of He...

"Relying on eyewitness testimony (most notably that of the uncannily observant diarist, Samuel Pepys) and official reports, Tinniswood succeeds in evoking the smoky horror of the fire and chaos. A fascinating narrative of Restoration London's great tragedy, loaded with dramatic anecdotes and captivating characters."

—*Minneapolis Star-Tribune*

"A heroic amount of research . . . interesting and informative."

—*The Washington Post Book World*

"There is no shortage of vivid detail. [Tinniswood] succeeds in elucidating the broader impact of the disaster: its consequences for English Catholics (widely blamed as the Fire's instigators); for the much harassed government of Charles II; and, in the longer term, for the present-day appearance and layout of the capital. As Tinniswood argues effectively, the widespread perception that Catholics were responsible for the destruction of London fueled the frenzied anti-Popery of the following decade. It is in discussing the Fire's consequences for London's urban planning that Tinniswood (whose background is in architectural history) comes into his own. The Fire created a tabula rasa for urban design that provided an unparalleled opportunity for architects and town planners, and the book offers a fascinating survey of the various Londons that might have been."

—*Sunday Telegraph* (London)

"Deeply satisfying . . . his is a diverting history, and our lives as Londoners are still marked by the event. We have post-1666 architecture, and the magnificent dome of St Paul's dominates the riverside, but does this flame-shaped city of ours mould our lives with aspirations and anxieties of which we are unaware? Its fireproof walls, broader vistas, and standardized buildings are, after all, the landscape of our urban psychologies. After 9/11, what might we learn from the psychic vibrations of London's distant disaster? Tinniswood draws no parallels, but perhaps he ought to. Blink and the fear of terrorism in London 1666 is America's today."

—*The Observer* (London)

continued . . .

"[Tinniswood's] strength lies in the rendering of the epic: of the Sisyphean task of fighting a bonfire the size of a city with a chain of buckets and hand pumps; of the courageous attempts of Charles II to mount a strategy for containment; and of the pogroms that followed when rumor, rushing like a backdraft, convinced locals it was a foreign arson attack. Reproducing selected street plans and architectural designs by Robert Hooker, John Evelyn, and Christopher Wren among others, Tinniswood accounts for how the city was largely fully functioning and inhabitable within ten years. *By Permission of Heaven* is a fine history, and few narratives could so vividly illuminate the enchanting mysteries and higgledy-piggledy inconsistencies of a city that perhaps had to become a 'Suburb of Hell' if there was ever to be a 'Wrenaissance.'"
—*The Spectator*

"A robust account . . . of the fire that reduced much of Wren's London to ashes in 1666. Tinniswood . . . sweeps from the political stage to the mob in the streets, analyzes social contracts and building styles, airs conspiracy theories, and examines local xenophobia. The author does particularly well in unraveling the many suspicions that flew in the fire's wake: It was Dutch revenge for the English bonfire at West-Terschelling, people speculated, or a popish plot, or the work of the Almighty pointing a finger at King Charles the Dissolute. Tinniswood is also adroit in drawing a sensible picture of the reconstruction of London, delineating its many players and their shifting intents within the broad context of the Rebuilding Act, the Fire Court, and the nasty eruptions of religious intolerance that kept cropping up like spot fires after the blaze. Covers the Great Fire like a blanket."
—*Kirkus Reviews*

"In this history of the 1666 fire that destroyed almost the entire city of London, Tinniswood focuses on the political, legal, and cultural significance of the catastrophe. He describes the blaze through the written accounts of both London's commoners and upper crust during the three-day blaze. Tinniswood's greatest achievement is his ability to re-create the wave of paranoia that engulfed London before, during, and after the tragedy. An architectural scholar, Tinniswood saves his best for last, outlining the myriad factors that went into creating the landscapes of modern-day London, including bureaucratic decision-making and the emergence of architect Christopher Wren, about whom Tinniswood wrote in *His Invention So Fertile*."
—*Publishers Weekly*

BY PERMISSION OF HEAVEN

The True Story of the Great Fire of London

Adrian Tinniswood

RIVERHEAD BOOKS

New York

THE BERKLEY PUBLISHING GROUP
Published by the Penguin Group
Penguin Group (USA) Inc.
375 Hudson Street, New York, New York 10014, USA
Penguin Group (Canada), 10 Alcorn Avenue, Toronto, Ontario, Canada M4V 3B2 (a division of
Pearson Penguin Canada Inc.)
Penguin Books Ltd., 80 Strand, London WC2R 0RL, England
Penguin Group Ireland, 25 St. Stephen's Green, Dublin 2, Ireland (a division of Penguin Books, Ltd.)
Penguin Group (Australia), 250 Camberwell Road, Camberwell, Victoria 3124, Australia (a division
of Pearson Australia Group Pty., Ltd.)
Penguin Books India Pvt. Ltd., 11 Community Centre, Panchsheel Park, New Delhi—110 017, India
Penguin Group (NZ), Cnr. Airborne and Rosedale Roads, Albany, Aukland, New Zealand (a
division of Pearson New Zealand, Ltd.)
Penguin Books (South Africa) (Pty.) Ltd., 24 Sturdee Avenue, Rosebank, Johannesburg 2196,
South Africa

Penguin Books Ltd., Registered Offices: 80 Strand, London, WC2R 0RL, England

Originally published in the United Kingdom by Richard Cape.
First Riverhead hardcover edition: January 2004
First Riverhead trade paperback edition: December 2004
Riverhead trade paperback ISBN: 1-59448-039-7

The Library of Congress has cataloged the Riverhead hardcover edition as follows:

Tinniswood, Adrian.
By permission of heaven : the true story of the
Great Fire of London / Adrian Tinniswood.
p. cm.
Includes bibliographical references and index.
ISBN 1-57322-244-5
1. Great Fire, London, England, 1666.
2. London (England)—History—17th century. I. Title.
DA681.T56 2004   2003058509
942.1'2066—dc22

PRINTED IN THE UNITED STATES OF AMERICA

10 9 8 7 6 5 4 3 2 1

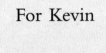
For Kevin

Here, by ye Permission of Heaven,
Hell broke loose upon this Protestant City

Inscription at the site of Farriner's bakery
in Pudding Lane, London

Contents

Illustrations

Plates

The author and publishers would like to express their gratitude to all the libraries and individuals who have helped with these illustrations; especially to the staff of the Guildhall Library in London and the National Maritime Museum. Acknowledgement for the reproduction of photographs or originals is gratefully made to the National Trust for 1 (Petworth House, photograph courtesy of the Courtauld Institute of Art); the Guildhall Library, Corporation of London for 2, 18, 19, 20, 21, 23, 29, 30 and *11*; The Bridgeman Art Library for 3 (Royal Academy of Art/Bridgeman), 14 (Private Collection/Bridgeman), 15 (Guildhall Art Gallery, Corporation of London/Bridgeman) and *10* (Guildhall Art Gallery, Corporation of London/Bridgeman); the National Maritime Museum for 5 (after Sir Peter Lely), 6 (by Richard Gaywood), 7 (by Pieter Nason) and *1*; the National Portrait Gallery, London for 10; the Courtauld Institute of Art for 24; the Warden and Fellows of All Souls for 25 and 26; and the British Museum (Sloane Collection) for 27, 28 and *14*. Although every effort has been made to trace the owners of copyright material reproduced herein, the publishers would like to apologise for any omissions and will be pleased to incorporate missing acknowledgements in any future editions.

Acknowledgements

Many people have helped me with this book. I owe a particular and personal debt of gratitude to my agents Felicity Bryan and Irene Skolnick, who between them have managed to shield me from harm and enrich my life (a combination which is hard to beat); to Dan Franklin at Jonathan Cape, who first suggested that I might like to write about the Great Fire of London; to Tristan Jones, whose editorial skills with a manuscript are positively alchemical; to Tricia Lankester, whose comments and suggestions have, as always, been more helpful and encouraging than I can say; to Kevin Simpson, who understands the psychology of the Fire so well, and understands his old friend even better; and to Martin Sparkes, without whom my working life would have been a lot more painful.

I'd like to pay tribute to the students and friends who did so much to clarify my thoughts on the seventeenth century during a series of seminars at Merton College, Oxford, in the summer of 2002; to Barry Gillions of the Paul Hamlyn Foundation; to map-maker Reginald Piggott and indexer Douglas Matthews; and to the staff at the many libraries I've haunted in the course of my research, including the Bodleian, the British Library, the Guildhall Library and the London Library. I am especially grateful to the library staff at Bristol University, who have borne the brunt of my enquiries over the last couple of years; time after time, their calm efficiency, unfailing kindness and superhuman patience have left me lost in wonder and admiration. I must also acknowledge a debt to past historians of the Fire, who have made my work so much easier than it might have been; and particularly to the late Walter George Bell, whose works on Restoration London created a standard of lucidity by which all historians of the period will be judged.

Last, first, always, thanks to Helen.

Bath, June 2003

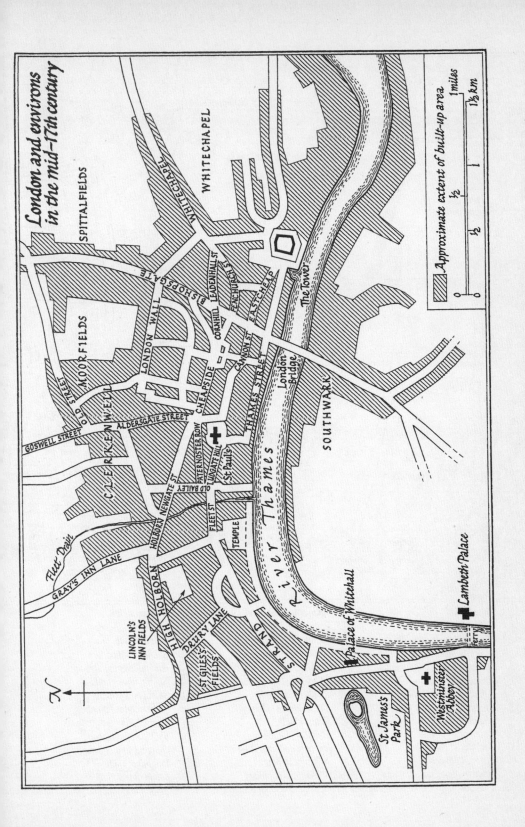

London and environs in the mid-17th century

SPITTALFIELDS

WHITECHAPEL

WHITECHAPEL

BISHOPSGATE

LEADENHALL ST

FENCHURCH ST

CORNHILL

EASTCHEAP

The Tower

LONDON WALL

MOORFIELDS

CANNON ST

THAMES STREET

London Bridge

OLD STREET

GOSWELL STREET

CLERKENWELL

ALDERSGATE STREET

CHEAPSIDE

PATERNOSTER ROW

NEWGATE ST

St Paul's

LUDGATE HILL

OLD BAILEY

SOUTHWARK

FLEET ST

HOLBORN

GRAY'S INN LANE

Fleet Ditch

HIGH HOLBORN

TEMPLE

River Thames

LINCOLN'S INN FIELDS

DRURY LANE

ST GILES'S FIELDS

STRAND

Palace of Whitehall

St James's Park

Westminster Abbey

Lambeth Palace

Approximate extent of built-up area

0   ½   1 mile
0   ½   1   1½ km

N

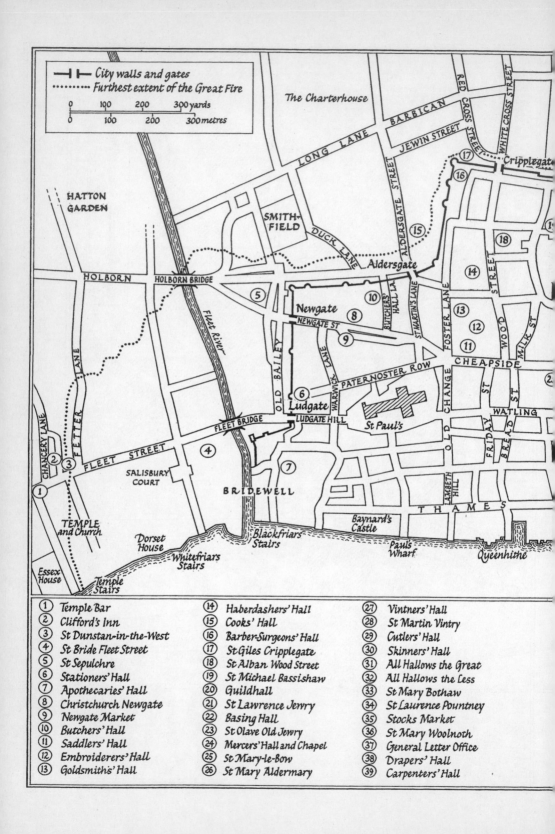

City walls and gates
Furthest extent of the Great Fire

0   100   200   300 yards
0 100   200   300 metres

The Charterhouse

HATTON GARDEN

LONG LANE

BARBICAN

JEWIN STREET

RED CROSS STREET

WHITE CROSS STREET

Cripplegate

⑰

⑯

SMITH-FIELD

DUCK LANE

ALDERSGATE STREET

⑮

⑱

HOLBORN

HOLBORN BRIDGE

Aldersgate

⑭

Fleet River

⑤

Newgate

NEWGATE ST

⑩

BUTCHERS' HALL LA.

ST MARTIN'S LANE

FOSTER LANE

⑬

WOOD STREET

⑧

⑨

⑪

⑫

MILK ST

CHEAPSIDE

PATERNOSTER ROW

OLD BAILEY

WARWICK LANE

OLD CHANGE

FRIDAY ST

BREAD ST

WATLING

⑥

Ludgate

St Paul's

FLEET BRIDGE

LUDGATE HILL

CHANCERY LANE

FETTER LANE

②

③

FLEET STREET

SALISBURY COURT

④

⑦

LAMBETH HILL

①

BRIDEWELL

Baynard's Castle

THAMES

TEMPLE and Church

Dorset House

Blackfriars Stairs

Pauls Wharf

Queenhithe

Essex House

Whitefriars Stairs

Temple Stairs

①	Temple Bar	⑭	Haberdashers' Hall	㉗	Vintners' Hall
②	Clifford's Inn	⑮	Cooks' Hall	㉘	St Martin Vintry
③	St Dunstan-in-the-West	⑯	Barber-Surgeons' Hall	㉙	Cutlers' Hall
④	St Bride Fleet Street	⑰	St Giles Cripplegate	㉚	Skinners' Hall
⑤	St Sepulchre	⑱	St Alban Wood Street	㉛	All Hallows the Great
⑥	Stationers' Hall	⑲	St Michael Bassishaw	㉜	All Hallows the Less
⑦	Apothecaries' Hall	⑳	Guildhall	㉝	St Mary Bothaw
⑧	Christchurch Newgate	㉑	St Lawrence Jewry	㉞	St Laurence Pountney
⑨	Newgate Market	㉒	Basing Hall	㉟	Stocks Market
⑩	Butchers' Hall	㉓	St Olave Old Jewry	㊱	St Mary Woolnoth
⑪	Saddlers' Hall	㉔	Mercers' Hall and Chapel	㊲	General Letter Office
⑫	Embroiderers' Hall	㉕	St Mary-le-Bow	㊳	Drapers' Hall
⑬	Goldsmiths' Hall	㉖	St Mary Aldermary	㊴	Carpenters' Hall

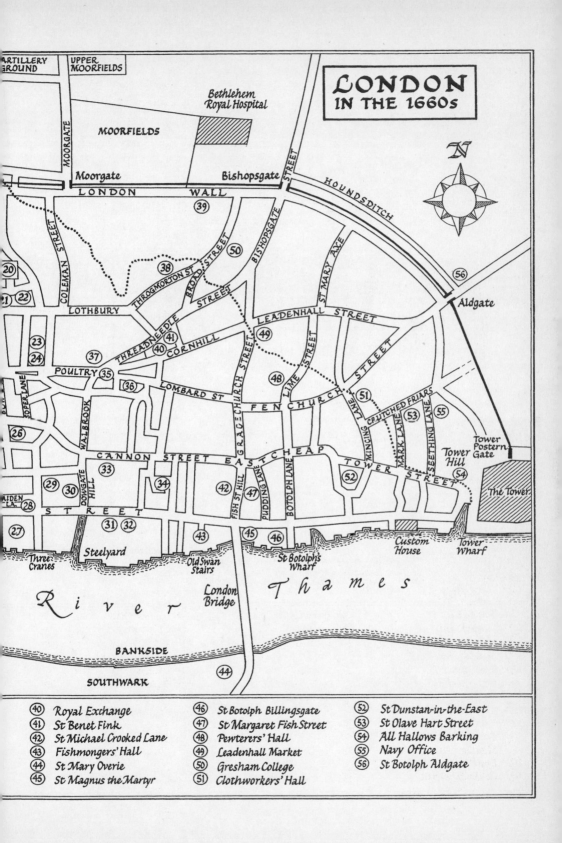

LONDON IN THE 1660s

N

ARTILLERY GROUND

UPPER MOORFIELDS

Bethlehem Royal Hospital

MOORFIELDS

MOORGATE STREET

Moorgate   Bishopsgate

HOUNDSDITCH

LONDON WALL

③⑨

⑤⓪

②⓪

COLEMAN STREET

BROAD STREET

THROGMORTON ST

③⑧

LOTHBURY

②① ②②

THREADNEEDLE STREET

④①

CORNHILL

④⓪

③⑦

BISHOPSGATE STREET

LEADENHALL STREET

④⑨

ST MARY AXE

Aldgate

⑤⑥

②③

②④

POULTRY ③⑤

③⑥

LOMBARD ST

GRACECHURCH STREET

FENCHURCH STREET

LIME STREET

④⑧

⑤①

MINCING LANE

CRUTCHED FRIARS

⑤③

MARK LANE

SEETHING LANE

⑤⑤

②⑥

SOPER LANE

WALBROOK

CANNON STREET

EASTCHEAP

③③

DOWGATE HILL

③④

②⑨ ③⓪

MAIDEN LA.

②⑧

STREET

②⑦

③① ③②

④②

④⑦

FISH ST HILL

PUDDING LANE

BOTOLPH LANE

TOWER STREET

⑤②

Tower Hill

⑤④

Tower Postern Gate

The Tower

④③

④⑤ ④⑥

Custom House

Tower Wharf

Steelyard

Old Swan Stairs

St Botolph's Wharf

Three Cranes

London Bridge

River   Thames

BANKSIDE

SOUTHWARK

④④

St Mary Overie

④⓪	Royal Exchange	④⑥	St Botolph Billingsgate	⑤②	St Dunstan-in-the-East
④①	St Benet Fink	④⑦	St Margaret Fish Street	⑤③	St Olave Hart Street
④②	St Michael Crooked Lane	④⑧	Pewterers' Hall	⑤④	All Hallows Barking
④③	Fishmongers' Hall	④⑨	Leadenhall Market	⑤⑤	Navy Office
④④	St Mary Overie	⑤⓪	Gresham College	⑤⑥	St Botolph Aldgate
④⑤	St Magnus the Martyr	⑤①	Clothworkers' Hall		

*A*fterwards, everyone swore they had been expecting it. They pointed to the prophecies of doom and the Popish plots that had been the talk of the city all through that long, hot August. They reminded each other about the harbingers of calamity: the great pyramid of fire which had hovered ominously over the sea earlier in the year; the monster which had been born in a tenement slum just days before it happened – a terrible thing with a wolf's tail, a goat's breasts, the ears of a horse and a birthmark in the shape of a human face on its chest. Such portents were signs of God's wrath, people said. England had been called to account. England's debauched King had been shown the error of his ways.

But that was afterwards, when it was too late.

As dawn broke bright and clear on the first day of September 1666, no one dreamed they were waking to the last sunrise the old city would ever see. No one dreamed that over the next six days God would blot out the heavens, or that hell would break loose as fear and flame turned the streets of London into Armageddon.

1

The Court of Vulcan

English ships burn West-Terschelling.

*U*nder a bright summer moon, the night watchman on the *Royal James* caught sight of a flash of fire in the distance. A second later the sound rumbled across the waves like thunder. Then there was another flash. While the crew of the *James* – 520 sailors and a hard-worked handful of wives and whores – lay restless and expectant, crammed into intimacy in a vessel just 124 feet long by 41 feet broad, the watchman called softly to rouse the ship's master, and the master woke the commander. The fleet was under attack.

It was just after midnight on Saturday 1 September 1666. For five or six miles around, the North Sea was spangled with a hundred warships, as a massive English battle-fleet lumbered down towards the Channel and what everyone hoped would be a decisive victory over the Dutch. The senior officer on board the seventy-gun *Royal James* was Sir Thomas Allin, Admiral of the White and a veteran whose career as a professional sailor and occasional privateer stretched back almost a quarter of a century.

In spite of his long experience, Allin was not sure what to make of the flashes. 'We judged [them] to be guns between the Dutch and the Blue,' he wrote in his journal that night;[1] but when he tacked and went in search of the enemy, there was no enemy to be found.

On board the *Royal Charles*, the two Generals-at-Sea who commanded the entire fleet were as puzzled as Allin. One was the 46-year-old Prince Rupert, the second cousin to Charles II. The other was George Monck, Duke of Albemarle, who, after proving himself one of Cromwell's most competent soldiers, had changed sides, restored the monarchy and, in Charles's own words, given the King his kingdom. Monck and Rupert also saw the flashes. Like Allin, they thought that the Dutch had launched a surprise attack on the tail end of the fleet under cover of darkness, and the *Royal Charles* tacked to go to the aid of its comrades. But whatever had caused the mysterious flashes of fire in the night, it wasn't the Dutch; and as dawn broke, the Generals gave the order to resume the journey southward to the French coast.

The sun came up at 5.30, and seventy miles to the west, Londoners woke to another working day. Many, in fact, had been awake for quite a while. Fourteen-year-old William Taswell, a pupil at Westminster School, had already dressed and said morning prayers. His Saturday-morning studies, which began at six, would consist of repeating and being examined in the passages from Horace he had learned the day before; the afternoon was given over to an assembly in the fourteenth-century Hall, at which the headmaster, Richard Busby, chose two or three boys to declaim on a given theme in Latin.

Across the city, in the streets and alleys beside Bear Lane, the smart residential area next to the Tower where Taswell's merchant father owned a grand house, salters and ironmongers were laying out their wares. The corn market on nearby Bear Quay was already open. Stallholders in the Leadenhall meat market, and the fishmongers and poultry-sellers in the neighbouring Greenyard, had been open for business since 5 a.m.; they were supposed to sell only to private citizens until 7 a.m., after which street traders were allowed in to negotiate for the produce they intended to sell on later in the day.

Traders in the three main shopping centres opened their shutters and began to lay out their goods at 6 a.m. The western suburbs had the Norman Westminster Hall, which the nation's Law Courts shared with trinket-sellers and toymakers, booksellers, print-dealers and seamstresses. (And with Oliver Cromwell, whose battered and weather-beaten head adorned the roof along with those of the regicides Ireton and Bradshaw.) On the Strand there was the New Exchange, built as 'Britain's bourse' in 1608–9; its double galleries were lined with booths selling luxury goods and the shops of high-quality drapers and mercers.

But the retail hub of London was to the east: the Royal Exchange on Cornhill. The brainchild and bequest of a powerful Elizabethan merchant named Sir Thomas Gresham, it had opened in the late 1560s as London's real answer to the Bourse at Antwerp, on which it was modelled. The merchant community conducted its business in the central courtyard, presided over by statues of English monarchs and a particularly grand figure of Sir Thomas himself; on the ground and first floors of the building, covered walks were occupied by traders and shopkeepers – 135 of them in all. The Royal Exchange was one of the City's most important landmarks, a cathedral of commerce to match the medieval St Paul's, which towered over the landscape half a mile away. Anyone who was anyone gathered at the Exchange not only to buy and sell, but to be seen, to pass on gossip and glean the latest news, to pick up women among the fruit-sellers who hung around at the entrance.

London in 1666 was by far the largest city in the British Isles. Indeed, it was the third largest in the Western world, surpassed only by Constantinople and Paris. Such statistics are relative, of course: this 'wooden, northern, and inartificiall congestion of Houses', as the diarist John Evelyn characterised it in 1659,[2] was home to around 300,000 people. In terms of population, that's about the same size as modern-day Coventry, or half as big as Milwaukee.

Most people lived in the suburbs and outlying parishes. Even Evelyn, whose interest in the welfare of the capital lasted his entire life, made his home at Sayes Court in Deptford, four miles to the south-east. The City of London proper – an area of about 677 acres, or just over one square mile – had a population of only around 80,000. It was more or less bounded by its old Roman walls to the north, east and west, and by the Thames to the south, although its jurisdiction had begun to creep over London Bridge – the City's only fixed river crossing – into parts of Southwark on the south bank. And commerce was at its heart.

London was the leading consumer in the kingdom, the busiest port, the biggest manufacturer, the largest market and distribution centre. There were hundreds of trades practised in the City and its outlying suburbs: maritime workers like ropemakers, anchorsmiths and shipwrights; glovers and cobblers and feltmakers; brewers and bakers and candlestick-makers. The clerks in the old Elizabethan Custom House which stood among the quays and wharves just below London Bridge welcomed goods from almost every part of the known world – pitch, tar and hemp from the Baltic to supply the naval dockyards, timber and tobacco from the plantations of Virginia, raw cotton and sugar from the Caribbean and spices from the Dutch East Indies.

And the City was literally ruled by trade and commerce. The centre of civic government was the Guildhall on Cateaton Street, 'a large and greate house' with an imposing Gothic entrance porch, stained glass in its windows and a massive paved hall.[3] It was here that the annually-elected Lord Mayor presided over the capital, assisted by a Court of Aldermen. Each alderman represented one of the City's twenty-six wards, and was usually elected for life. Each year the wards also elected a number of councilmen to the Court of Common Council, members of the 'commonalty' who shared the task of government with the aldermen.

However, both the franchise and the candidature were effectively limited to members of the sixty-odd Livery Companies, descendants of the craft guilds which had once exercised a draconian control over the practice of their respective trades. Unless you were 'made free' of your Company to practise your trade, you could not be 'made free' of the City to work there. And only freemen could vote in the annual elections and stand for office.

The economic power of the Companies had declined since their heyday in the late Middle Ages. By the 1660s, of the twelve 'Great Companies' – the Mercers, Grocers, Drapers, Fishmongers, Goldsmiths, Skinners, Merchant Taylors, Haberdashers, Salters, Ironmongers, Vintners and Clothworkers – only the Fishmongers and Goldsmiths still maintained close connections with their trades. The other ten were fast becoming little more than charitable societies. Nevertheless, they appealed to wealthy merchants who either saw membership as a necessary stepping stone to a political career, or simply enjoyed the status and prestige that went along with belonging to an exclusive club. There were three routes to entry: apprenticeship; patrimony, where a son had a right by virtue of his father's membership; and redemption, a straightforward cash transaction. Redemption was, understandably, an attractive option for City merchants who had no connections with the relevant trade.

Most of the minor Companies still did their best to exercise their monopolies. Bricklayers, masons and carpenters tried to regulate the building trades, even though – rather confusingly – many of the bigger contractors were freemen of other, unrelated Companies such as the Painter-Stainers or the Leathersellers. No one could make or sell a wax candle in the City unless they were a freeman of the Wax Chandlers' Company; no one could make or sell a tallow candle unless they belonged to the Tallow Chandlers. But it was the *political* power that the Companies still wielded, the way in which they shaped and defined civic government, that really made them such a force in the capital.

That force was also demonstrated by a significant physical presence. Fifty-two of the Companies ran their own Halls, clubhouses in which they met to hold meetings, conduct business and entertain the great and the good. Those Companies influential enough to put forward a successful candidate for Lord Mayor also offered their Halls for the Mayor's use during his year in office, since London had no official mayoral residence.

Some of these buildings were fairly modest. Butchers' Hall, for example, was a converted parsonage in the yard of a redundant – and demolished – church, St Nicholas by the Shambles in Newgate Street. Other Companies occupied old mansions and merchants' houses. The Apothecaries used Cobham House in Blackfriars, once the guest house of the Dominican friary which gave the district its name. The Haberdashers had put up a purpose-built Hall in Ingen Lane (now part of Gresham Street) in 1459–61: it consisted of a great hall, a parlour, a kitchen, an armoury and an upper room called the Raven Chamber. Cutlers' Hall on Cloak Lane – a rather decrepit medieval building which had been acquired in the middle of the fifteenth century – had just been rebuilt after a chimney collapsed and fell through the roof. The work, which began in 1661, took four years to complete; and the bill – a hefty £2,733 2s 7d – was finally paid off in June 1666. The premier Livery Company, the Mercers, had a spectacular Hall and chapel on Cheapside, originally part of the medieval Hospital of St Thomas of Acon which had been founded in 1190 by St Thomas Becket's sister Agnes on the site of his birthplace. (The Beckets' father was an important mercer.) The Vintners were based in a substantial late-fourteenth-century house just south of Thames Street, which had been their home for two centuries.

The Vintners were currently riding high in City life. The previous October one of their members, Sir Thomas Bludworth, had been elected Lord Mayor – the first time in the seventeenth century that a Vintner had achieved that honour. Bludworth was forty-six, a past Master of the Company and the son of a past Master. Like his father, he was a merchant specialising not in wine, but in the timber trade with Turkey and the Near East; even so, when he entered the Vintners in 1643 he did so not by patrimony but by serving his apprenticeship.

Bludworth was an astute businessman, with an income which was reckoned to be around £3,000 a year. He was also politically ambitious, if not particularly brilliant. A fellow Royalist later described him as 'a zealous person in the king's concernments: willing, though it may be, not very able, to do great things'.[4]

After a period as a colonel in the local militia during the Civil War, he had become an alderman in 1658. Two years later he rushed to the Hague to congratulate Charles on his restoration to the throne and help escort him back to England. He received a knighthood for his pains and that same year he was elected MP for Southwark. In 1662–3 he served as Sheriff for the City, an ancient judicial role and a prerequisite for anyone aspiring to the office of Mayor. Finally he achieved his goal, following on from Sir John Lawrence, a Master of the Haberdashers' Company whose heroic efforts to control the plague during his year in mayoral office had earned him universal acclaim for the way in which 'throughout this dreadful visitation he has, in spite of all hazards and mistakes, persisted in his duty'.[5]

Unfortunately for Thomas Bludworth, the death and disruption caused by the 'dreadful visitation' meant that it was not an auspicious time to be Mayor – as he found out when he took office on 29 October 1665. The usual custom was for the new Lord Mayor to sail in triumphal procession at the head of a flotilla of Company barges up the Thames to Westminster, where he presented himself to the monarch or his justices to swear fealty. He then returned to the City, landing at St Paul's Wharf and processing to the Guildhall on horseback, escorted by the rest of the aldermen with trumpeters, standard-bearers and highly theatrical pageantry. (In 1612, for instance, the Pageant of the Triumphs of Truth in honour of Sir Thomas Middleton involved the creation of five islands on the Thames, 'artfully garnished with all manner of Indian fruit trees, drugges, spiceries and the like, the middle island having a faire castle especially beautified'.[6]) Everyone who was anyone was invited to the feast which followed at the Guildhall. Guests at Lawrence's banquet in October 1664, which was reckoned to have cost £1,000, had included Secretary of State Lord Arlington, Lord Chancellor Clarendon, the Lord Treasurer, the Lord Chamberlain, the Dukes of Albemarle, Buckingham and Ormond and the French Ambassador. 'The cheere was not to be imagined for the plenty and raritie, with an infinite number of persons at the rest of the tables in that ample hall.'[7]

Thomas Bludworth's big day took place when 'Death's writt

[was] in bloud on every doore, [and] Red characters upon our posts are signs of life no more'.[8] With around a thousand people dying every week, it was understandably a restrained affair. There was no state barge, no procession down Cheapside, no pageant, no Lord Mayor's banquet. Charles and his court had run away to Oxford; no judges had sat in Westminster Hall since June. So Sir John Robinson, Lieutenant of the Tower of London and a past Mayor, stood in for the King. Bludworth met him just outside the Tower at a barber's shop, which had been rather desperately hung with festive draperies to mark the occasion. Afterwards everyone went back to dinner at Bludworth's house in Gracechurch Street. That was it.

Of course the plague did rather more than cast a dampener on the new Lord Mayor's social aspirations. It had turned London into a wasteland; and in the summer of 1666 it was still having a profound effect on the life of the capital.

There had been many outbreaks of plague in recent years, so the first recorded fatality of 1665, in the parish of St Paul's Covent Garden in the second week of April, hadn't attracted any attention. There were two more a fornight later, this time among the poor of St Giles-in-the-Fields, an underprivileged area to the north of Covent Garden. In May, the weekly Bills of Mortality, which published figures and causes of death for London and the surrounding area, noted nine plague deaths in the City itself, and eight in the suburbs.

The mortality rate climbed rapidly. By the week ending 27 June 1665 it had reached 267. Richard Busby evacuated Westminster School, taking William Taswell and his fellow students out to a safe house in Chiswick before giving up the struggle and ordering them all to return to their homes. (William stayed at his father's country house in Greenwich for the next ten months.) The Lord Chamberlain ordered the closure of all playhouses in the capital to prevent the spread of the disease, and a couple of days later Samuel Pepys arrived at Whitehall to find 'the Court full of waggons and people ready to go out of towne'.[9] The King, together with the Duke of York and Prince Rupert, decamped to Hampton Court, then to Salisbury and, in

September 1665, to Oxford. His mother, Henrietta Maria, fled to France, never to return.

It is hard for a society which greets every winter with hysterical headlines about 'killer flu epidemics' to understand the effects of the plague. The annual death rate from infectious and parasitic diseases in the United Kingdom currently runs at about 5 per 100,000 of the population; in the United States it is around 24 per 100,000. Recent World Health Organisation statistics on AIDS in Zimbabwe, which has one of the highest HIV rates in the world, suggest an annual death rate from AIDS-related illnesses of one in sixty-four of the population.

In the epidemic of bubonic plague which broke out in May 1665, the mortality rate was *20,000* per 100,000 of the population. One in five Londoners died. 'Now death rides triumphantly on his pale horse through our streets', said Thomas Vincent, 'and breaks into every house almost where any inhabitants are to be found. Now people fall as thick as leaves from the trees in autumn, when they are shaken by a mighty wind.'[10]

Vincent, a young Nonconformist preacher in the north-eastern suburb of Hoxton, could speak about the Pale Rider with such graphic intensity because he was there, watching the Rider's terrible progress from house to house.★ Like many Dissenting ministers, Vincent remained in London throughout the summer and autumn of 1665, offering spiritual comfort and ministering to the sick. He later recalled some of the horrors he witnessed: naked plague victims running screaming down the street; a bleeding man who had collapsed and fallen on some railings and who, when Vincent went to speak to him, could only rattle in his throat; a weeping woman carrying a little coffin under her arm. 'Multitudes! multitudes! in the valley of the shadow of death, thronging daily into eternity; the church-yards now are stufft so full with dead corps, that they are in many places swell'd two or

★Vincent was educated at Westminster School, and had a brief spell as a master there in the 1650s. Apparently he was 'a sensitive scholar, on whose nerves the mistakes of the fourth form so jarred that he retired to die of their false Latin' (John Sargeaunt, *Annals of Westminster School* [1898], 85).

three foot higher than they were before; and new ground is broken up to bury the dead.'[11]

While highly principled Dissenters like Vincent stayed at their posts, most of the Anglican clergy deserted their congregations and, like the gentry and the merchant class, followed the example of their sovereign and joined the general exodus. The practice of quarantining entire families in their homes as soon as a single case was suspected led many people to lie about causes of death, so official figures must be treated with caution, but the Bills of Mortality show a peak of 7,165 plague deaths in London in the week ending 19 September 1665. They fell steadily over the autumn and winter, and the King felt it safe to return to the Palace of Whitehall on 1 February 1666. Catherine of Braganza followed him ten days later.

The hot summer of 1666 showed that although the plague was declining in London, it was far from over. The disease claimed 38 deaths in the last week of July, and 162 in August. Playhouses remained closed; the annual Bartholomew Fair at Smithfield was cancelled 'for fear of a renewal of the contagion'.[12] And all through August, reports of the epidemic poured in from around the country: 'In Northamptonshire the sickness rages extremely, especially in Peterborough, Oundle, and Newport Pagnell, in which last, though a market town, only 700 or 800 people are left. At Cambridge it is so sore that the harvest can hardly be gathered in.'[13] The east of England was badly hit – 'all parts in Norfolk are very sickly with agues and fevers'[14] – and Norwich's market was moved half a mile from the city in an attempt to prevent the spread of the disease. On the Kent coast, the situation in the Cinque Ports was desperate: by the end of the month, three-quarters of those who had stayed in Deal and risked infection were reported dead; Dover and Sandwich were affected; and the plague had moved inland to Canterbury and Maidstone. There were signs of hope, however: 'formerly it scarcely left one in a house; now most live and have sores'.[15]

In the capital itself, the most recent Bills of Mortality, for 28 August 1666, showed that there had been 266 deaths in total in the past week. Only thirty were attributed to the plague. Forty-eight people succumbed to consumption, and twelve died from convulsions. Two people drowned in the parish of St Katherine-by-the-Tower, one plunged to his or her death from a window in St Botolph Aldgate, and someone had a fatal fall down some stairs in Stepney. One Londoner died of lethargy, one of French pox. One poor soul died of grief.

Even without the plague, London was not a pleasant place in which to live in 1666. It was noisy, filthy and smelly, and most Englishmen agreed that only Paris was worse. Charnel houses stood side by side with stately mansions; butchers' offal lay rotting in the narrow streets, and human waste blocked open drains. Commentators cursed the constant traffic jams and marvelled at the way in which the smoke from brew-houses hung like a great cloud over the houses and gardens of the nobility that lay between the City and the centre of government in Whitehall. There was no sense of order, no symmetry to the houses. In spite of the best efforts of the authorities – and in marked contrast to, say, the elegant planned vistas of Sixtus V's Rome – street-architecture in the capital seemed completely unregulated. As John Evelyn pointed out in 1659:

> The Buildings . . . are as deformed as the minds & confusions of the people, for if a whole street be fired (an accident not unfrequent in this wooden City) the Magistrate has either no power, or no care to make them build with any uniformity, which renders it, though a large, yet, a very ugly Town, pestred with Hackney-coaches, and insolent Carre-men, Shops and Taverns, Noyse, and such a cloud of Sea-coal, as if there be a resemblance of Hell upon Earth, it is in this Vulcano on a foggy day.[16]

The smoke pollution which disfigured the metropolis continued to play on Evelyn's mind, and two years later he returned to the theme in *Fumifugium, or The Inconveniencie of the Aer and Smoak of London Dissipated*, in which he advocated the removal of environmentally hazardous trades such as brewers,

11

dyers, lime-burners and soap-boilers. Such industries, he said, polluted the air; the smoke from their chimneys corroded the stonework of buildings, ruined furniture and textiles, and bred consumption and other lung diseases. While they remained uncontrolled, 'the City of London resembles the face rather of Mount Ætna, the Court of Vulcan, Stromboli, or the Suburbs of Hell, then an Assembly of Rational Creatures, and the Imperial seat of our incomparable Monarch'.[17]

These were advanced views. They were also prophetic. Evelyn, who spent Saturday 1 September at home with his family in Deptford, was about to find out just how much his dear city might come to look like the Court of Vulcan. The next time he visited London he would indeed be entering the Suburbs of Hell.

The most charismatic commander in the fleet which had entered the English Channel at daybreak on Saturday 1 September 1666 was undoubtedly Sir Robert Holmes, Rear-Admiral of the Red.★ Born in 1622 in Mallow, County Cork, Holmes had fought side by side with Prince Rupert and his brother Maurice during the Civil War, and later served against the Spanish at Armentières, when the Prince saved his life during an ambush after his leg had been shattered by a Spanish musket ball. When Rupert turned to piracy in the early 1650s, Holmes went with him, acquiring a taste for the seafaring life which after the Restoration took him to the coast of West Africa. His orders on that mission were to support the Royal African Company against Dutch encroachments – but to avoid hostilities if at all possible.

Holmes, who wore a gold-lace suit and kept a pet baboon he had adopted during his expedition to the Guinea coast, was something of a dandy. With his hair tied back, his dark beard and his pointed moustaches, he looked more like an Elizabethan adventurer than a rear-admiral in Charles II's navy. And he behaved

★The fleet was organised into three squadrons: the Red, headed jointly by Rupert and Albemarle in the *Royal Charles*; the Blue; and the White. Each squadron had its own admiral, vice-admiral and rear-admiral.

like an adventurer, wreaking havoc among the Dutch, looting their merchant ships and capturing every one of their trading stations he could find, before returning to England at the end of 1664. For appearance's sake, an embarrassed Charles ordered Holmes to the Tower of London, where he remained for several months until the King gave him a full pardon and indemnified him against all felonies and offences committed in England or elsewhere.

Holmes's escapades were the final straw for the Dutch, or the 'Hogen Mogens', as the English contemptuously called them. (The phrase is an ironic corruption of *Hoogmogendheiden*, 'High Mightinesses', which was the formal title of the States-General, the Dutch national assembly.) The Hogens declared war on 14 January 1665, with England responding in kind five weeks later. Both declarations were formalities, because the two nations had been skirmishing for months, neither emerging with much credit. In the autumn of 1664, Admiral Michiel Adrienszoon De Ruijter had retaken most of the African colonies lost to Holmes's squadron, and tales of atrocities he committed against English settlers there caused outrage at home. (According to rumour, one of his favourite tricks was to bind men, women and children back-to-back and throw them into the ocean.) Then, in December 1664, Sir Thomas Allin and his squadron were cruising off the Straits of Gibraltar when they came across a Dutch convoy returning from Smyrna. Reasoning that war was bound to be declared pretty soon anyway, Allin attacked the convoy without warning, sinking one ship and capturing three others.

The first year of the war had gone well for England – and for James, Duke of York, who as Lord High Admiral insisted on taking personal command of the fleet. The only major action was the Battle of Lowestoft, which took place at the beginning of June 1665; and it was a famous victory, with 32 Dutch sail sunk or taken, 4,000 of the Hogen Mogens killed and 2,000 captured. English losses amounted to 2 ships and around 600 men killed or wounded.

But a vice-admiral, a rear-admiral and three captains were among the English casualties, and the fact that the Duke of York was not was little short of a miracle. His flagship, the *Royal Charles*, was involved in a vicious one-to-one battle with the Dutch commander-in-chief, Jacob van Wassenaer, in the *Eendracht*. The *Eendracht* tried to board the *Charles*, and fired broadside after broadside into her from terribly close range. James, who was on deck with a group of officers and friends, saw those friends explode into pieces beside him as a single Dutch chain shot ripped apart the Earl of Burlington's son, Richard Boyle; Lord Muskerry; and Charles Berkeley, Earl of Falmouth, who had been one of James's closest companions for more than a decade. James himself was drenched in their blood, although his only wound was a cut to his hand. It was caused by a bone fragment from Boyle's skull.

As the Dutch moved in for the kill, the Duke's capture or death seemed a foregone conclusion. Then without any warning, the *Eendracht* suddenly blew up in front of him, killing all but 5 of her 409-strong crew.

King Charles, Parliament and the Duchess of York all insisted that James must plan the future conduct of the war from the safety of London. 'For the Duke's honour and safety, it were best, after so great a service and victory and danger, not to go again.'[18] Prince Rupert considered himself the best candidate for the new job of commander-in-chief of the fleet, but Rupert was 'a man of no government and severe in council, [so] that no man can offer any advice against his'.[19] The stakes were raised at the beginning of 1666 when the French pitched in – albeit rather reluctantly – on the side of the Dutch; and George Monck, the dependable Captain-General of the Kingdom, was given joint command in the hope that his natural caution would temper Rupert's rashness.

The English navy fought two major battles against the Dutch in the summer of 1666. At the beginning of June the Four Days' Fight had resulted in a Dutch victory and left the English with 10 ships lost, more than 2,000 men taken prisoner and at least twice that number killed.

In contrast, the St James's Day Fight of 25 July was a resounding English victory. Rupert and Monck lost just one ship of the line, the 58-gun *Resolution*, and about 300 men; the Dutch fleet, commanded by De Ruijter, lost 4 flag officers, 20 ships, 4,000 men killed and 3,000 wounded. That was not enough for Robert Holmes: when the Admiral of the Blue, Sir Jeremiah Smyth, failed to pursue the Dutch fleet with sufficient enthusiasm, the Irishman fired on his superior in an attempt to persuade him to change his mind; and when Smyth still refused to fight, he publicly called him a coward.

Holmes was a friend of Prince Rupert; Smyth was Monck's man. There was talk of a duel; of mediation by Secretary of State Lord Arlington, or Treasury Commissioner Sir Thomas Clifford. Rupert and Monck exchanged words, and the fleet was split by factional in-fighting.

But within days the feud was overtaken by events and Holmes was a national hero, with everyone in the country talking about how he had carried out the most audacious action of the war. At the beginning of August a Dutch defector called Lauris van Heemskirck offered to show where magazines and stores were kept on Vlieland and Terschelling, two of the West Frisian Islands which lie about ten miles off the coast of Holland. Holmes was told to take Heemskirck and 900 men and to plunder the islands, destroying provisions, killing cattle and taking or burning any ships they found in the harbour; and to 'perform such acts of hostility as is usual against a professed enemy'.[20] So on the morning of 8 August he sailed a small squadron of nine men-of-war with five fire ships and seven ketches into the natural harbour formed by the Frisian Islands, where – to his surprise and delight – he found around 150 Dutch merchantmen lying at anchor. Many of them were richly laden and homeward bound from Guinea, the West Indies and the Mediterranean.

Two Dutch men-of-war sailed out to meet the raiding party, guns blazing. The first was promptly grappled and set alight by the lead fire ship, and in the smoke and confusion the crew of the second thought their vessel had also been fired – which it hadn't – and took to their boat. After a moment or two they realised their mistake, and a frantic race for the ship took place. The English got there first, turned the Dutch ship's guns on its own crew, and burned it.

The crews of the 150 merchantmen abandoned ship as soon

as they saw what had happened to their protectors, and rowed hard for Amsterdam in their boats. They were followed by 'an infinite number of boats from the Vlie; the people running away thence as fast as they could'.[21] Holmes and his men were left to spend the afternoon and evening burning every ship they could find.

Then they went to sack the town of West-Terschelling, with Holmes leading the way in the little four-gun *Fanfan*. As they approached land, expecting at any minute to meet with an ambush among the hillocks and sand dunes, they saw a single horseman watching them from the shore. Holmes fired at him and missed – but the Dutchman's horse reared, and he fell off. That was the end of any Dutch resistance.

The raiders marched through an almost deserted town, commenting on the new Town Hall, the single-storey homes 'well contrived and very clean and sweetly kept', the gardens with their vines and apple trees.[22] One party went from house to house, taking whatever they could find, while another was ordered to set fire to some of the buildings on the edge of the town, to cover the English retreat. Strong winds blew the flames across West-Terschelling, so that as the English pulled back half an hour later the whole town – around one thousand houses – was ablaze and there was a huge pall of smoke rising into the sky. 'Make all haste as soon as weather and wind will permit to return back to the fleet again,' ordered Rupert and Monck; 'for we presume by the smoke which we ourselves have seen, that the country by this time may be alarmed to such a degree, that they may possibly pour over some sudden forces upon you.'[23] Holmes was trying his best to do just that, but some of his men were so preoccupied with plundering the town that they ignored the drums calling them back to their boats. Others marched back to the waterside as well as they could, loaded down with household goods. They were 'missing many of our number, who were gone before to the sea side with burthens and were ready to go back again for more'.[24] In the end, Holmes turned his ships' guns on Terschelling, and this was enough to persuade sailors and marines that it was time to take their leave of the town.

Coming only a fortnight after De Ruijter's defeat in the St James's Fight, the news of the firing of West-Terschelling was greeted with horror in Amsterdam and the Hague. The Dutch had lost goods and property worth nearly a million pounds, and God knew how many lives; Holmes, who admitted to a few aches and bruises, reckoned he had lost twelve men killed or wounded. There were rumours of mass desertions in the ranks of the Dutch fleet; and the Venetian Ambassador to France told the Doge that there was a universal air of desperation throughout Holland, and that as for the inhabitants of Terschelling, 'the tears and lamentations of those poor wretches are indescribable'.[25]

At home, the news of 'Sir Robert Holmes his bonefire', as everybody called it, was greeted with wild jubilation. The days appointed for public celebration of the St James's Fight – 14 August in London, and 23 August in the rest of the country – turned into a triumphal victory parade, with civic dinners, peals of bells, fireworks and bonfires. From Truro to Leith the people turned out into the streets to exult in the destruction of West-Terschelling. The authorities in Edinburgh reported that the action had raised everyone's spirits, and was being celebrated with guns firing and church bells ringing; at King's Lynn in Norfolk, the mayor and aldermen processed in their scarlet from the town hall to the parish church, with the town band playing before them:

> Our streets were thick with bonefires large and tall,
> But Holmes one bonefire made was worth them all.[26]

The immediate consequence of Holmes's bonfire was to convince Monck that the Dutch were too demoralised to put to sea again before winter set in. Prince Rupert disagreed, and wagered five pieces of gold that De Ruijter would want to taste English blood.

He won his bet. As dawn broke on the morning of Saturday 1 September 1666, and a hundred English ships moved southward in a stately procession towards the coast of Holland, it was common knowledge that the Dutch fleet was out again, eager to avenge the sacking of West-Terschelling. No one dreamed that within twenty-four hours a fire would be lit in London that would burn a thousand times more brightly than Sir Robert Holmes's bonfire.

2

The Future Condition of the English Nation

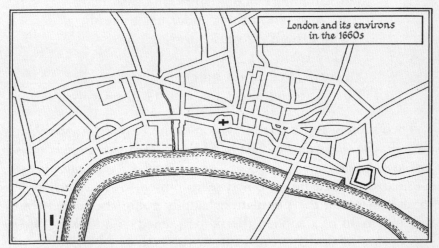

London and its environs
in the 1660s

A vague foreboding about what 1666 might bring had been in the air for decades, and most of the population felt the frisson of unease expressed by mathematician George Wharton in his *Calendarium Carolinum* for the fateful year: 'Now Sixtene Hundred Sixtie Six is *come: / When (as some say) shall be the* Day of Doome.'[1] London itself had been the subject of several vague but dramatic prophecies. In *Monarchy or No Monarchy* (1651) the eminent astrologer William Lilly published nineteen cryptic emblems which he said represented 'the future condition of the English Nation and Commonwealth for many hundreds of years yet to come'.[2] One showed a burning city beside a river, and another depicted the Gemini twins falling head first into a flaming bonfire. Gemini was the zodiacal sign associated with the capital.

London's role in Charles I's downfall was the subject of a broadside ballad, 'Mourne London Mourne'. The anonymous author

dwelled at length on the fate which awaited its citizens for daring to kill their King:

> Fire raging fire
> Shall burn thy stately towers down
> Yet not expire,
> Tygres and Wolves, or men more savage grown,
> Thy Children's brains, and thine shall dash,
> And in your blood their guilty tallons wash,
> Thy Daughters must
> Allay their lust,
> Mischiefs will be on mischief thrust,
> Till thy Cap tumble as thou mad'st the Crown.[3]

Then there was the terrible vision of the Royalist mystic Walter Gostelo. In *The coming of God in Mercy, in Vengeance; Beginning with fire, to Convert, or Consume, at this so sinful City London* (1658), Gostelo described how he had seen himself to the north of the capital, watching the population happily going about their business, when all of a sudden the sky darkened; and looking up he saw hordes of devils flying in from the east. There was a stench of fire and brimstone, and the air grew unbearably hot; and through the darkness an invisible army marched on London carrying black and white ensigns. 'I looked again upon the City,' he wrote:

> and then I saw *Lights* shining in most parts of it, which *Lights* clearly discovered to me the Ruinous condition of the *Cathedral Church* dedicated to Saint Paul; these lights were placed to so wonderful advantage, That they laid open to me, *Close Corners, Ware-houses, Shops, dark places, places of Sacriledge, Theft, Murder, damnable uncleannesses, Hypocrisies as deep as Hell.*[4]

People in Restoration England took their portents and prophecies seriously. As the fleet was sailing round the North Foreland on the morning of 1 September, for example, a letter was on its way from the port authorities at Margate on the Kent coast to Lord Arlington's office at Whitehall. They were anxious to inform the Secretary of State that the inhabitants of Middleburg in the Netherlands had seen a vision in the air of the English and Dutch fleets; and that the Dutch had been wholly destroyed by burning and sinking. (With equally misplaced optimism, the same intelligence reported that a disaffected Dutch admiral, Cornelis Tromp, had just landed at Dover, intent on enlisting in the English navy.)

Anxiety over the presence in the date of three sixes – 'an Apocalyptical and mysterious number', as the renowned astrologer John Booker pointed out in his *New Almanack and Prognostication* (1666) – stemmed from St John the Divine's cryptic revelation that the number of the beast is the number of a man, and his number is six hundred threescore and six; and doom-mongers had been predicting a catastrophe of apocalyptic proportions for most of the century. In 1610, for example, the anonymous author of *Babylon is Fallen* identified the Pope as Antichrist and predicted that he would be overthrown in 1666. In the 1620s a Wiltshire cleric pointed out that all the Roman numerals placed in order – MDCLXVI – added up to the fatal year, 'so that when the odd 666, are completed in the Year of Christ, it may bode some ominous Matter, and perhaps the last End'.[5]★ And Francis Potter, a numerologically inclined rector of Kilmington in Somerset, reckoned to have a cast-iron mathematical argument for the Pope as St John's beast in his *Interpretation of the number 666*, which had first appeared in 1642 and was now enjoying something of a vogue. His reasoning went thus: 144 was chosen 'to be the measure of the wall of the celestiall Jerusalem' (Revelation 21:17) because it is the square of twelve, and this is obviously a special number since there were twelve apostles, twelve tribes of Israel, twelve angels, and twelve gates in the new Jerusalem. If the holy number of 144 provides such insights, then the number of the beast demands further investigation. So we

---

★Oddly enough, that cleric was the father of Christopher Wren, for whom 1666 turned out to be a beginning rather than an end.

must look for the square root of 666, which, said Potter, was more or less 25, 'a fatal and unfortunate number'.[6] There were twenty-five cardinals and twenty-five articles in the Roman Catholic creed; twenty-five sessions of the Council of Trent and, originally, twenty-five churches in Rome. Ergo, Rome is Babylon and the Pope is Antichrist.

Potter's arithmetic may have been open to question, although when it was pointed out to him that 25 was not actually the square root of 666, he replied that it ought *not* to be the true root, since that agreed better with his purpose; presumably Catholicism's distortion of the truth extended even to simple arithmetic. But his book was endorsed by renowned Millenarians like Joseph Mede, author of *Clavis Apocalyptica* (1627), who wrote the foreword to Potter's *Interpretation*, in which he claimed that 'this discourse or Tract of the number of the Beast is the happiest that ever yet came into the world'. It was translated into Latin and French, and distributed widely by London booksellers all through the spring and summer of 1666. Potter's admirers included John Aubrey and also Samuel Pepys, who bought a copy of the *Interpretation* in February and thought it 'mighty ingenious'.[7]

Another cause for foreboding was the story of Sabbatai Zevi, a prophet of Smyrna whose fame as the professed Messiah had recently spread from Asia Minor across the whole of Europe. Tales of the self-proclaimed King of the Jews and his strange powers had reached England earlier in the year: it was said that a starry pillar of fire was seen hovering over his lodgings in the palace of the Grand Seignior in Constantinople, and that when the Vizier's men had tried to sneak in and strangle him, they had been struck down dead. Odds of ten to one were being offered – and accepted – in London on whether or not Zevi really was the returned Messiah.

The professional prophets whose almanacs were read in thousands of English homes – William Lilly, John Gadbury, Vincent Wing, William Andrews and the dozens of astrologers who, like them, made a good living from foretelling the future – were all pretty sure that 1666 was going to be a difficult year. As far back as 1648 Lilly had predicted that in the mid-1660s there would appear in this kingdom so strange a revolution of fate, so grand a catastrophe and great mutation unto this monarchy and government as never yet appeared of which as the times now stand, I have no liberty or encouragement to deliver my opinion – only it will be ominous to London, unto her merchants at sea, to her traffique on land, to her poor, to all sorts of people, inhabiting in her or to her liberties, by reason of sundry fires and a consuming plague.[8]

And though the resonance with Revelation was bad, recent and forthcoming celestial phenomena looked set to make matters even worse. A partial solar eclipse took place at 6.37 a.m. on 22 June 1666, and another – visible only in the southern hemisphere, but an eclipse nevertheless – was predicted for 15 December. There were also two eclipses of the moon, on 6 June and 1 December. And, in the words of Richard Saunders, a baker-turned-astrologer who practised in Chancery Lane,

> Universal experience certainly informs us, that *Eclipses* presig-
> nifie (as well as *Conjunctions* and *Comets*) many and great evils,
> troubles, damages, and discommodities to the World, and prin-
> cipally to those Regions thereby signified, with death and
> mortality of Princes and persons of renown. I could easily
> demonstrate, that all the great changes and mutations in the
> World, as, *sickness, famine,* and *grand evils,* have in all ages, been
> the sad consequences of these secondary and presignifying
> causes . . .[9]

Saunders' mention of comets reminded his readers that in the first week of December 1664 a fiery comet had been seen over Europe, a blazing star which abruptly vanished, only to appear again towards the end of the month, and yet again in late March and early April 1665. These heavenly apparitions were accompanied by some disturbing aberrations of nature: a coffin appeared in the sky over Vienna, 'which causes great anxiety of thought amongst the people';[10] and in Warsaw a hen laid an egg marked with a flaming cross, a sword, a rod and a drawn bow.

While astronomers in the academic community disputed whether there were one, two or three separate comets, struggled to establish the path it – or they – took through the heavens, and argued over whether a blazing star emanated from the sun or intruded on the solar system as a stranger, the majority of ordinary folk were worried. Traditionally, such phenomena were omens of doom; and astrologers were ready and willing to confirm traditional thinking.*

All agreed that the appearance of a blazing star could only mean that something very, very bad was going to happen. The uninitiated might argue that it already had, in the form of the plague. But Restoration almanac-writers were concerned to a man with selling the future rather than recycling the past. Since the deadline for their copy arrived each autumn, their 1665 offerings were already on sale by the time of the first comet, and it was not until they came to write their almanacs for 1666 that they had an opportunity to muse on the meaning of these strange phenomena. (An exception was John Gadbury, who rushed out his *Brief (yet full) Account of the III late Comets, or Blazing Stars . . . And what (in a natural way of Judicature) they portend* in the summer of 1665.) 'Without all doubt [the comets] portend very great Calamities,' warned William Lilly;[11] Richard Saunders believed they showed 'the immediate *Finger of God*, and the *Brandisht Sword* of the *Almighty*, denunciating his wrath upon the World for sin';[12] and John Tanner listed the considerable consequences for the world with relish: rapines, slaughters, dryness, heat,

---

*Astrologers were disarmingly honest about the difficulties of observing and interpreting the comets. Lilly, who had fled the plague for a rural retreat at Walton-on-Thames, confessed in his *Merlini Anglici Ephemeris* for 1666 that he had left his detailed observations in London, and subsequently lost them. John Tanner, an astrologer and physician from Amersham in Buckinghamshire, wrote of how he had caught only a glimpse of the April comet through his chamber window, 'by reason of the coldnesse of the weather, and the indisposition of my body' (*Angelus Britannicus*, 1666). And John Booker admitted that he had missed the blazing star completely because 'it pleased God to visit me then (and some years before, and yet not free) of a tedious Dysentery, by which means I was disabled from making such Observations as were requisite' (*A New Almanack and Prognostication*, 1666).

pestiferous and horrid winds and tempests, destruction of the fruits of the earth by vermin and putrefaction; prodigious and frequent lightnings and thunders; shipwrecks and sea-fights, chronic and long-lasting diseases, snows, earthquakes, plague, famine, exile, penury, grief, trouble and vexation.

There was, however, some disagreement over the likely recipient of all this mayhem. The current favourite was Pope Alexander VII, who was so sick that the London *Gazette* of 30 August 1666 predicted an imminent conclave. (In a snide reference to Alexander's notorious nepotism, the *Gazette* also noted that 'his near Relations are in great apprehensions of his, but especially their own condition'.) This was not only in line with long-held Protestant thinking, but a consummation devoutly to be wished by most Englishmen: '*Rome* must down, and . . . the Roman Catholick Religion must of necessitie have its final period even in this very year.'[13]

Closer to home, adherents to the 'Good Old Cause' of Republicanism hoped to see not only the fall of the Papacy, but also the destruction of the restored monarchy and the creation of a new world order. The Fifth Monarchy Men, Millenarian extremists who took their name from the prophet Daniel's vision of a world-empire of the righteous which, according to contemporary interpretations, would follow on from those of Babylon, Assyria, Greece and Rome, preached that 1666 would see the fall of the ungodly as the Lord took vengeance on England for its failure to build the new Jerusalem. It was six years since Charles II had come home as the conquering hero, riding through ecstatic London crowds, 'the ways strewed with flowers, the bells ringing, the streets hung with tapestry, fountains running with wine . . . trumpets, music and myriads of people.'[14] The honeymoon was short-lived, and disaffected Dissenters and Republicans had been making haphazard attempts at revolution ever since. For three days in January 1661 a group of fifty rebels caused havoc in London with a desperate and hopeless attempt at insurrection in which, it was rumoured, they expected Christ himself to come down to earth and direct them. Led by a Fifth Monarchist and Nonconformist preacher, Thomas Venner, they engaged in some vicious street-fighting with troops from the

King's personal household, the Life Guards. Detachments from the local militia, the trained bands, were sent to aid the Guards, and twenty soldiers and twenty-six rebels died before they were overpowered. The rebels' battle-cry, 'King Jesus, and the heads upon the gate', was prophetic: it was the heads of Venner and twelve of his comrades that ended up on London Bridge.

The next year a plot was uncovered in which two of the royal guard were to admit Cromwellian veterans into the Palace of Whitehall so that they could assassinate the King. Then in 1663 a much more elaborate scheme was hatched – again by old Republicans – in which towns in the north, the Midlands and the west would be taken by rebels, causing Charles to dispatch the Life Guards to put down the risings; with the Guards out of the way, Londoners would rise up and over-throw their tyrannical King. It was absurd, of course: popular support for the revolutionaries was largely a figment of their imagination, and thirty of the ringleaders were duly captured and executed. Others committed suicide, or turned King's evidence, or fled abroad.

As relations with Holland deteriorated, dissidents understand-ably, if unpatriotically, looked to the Dutch for arms, money and moral support. Several hundred ex-army officers enlisted with the Hogens, who were happy to play along with the rebels' dreams of revolution, although they had no real intention of following them through. As war was declared early in 1665, English defec-tors in Holland were writing to their comrades at home that an army of 30,000 men, many of them in regiments led by old Republican officers, were ready to overthrow the monarchy and restore the Commonwealth.

That was wishful thinking. But if it was meant to stir Republicans into action, it had the desired effect. In the early summer of 1665, an old army colonel named John Rathbone conspired with seven others – all 'formerly Officers or Soldiers in the late Rebellion' – to kill the King and depose the govern-ment. They were involved, it was said, with 'a Council of the great ones that sat frequently in London';[15] and this council received its orders from another in Holland. Rathbone's plan was to storm the Tower of London by sailing across the moat and scaling the walls. This would take place on 3 September, the anniversary of Cromwell's death, and also of his victory over the Royalists at the Battle of Worcester in 1651. The date was found in Lilly's *Merlini Anglici Ephemeris*, which suggested it was a lucky day for the purpose, 'a Planet then ruling which prognosticated the Downfall of Monarchy'.[16] The Lieutenant of the Tower, Sir John Robinson, was to be summarily executed along with Major-General Sir Richard Browne, an alderman and former Lord Mayor who had played an important part in suppressing Venner's rising; and once in control of the Tower, the rebels hoped to surprise and overpower the Life Guards and provoke a general insurrection.

An effective network of informers and government agents meant that Rathbone and his seven conspirators were caught several months before they could put their plans into operation. As a precautionary measure Monck, as Captain-General of the Kingdom, ordered all old soldiers to leave the City. Hundreds of arrests were made, the Tower was reinforced, and several counter-terrorist measures were passed by Parliament, including the so-called Five Mile Act, which prevented Dissenting ministers from coming within five miles of a city or town unless they had permission. Parliament also voted to recall all Englishmen still in service with the Dutch. Anyone who refused to return would be declared a traitor. In the spring of 1666 the eight plotters were tried at the Old Bailey and found guilty of high treason. They were all executed at Tyburn on Monday 30 April.

On 1 September these events were all fresh in the memory of Londoners. As each discovered plot erupted into the public domain, its importance had been talked up by government ministers, who felt genuine anxiety over the future of the monarchy – and also understood that a threat to the status quo could create a sense of solidarity and thus help to maintain loyalty. As a body of people, Londoners were not particularly enamoured of the King. Like the country as a whole, many of them were fiercely anti-Catholic, and mistrusted the fact that Charles had a Catholic mother, Henrietta Maria, who insisted on living in France with her nephew and their enemy, Louis XIV; and a Catholic wife, Catherine of Braganza. But it was only twenty-four years since Charles I had raised his standard at Nottingham; most adults remembered the miseries of the Civil War and, perhaps more importantly, the chaos and confusion which had followed Oliver Cromwell's death in 1658. They may not have wanted monarchy, but they wanted stability; and if they thought that it was threatened they closed ranks behind the government.

And threats to the nation's stability *had* continued throughout the summer. On 1 August reports started to circulate about a mysterious figure called the Precious Man. No one knew his name or his whereabouts or even his precise intentions, but government informers said that there were 1,800 armed conspirators ready to act on his orders. Ten days later an agent in Exeter told Lord Arlington that dissidents were spreading rumours that the Queen Mother intended to bring in Popery, and that King Charles supported her. Cromwellian veterans in the south-west – influential characters who could raise 2,000 men in an hour or two – were saying that 'the good old cause will be the cause again before a year is over'.[17] By the end of August Quakers in Westmorland were advocating rebellion and stirring up anti-government support; and a group of subversives who had recently travelled to Dublin were giving cause for concern. They included a shadowy character codenamed Mene Tekel, after the words which the moving finger wrote in the plaster at Belshazzar's feast: 'Mene, Mene, Tekel, Upharsin' (Daniel 5:25). This was a favourite text among Quakers, Millenarians and Nonconformists generally, and was the title of several anti-government tracts. The authorities were also anxious to find the adventurer Captain Thomas Blood, who had tried to seize Dublin Castle in 1663, and who would kidnap and try to hang the Duke of Ormond in the centre of London in 1670, and the following year steal the Crown Jewels from the Tower.

Most Londoners were neither politically active nor politically sophisticated. They didn't live in a democracy; and when they thought about Charles and the government at all, then of course they complained, like the merchant tailor who reckoned that 'wee were made to believe when the King came in that we should never pay any more taxes', and that 'if wee had thought that he would have taxed us thus, hee should never have come in'.[18] But in general they did their best to get through life without causing any trouble. After the Civil War, the Commonwealth and the Restoration, they mistrusted anyone who wanted to turn the world upside down again and, rightly or wrongly, they subscribed to the sentiments of a song which went the rounds immediately after Charles's return from exile: 'All wise Men and Good, say it is a mischievous Fate, / A Kingdom to turn to a popular State'.[19]

As far as most people were concerned, the real threat came not from the Precious Man or Mene Tekel, but from the Hogen Mogens and their French allies. And it was very real indeed. There had been fears of invasion all summer. Early in August the captain of an English warship, the *Constant Warwick*, caused panic when he landed a press gang on the Sussex coast in the middle of the night – the locals mistook it for a French expeditionary force and fled for their lives. And the Isle of Wight had been in a state of alert for some weeks, with three foot companies of militia stationed there as a precaution after a group of Dutch engineers working in England happened to mention that the island was the most likely spot for a landing by their countrymen.

The news in August that the Dutch fleet was out again had led to renewed anxieties, and a fresh spate of rumours and defensive preparations. In the east of the country, the Lord Lieutenants of Essex, Suffolk and Norfolk were told to look to their towns and coastline; in the south, the Ordnance Commissioners were instructed to send twelve extra cannon down to Deal Castle in Kent, for the defence of the Isle of Thanet.

Joseph Williamson, Lord Arlington's Under-Secretary of State, had the job of collating intelligence as it came in from around the country. Over the three-day period from 29 August to 1 September Williamson had a flood of reports of Dutch and French activity around the English shores. On Wednesday 29th a French man-of-war sailed right into Lyme Bay and fired on the Isle of Portland, blasting a hole in the roof of a small thatched house. The following day the whole north-east coast prepared for an enemy assault, as a convoy of 300 colliers bound for London out of Newcastle was mistaken for the Dutch fleet. The garrison of Scarborough Castle was mobilised to defend the town, and further down the coast, the country people set fire to hilltop gorse all along Bridlington Bay, in the hope that it would serve as a beacon to warn those inland that the enemy was coming. On Friday at Kingsdown on the Straits of Dover – less than three miles south of the heavily fortified Deal Castle – fifty Hogens came ashore in an abortive attempt to fire and plunder the village in revenge for Holmes's bonfire. Williamson was informed that 'the rogues grow bold'.[20]

Williamson was responsible for publishing the London *Gazette*, the twice-weekly news sheet he put together using the intelligence he received from Britain and abroad. On 1 September the most recent issue, which was two days old, showed that he was very aware of the importance of propaganda in boosting confidence. Alongside the report of the Pope's imminent demise, there was a story from Ratisbon in Bavaria explaining that the Dutch envoy had gone into hiding after a plot to spread a false version of the St James's Day Fight had been exposed. The English expatriate community in Ratisbon, on the other hand, 'testifie their joy by their Bonefires, and other signes of extraordinary satisfaction'. At Flushing the plague was apparently on the increase, causing all houses of entertainment to close, which in turn had led to 'many contentions and quarrels, and oftentimes fighting and killing'. Dutch morale was now so low that it was impossible to find new recruits, and many seamen were quitting the service; in fact sailors on De Ruijter's own flagship had actually mutinied at his inept handling of the war, and could only be placated by senior officers 'raigning down Ducatoons on them'.[21]

It was not only the English who were waging a propaganda war: discussing Robert Holmes's recent exploits at Terschelling, Sir Thomas Clifford, who was with the fleet, told Lord Arlington that the burned Dutch merchantmen had been carrying 'scandalous pamphlets of their power and our weakness, which they intended to spread into all parts of the world'.[22] But Williamson was really very good at it. The current issue of the *Gazette*, for instance, closed with a long account of a recent atrocity. At the beginning of the week a Hamburg vessel had arrived in Bristol from La Rochelle, bringing with it an Englishman named Richard Williams. Williams had no tongue, and when he was brought before the local justices, he signed to them that he had been a merchant seaman on board the *Mary of London*. The *Mary* had been on its way home from Malaga when it was chased, fired on and boarded by the French. They tied the sixty-two surviving crewmen together, back to back, and tipped them overboard – all except for Williams, whose tongue they cut off close to the root with a pair of pincers before putting him ashore in France. In a masterly touch the *Gazette* declared this 'an instance of so great inhumanity, that we are not willing to believe it, with all its circumstances, even of the most Savage Enemy, and will therefore expect a further confirmation'.[23]

The conflict with Holland and France was hardly total war in the modern sense of the phrase. Trade with the enemy carried on much as it had during peacetime. Hostile nationals were not interned – Charles II's own firework-maker was a Frenchman – and prisoners-of-war were free to come and go pretty much as they wished. Two weeks after Sir Robert Holmes's bonfire, for instance, a group of Dutch prisoners who were lodging in Bristol plotted to set fire to a woodpile on Bristol quay, in the hope that it would destroy the ships in port and burn most of the town. By chance, the maid at their lodgings understood Dutch; she overheard their plans, and reported them to the authorities. Only then were they committed to prison.

Geography, technology and circumstance meant that the major set-piece battles of the war had all been fought at sea – which was one reason why the Hogens were so shocked at the firing of West-Terschelling. Until now, English civilian casualties had been largely confined to unwary fishermen who were unable to outrun Dutch sloops, or hapless merchant seamen like Richard Williams and his crewmates. In the capital, the war made itself known in unexpected ways. There were few men 'of mean sort' to be seen on the streets, either because they had been pressed into service with the navy, or because they were frightened to walk out in case they met with a press-gang. All summer long it had been difficult to find a waterman: although they were nominally exempt from the press, their knowledge of ships and sailing made them prime targets for the gangs, so they also tended to keep a low profile. There were crippled servicemen begging on the streets of London, and navy wives and widows driven to whoring by poverty and the reluctance of the Navy Office to pay sailors' wages.

Occasionally reminders of the war came uncomfortably close. During the St James's Day Fight in July, for instance, the King and the Duke of York were at divine service in the Chapel Royal at Whitehall when word was sent that the rumble of cannon could be heard nearby. Charles and his brother went out onto the bowling green which lay next door to the royal lodgings and then up onto the leads of the roof, where they stood for some time with the court listening to a distant low thunder – a sound which meant the death of men in the North Sea seventy miles away.

The Palace of Whitehall was not exactly a thing of beauty – the Frenchman Samuel Sorbière, who saw it in 1663, dismissed it as 'nothing but a heap of houses erected at divers times'[24] – and the only architectural jewel in its crown was the Banqueting House designed by Inigo Jones, which had acquired iconic significance as the scene of Charles I's execution in January 1649. But what the Palace lacked in good looks it made up for in bulk. The sprawling labyrinth of lodgings, offices and kitchens stretched for more than 250 yards from St James's Park down to terraces on the Thames, and straggled along the river for over a quarter of a mile, starting beside Westminster Palace and ending at Charing Cross and the Strand.

The medieval Palace of Westminster lay only a hundred yards or so away from the gated entrance to Whitehall, so that on those somewhat infrequent occasions when Parliament was summoned, King and Commons were within hailing distance of each other. But by an anomaly of history, neither was actually *in* the capital. Anyone riding into the City of London from Whitehall in 1666 had to travel along the Strand, past the battered tenements of the old Savoy Hospital and the elegant street façade of the Queen Mother's Somerset House (where their coach would have to negotiate the tallest maypole in England, which stood smack in the middle of the thoroughfare). From there, the route led along Fleet Street and over the narrow bridge that spanned the foul-smelling Fleet River, before climbing Ludgate Hill and finally passing through Ludgate, one of eight guarded gates in the City wall and the principal entrance from the west. Travellers had to time their arrival and departure with care: all the gates were closed and secured at ten o'clock each night.

In spite of Whitehall's separateness, its existence outside the commercial mainstream of the City, it had been at the heart of court life ever since Henry VIII had acquired it from the hapless Cardinal Wolsey in 1530, and to all intents and purposes, that meant it was at the heart of the nation's social and cultural life. It was the favourite residence of Charles II, who much preferred it to the only real alternative, St James's Palace. Charles had a regally furnished set of apartments at Whitehall overlooking a big, statue-filled formal garden, while Catherine of Braganza had separate lodgings on the river, at a convenient distance from those of her husband. The convenience was for Charles's benefit. His current mistress, Barbara Villiers, the Countess of Castlemaine, had moved into an apartment next door to his own several years previously, after the King's habit of returning alone in the early dawn from her nearby house caused even the palace guards to comment on his lack of discretion. Her lodgings had recently been refitted at vast expense.

The Duke of York also had sizeable lodgings at Whitehall, although he and his Duchess usually spent their summers at St James's Palace, where they held court with a separate establishment around 130 strong. According to one contemporary, they were 'better lodged than the king or queen'.[25] Their annual migration to the far side of St James's Park usually took place in early June; but this year the Duke had found a good reason to spend more time at Whitehall. James, who was at once a more serious character, a more religious soul and a more obsessive womaniser than his elder brother – he was described as 'the most unguarded

ogler of his time'[26] – was currently obsessed with a palace beauty:
the nineteen-year-old Margaret, Lady Denham.

Lady Denham had just married Sir John Denham, a Cavalier
and poet whose loyalty to Charles in his exile had been rewarded
with the post of Surveyor-General of the King's Works. This
placed Denham in charge of all royal building works; and the
newly-weds lived in the Surveyor's official residence in Scotland
Yard, then an important part of the Whitehall complex. Lady
Denham was happy to accept the Duke into her bed, but she
refused to creep around like a tuppenny whore, with the result
that he frequently strolled over to Scotland Yard with his entourage
in the middle of the day – when Sir John was absent, presumably. Running against the conventions of the time, the latter was
none too enthusiastic about the honour done to his wife, and
that summer he had lost his wits in spectacular fashion, bursting
into the King's chamber and announcing that he was the Holy
Ghost.

Besides the King, the Duke, their wives and their mistresses,
Whitehall was also home to the Duke of Monmouth, Charles's
illegitimate seventeen-year-old son by a previous mistress, who
lived with his new wife in an opulent set of apartments which
consisted of more than forty rooms. When he wasn't on the high
seas, Prince Rupert had lodgings on three floors next door to
the Duke of York. George Monck, Duke of Albemarle, also had
a rather splendid set of lodgings with its own presence chamber,
chapel and walled gardens, on the site of the Tudor Cockpit overlooking St James's Park. (One of Albemarle's roles, apart from
being Captain-General of the Kingdom and joint General-at-
Sea, was Chief Keeper of the Park.)

In fact an army of courtiers, officials and servants lived at
Whitehall, ranging from Sir Alexander Frazier, Physician to the
King's Person, to the Paymaster-General of the Army, Sir Stephen
Fox. Lord Arlington had his office here; so did the Earl of
Lauderdale and Sir Robert Murray, the Secretary and Deputy
Secretary of State for Scotland; the Queen's Apothecary; the King's
Barber; the Locksmith of the Household and Thomas Duppa,
who had the title of Assistant Gentleman Usher Daily Waiter. In

total, more than 1,500 rooms – including 18 kitchens and 2 shops – were set aside for lodging the royal household, its officials and their various hangers-on.

Charles was in residence at Whitehall on that September Saturday afternoon, anxiously waiting for news of his fleet. Lord Arlington, who was receiving intelligence from lookouts all round the south-east coast, was keeping him informed; and in any case a letter personally directed to His Majesty had just arrived from Rupert and Monck to say that they intended to intercept De Ruijter's ships before the Hogens had the chance to rendezvous with the French. They begged him to order provisions and rein-forcements to be on hand at Dover, Portsmouth, Dartmouth and Plymouth. 'We shall have need enough of all the strength that can be given us to contend with the united powers of both these nations,' they said; 'and if we can but be supplied, as we think we may be, we do not doubt, but to have a good day for it, and return with a good account to your Majesty of this great expedition.'[27]

At the Navy Office, which was housed in half of a large mansion on Seething Lane, just to the north-west of the Tower of London, everyone was understandably anxious about what the day might bring. The Office, and the Board members who ran it, was responsible for the administration of the navy – the repair and building of ships, the payment of seamen, the supervision of victualling and the control of the four royal dockyards at Deptford, Woolwich, Chatham and Portsmouth. In wartime, especially, this required plenty of ready money, and all too often the Treasury was unwilling or unable to supply it, leaving the Board's officials to bear the brunt of frequent complaints from Rupert and Monck.

Relations had been particularly strained over the past couple of weeks. The previous Sunday afternoon two of the principal offi-cers, the Treasurer, Sir George Carteret, and the Clerk of the Acts, Samuel Pepys, had been peremptorily summoned to Whitehall, where they were brought before a formidable Cabinet Council which gathered in the Green Chamber at the Palace. The King was there, and the Duke of York. So were the Earl of Clarendon,

Lord Chancellor and father-in-law to the Duke, along with two Navy Commissioners and the Secretaries of State for the North and the South. A letter to James from the Generals-at-Sea, anchored with the fleet in Southwold Bay, was read to the Board officers – or, more specifically, to Pepys, who effectively ran the Navy Office.

Rupert and Monck complained that Pepys had failed to send enough beer for the seamen; if more supplies weren't forthcoming, 'and that very suddenly, we shall not be in a condition to visit the Dutch coast again at this season, though we much desire it'. Moreover, in spite of repeated requests, an extra five fire ships which the Generals needed had still not turned up. 'We doubt not but your Highness hath been very careful in giving out your orders, but there hath been great neglect somewhere else, otherwise we could not thus long have been without supplies in this kind after so many weeks importunity.'[28]

Of necessity, Pepys was well used to fending off such criticism. He promised he would look into the complaint, and said the Office would do everything possible to meet the fleet's requirements. Then, like the experienced civil servant that he was, he left the room and did nothing, so that on Monday the Generals fired off an even angrier letter direct to the King – 'a most scurvy letter', Pepys wrote in his diary.[29] However, when the news came on Thursday that the Dutch had put to sea, and the fleet set sail out of Southwold to meet them, the beer still hadn't arrived. Nor had the fire ships.

The rest of Pepys's week had been spent in watching his back and helping Sir William Coventry, his mentor and Secretary to the Lord High Admiral, to respond to the Generals' complaints. He and his young wife Elizabeth lived at Seething Lane; so when he rose early on Saturday he could begin work in his office without leaving the building. He spent the morning there, before returning home for his midday meal and then supervising preparations for the following day, when he had guests arriving. Pepys often had company for Sunday dinner, and at the moment he was particularly keen to show off a new closet which had been decorated (in purple) only that week. An acquaintance named Moone, who was secretary to Lord Belasyse, a prominent Catholic courtier and Governor of Tangier, was coming expressly to view it.★ The other guests were to be William Wood, the son of a wealthy mast-maker and timber merchant, and his new bride Barbara, whose uncle William Sheldon was Clerk of the Cheque at Woolwich.

While the closet was being 'made mighty clean against tomorrow',[30] Pepys took the rest of Saturday off and went up to Moorfields, just north of the City wall. He was accompanied by Elizabeth, her waiting-woman Mary Mercer and Sir William Penn, one of the Navy Commissioners. Their object was to see *Polichinello*, the popular Italian puppet-play and direct ancestor of Punch and Judy; and it must have been good, because Pepys had already seen it twice in the past ten days. So had Elizabeth.

Perhaps the Clerk of the Acts to the Navy Board left his office at this crucial moment in the nation's naval history because he needed to take his mind off the events unfolding in the English Channel. Whatever the reason, he certainly did not want word of his truancy to get back to Whitehall: he and Sir William were 'horribly frighted' to see a member of the Duke of York's house-hold, Henry Killigrew, come into the playhouse with a group of friends. 'But we hid ourselves, so as we think they did not see us.'[31] After Killigrew had left, the foursome went drinking in Islington and sang all the way home.

Early on Saturday afternoon the inhabitants of Dover heard the roar of a massive explosion out at sea towards the French coast. It was so violent that the buildings in the town shivered as if there had been an earth tremor. The story immediately went round that one of the Dutch flagships had fallen behind the rest of the fleet and suddenly blown up without warning; and the news was duly sent up to London by post-horse. The Dutch always denied that they lost a ship in this fashion, and no one ever did find out what caused the explosion. But watchers all along the south-east coast

★On top of his duties at the Navy Office, Pepys was Treasurer to the Committee for Tangier, which had been ceded to England by Portugal in 1661 under the terms of Charles II's marriage treaty with Catherine of Braganza. The post was a lucrative one, and Pepys was eager to keep in with Belasyse.

were put on the alert for signs of battle, and very soon a lookout posted on the battlements of Dover Castle caught sight of De Ruijter's ships on the French side of the Straits, with Rupert and Monck bearing down on them from the north-east as fast as they could. At four in the afternoon, while Samuel and Elizabeth Pepys were laughing at Punchinello's antics in Moorfields, while the stalls in Leadenhall and the Greenyard were shutting up for the day, while news of the strange vision at Middleburg was on its way to Whitehall, the English battle fleet finally closed on the enemy.

Eighty-one Dutch ships were lying at anchor in St John's Road, south of Cape Gris Nez and halfway between Calais and Boulogne. As soon as they saw the English approaching, they got under sail and stood for Boulogne, where they hauled in close to the shore in the hope that the north-easterly winds, which were gathering strength by the minute, would carry the enemy past them and give them the windward station. Having the weather gage, as this was called, was vitally important in battle, since it was so much easier to bear down on the enemy than to move upwind to meet them; although in fierce weather there were definite disadvantages. When a ship with the weather gage prepared to fire a broadside at an opponent, it was often unable to bring its lower tier of guns to bear, because the wind made it list to one side and there was a risk that water would pour in through the hatches.

The Red Squadron, with Rupert and Monck in the *Royal Charles* supported by Vice-Admiral Sir Joseph Jordan and Holmes, was now in the van. The Generals decided sensibly to wait while the rest of the English ships caught up. Naval warfare in the seventeenth century was a stately, terrible business, and by six o'clock that evening the two fleets were still manoeuvring for position, with the English trying to get between the Dutch ships and the French shore, thus driving the enemy to seaward; and the Dutch hugging the shoreline and trying to maintain their advantage. Then De Ruijter raised the red flag of defiance on his mizzen masthead, indicating that he was ready for battle. Rupert and Monck did the same. The signal went up for the fire ships to move in among the Dutch.

But the weather didn't favour a fight. The winds had been strong all afternoon, and by now they were approaching gale force.

It was impossible to prevent the little fire ships from careering around and taking in far too much water, so they were recalled. As the English milled about in the crashing seas, disaster struck. The 58-gun *York* suddenly lost its mainmast in the gale and broke off the engagement. It was followed by the 50-gun *West Friesland*.

Daring his enemy to fight, De Ruijter moved out into open sea to fire on two English vessels, the *Assurance* and the *Guinea*, before tacking to rejoin his main fleet in the shelter of the shore. That was enough: as he turned, Sir Robert Holmes in the *Henry* went after him, followed by Sir Thomas Tyddiman, Vice-Admiral of the White.

All of a sudden the full force of the storm hit, and hell broke loose among the English vessels without the Dutch having to fire another shot. As Rupert and Monck tried to follow Holmes into battle, the *Royal Charles* lost a topsail; its sailors struggled desperately to hoist another, only for that to blow into pieces while it was half-mast high. Tyddiman also lost his fore topsail; the *Plymouth* lost two sails, which blew off and flew away together. The *Dover* lost its foremast, bowsprit and main topmast; while Sir Thomas Allin in the *Royal James*, one of the finest ships in the navy, had four sails torn to shreds. The main body of the English fleet could do nothing without running the risk of colliding with each other. In more than twenty-five years at sea, wrote Allin in his journal that night, 'I never saw the like'.[32]

Holmes wouldn't give up the chase, even though his comrades were now running for the shelter of the English coast. The *Henry* continued after De Ruijter, and its crew tried desperately to bring their guns to bear in the towering seas. On the crowded deck of the *Royal Charles*, the Generals struck their flag of defiance and fired a signal gun ordering Holmes to break off the engagement, 'it being impossible for us to do the enemy any damage, having work enough to keep our sails to the yards and our masts standing.'[33] Only then did he reluctantly turn for home.

The battle which was to have ended Dutch naval ambitions once and for all had exploded into chaos; and the scattered and demoralised English navy was blown westward, past Dungeness and Fairlight, towards the safe haven of St Helen's Point on the Isle of Wight, taking small consolation from the fact that they had left the Dutch to the storm, 'which was able to do them greater mischief than we could'.[34]

Late that night, the gales crossed the Channel. They began to move across south-east England, reaching London in the early hours of Sunday morning. And as they swept through the capital, toppling chimneys and lifting thatch, a fire broke out on the ground floor of a baker's house in Pudding Lane.

3

God's Bellows

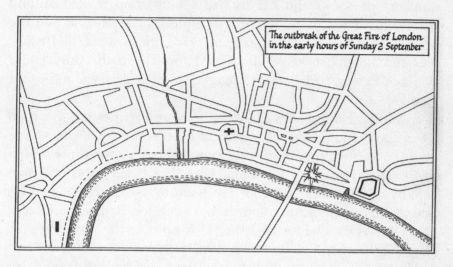

The outbreak of the Great Fire of London in the early hours of Sunday 2 September

fterwards, Thomas Farriner was always quite clear about one thing. The events of that Saturday night were not his fault.

Farriner was an ordinary tradesman. His main source of income was a contract to produce ship's biscuit, an unleavened bread which was baked, sliced and then oven-dried. His client was the Navy's Victualling Office, which is why he was occasionally referred to in contemporary accounts of the Fire as 'the King's baker'; and his premises were on Pudding Lane, a narrow thoroughfare less than 100 yards long which ran north-to-south from the meat markets and butchers' stalls of Little Eastcheap down to Thames Street with its riverside wharves and warehouses. The parish church, St Margaret Fish Street, had been the site of a large fish market in the Middle Ages – a 1311 ordinance required French lampreys to be set out for sale under its walls immediately on their arrival in England – and according to John Stow, whose famous *Survey of London* first appeared in 1598, Pudding

Lane had acquired its name because the Eastcheap butchers had a scalding-house for hogs there, 'and their puddings, with other filth of beasts, are voided down that way to their dung boats on the Thames'.[1] 'Pudding' is a medieval word for entrails or bowels.

The area also had a more appetising reputation. Over the years, numbers of cooks and bakers had set up shop in and around Eastcheap, drawn there by the easy supply of fresh meat and the proximity of the Victualling Office near Little Tower Hill. Breads, pies and hot meats were all offered for sale to the public, and traders 'cried hot ribs of beef roasted, pies well baked, and other victuals'.[2]

As well as baking hard tack for the navy, Farriner ran just such a business, making and selling bread (few households baked their own), and cooking both his own pies and pasties and those which had been prepared by his neighbours. His bakery was less than halfway up Pudding Lane; it lay behind the Star Inn on Fish Street, the main northern approach to London Bridge, which ran more or less parallel to the lane. He lived over the shop with his daughter Hanna, a maid and a manservant.

Thomas Farriner closed for business at the usual time on Saturday evening, around eight or nine at night. His oven was probably of the beehive type, a brick structure which was brought up to temperature by laying bundles of faggots directly on its floor and kindling them with a light from the bakehouse hearth. The faggots were raked out when the baker judged the oven to be hot enough; loaves were baked when it was at its hottest, and then as it cooled down their place was taken by pies and pasties.

So the oven should have been virtually cold by now. Thomas checked it and filled it with faggots ready for the morning. He prepared several pots of baked meat for Sunday dinner, raked up the coals in the hearth and went to bed. A couple of flitches of bacon were left beside the oven.

Hanna checked on the bakehouse around midnight, when she also took a last look round the house to make sure all was well. Then she too went to bed.

About an hour later the Farriners' manservant woke up. Smoke filled the ground floor of the bakery, and he could hardly breathe with the fumes. But he managed to climb the stairs and rouse Thomas, Hanna and the maid. Only now there was no way down, and the four found themselves trapped on the upper floor.

Someone, either Thomas or his manservant, hit on the idea of clambering out of one of the upstairs windows, crawling along the guttering and climbing back in through their neighbour's window. They were shouting as loud as they could to raise the alarm:

> And now the doleful, dreadful, hideous Note
> Of FIRE, is screem'd out with a deep-strain'd throat;
> Horror, and fear, and sad distracted Cryes,
> Chide Sloth away, and bids the Sluggard rise;
> Most direful Exclamations are let fly
> From every Tongue, Tears stand in every Eye.[3]

At some point Hanna was badly burned. But she managed to scramble to safety along the eaves with her father. They were followed by the manservant. Only the maid was left in the house, too frightened of heights, or too confused by the noise and the smoke to escape. As the easterly gales whipped across the rooftops, she died there – the first victim of the Great Fire of London. No one even knows her name.

Like most London streets, the houses in Pudding Lane were timber-framed and linked so that two haphazard terraces faced each other, almost touching eaves in the centre of the lane where their upper storeys had been jettied out. People were hardly alert: the early hours of Sunday morning were a time when, as one contemporary put it, 'Slothfulness and the Heat of the Bed have riveted a Man to his Pillow, and made him almost incapable of waking, much less of acting and helping his Neighbours.'[4] But community action was the normal and expected response to an accident of this sort, and the neighbours did stir themselves, roused by the Farriners' cries – and, in one case at least, by their abrupt arrival through a bedroom window. They threw on clothes and ran out into the street to see what was happening. Within minutes, there must have been dozens of anxious and bleary-eyed people milling around in the driving wind, shouting to make themselves heard over the crackling flames and using whatever came to hand to extinguish the blaze: buckets of water; shovelfuls of earth and dung; milk, beer and urine.

For nearly an hour, it looked as if the blaze could easily be confined to the bakery, with minor damage to the homes on either side. As a precaution, neighbours began to bundle up their valuables and drag them out into the street; the summer had been extraordinarily hot and there had been little rain, so that the timber and plaster were very dry, and the wind was obviously fanning the flames. The parish constables arrived, and decided that the situation warranted the presence of the Lord Mayor. As chief magistrate of the City it was Sir Thomas Bludworth's job to authorise any radical measures involving citizens' property; and the constables, uneasy at the speed with which the flames were consuming Farriner's bakery, were looking for permission to override the wishes of neighbours and pull down buildings in the street, so as to prevent the spread of the fire.

But Bludworth, whose success in City politics was due to his Royalist sympathies rather than any innate ability, was a weak man. Although he was coming to the end of his year in office, he didn't have the experience, the leadership skills or the natural authority to take command of the situation. True, he was prompt to arrive on the scene; but what he saw there – the raging fire, the chaos and confusion and heat and noise that always accompany such accidents – terrified him. As the fire moved from the bakery to the adjoining houses, creeping along the lane towards the warehouses of Thames Street, more level-headed men among the firefighters wanted to form firebreaks by demolishing several untouched houses. But Bludworth simply said that he dared not do it without the consent of the owners. Most of the shops and homes were rented, so those owners were God knew where. Not in Pudding Lane, for sure.

Pressed to reconsider, Sir Thomas took refuge in bluster. The fire wasn't all that serious, he said. 'A woman could piss it out.' And with that he went home to bed and a place in the history books.

1. Hell breaks loose on the capital of England in this nightmarish *Allegory of London* by a follower of Jan II Breughel. The painting in the foreground shows the execution of Charles I, while the City burns in the distance.

2. Buckets and fire-hooks being used to fight a fire at Tiverton in Devon in 1612.

3. Seventeenth-century fire engines in action. At the time of the Great Fire, hoses like those shown here were still a thing of the future.

4. Samuel Pepys.

5. George Monck, 1st Duke of Albemarle.

6. Charles II.

7. James, Duke of York.

Parliament House the Hall the Abby

8. Westminster from the Thames, with (*from left to right*) the Parliament House, Westminster Hall and the Abbey (Wenceslaus Hollar).

9. The river frontage of the Palace of Whitehall (Wenceslaus Hollar). The complex is dominated by Inigo Jones's Banqueting Hall, one of the most admired buildings in England in the 1660s.

SIR CHR: WREN.
Late Surveyor General of
the Royal Buildings .
He died the 2ª of Feb. 1722 aged 91.

10. Sir Christopher Wren, painted in 1711 by Sir Godfrey Kneller.
A plan of St Paul's Cathedral is draped over the table.

11. The Royal Exchange on Cornhill, London's cathedral of commerce and the retail hub of the City (Wenceslaus Hollar).

12. Wenceslaus Hollar's panorama of London before the Great Fire.

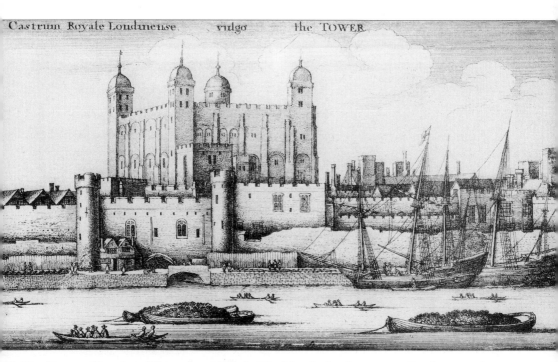

13. The Tower of London (Wenceslaus Hollar). Climbing its battlements on Sunday morning, Pepys first understood the true scale of the fire.

14. *The Great Fire of London*, print after Lieve Verschuier (1630–86).
Contemporary Dutch artists tended to focus on the apocalyptic nature of the disaster
which had befallen their enemy. Although one or two may have witnessed the Fire,
most simply adapted published engravings of London.

15. *The Great Fire of London* by Waggoner (seventeenth century).

Bludworth wasn't alone. In Seething Lane, seven streets away, Samuel and Elizabeth Pepys were woken abruptly at 3 a.m. by their favourite maid, Jane Birch. The servants had stayed up late to prepare for the dinner which the couple were giving that day; as Jane was going to bed she happened to look out of her window and catch sight of an unmistakable glow in the west. As soon as she told him that there was a fire, Samuel leaped out of bed, threw on his dressing-gown and followed Jane to her chamber. The blaze seemed close – just beyond the next street, in fact. But sights like that were not uncommon, and Samuel decided there was nothing to worry about. Like Sir Thomas Bludworth, he shrugged and went back to bed.

When he got up four hours later, the fire seemed further away. He also thought, presumably because the daylight took away from the drama, that it was 'not so much as it was'. Jane soon disabused him; she had heard that 'above 300 houses have been burned down tonight by the fire we saw, and that it was now burning down all Fishstreet by London Bridge'.[5]

Feeling anxious, Samuel left the Navy Office in Seething Lane and walked the hundred yards or so to the Tower of London. The Lieutenant of the Tower, Alderman Sir John Robinson, was an old acquaintance (although not a friend – Pepys thought him a fool, a glutton and 'a talking bragging Bufflehead');[6] and accompanied by Robinson's little son, he climbed to the battlements and surveyed the scene.

What he saw appalled him. Thanks to Bludworth, an ordinary house-fire had turned into a street-fire; and that street-fire now threatened to engulf the entire south-eastern corner of the City. During the night the easterly gale carried sparks and burning embers from the bakery across into Fish Street, where they ignited hay in the yard of the Star Inn. The trail of destruction had crept down Fish Street Hill, destroying St Margaret's and the neighbouring church of St Magnus the Martyr, which had presided over the northern end of London Bridge since before the Norman Conquest. Worse, it had reached Thames Street, where it found the wharves and met 'nothing but old paper buildings and the most combustible matter of Tarr, Pitch, Hemp, Rosen, and Flax which was all layd up thereabouts'.[7] Now the houses which lined the bridge itself were in flames.

Pepys spent a few moments talking to Sir John, who told him where the fire had started and how fast it was moving. Then he decided to see for himself at close quarters, and hired a boat to take him upriver, through the piers of the bridge.

What Samuel saw was worse – much worse – than the prospect of smoke and flames and burning streets that the battlements of the Tower had offered. About a quarter of a mile of the north bank of the river was on fire. Lighters and small boats were clustering round the stairs at Old Swan Lane beside the bridge while everyone in the neighbourhood frantically tried to save their goods from the flames which marched from house to house, and street to street. They threw their belongings into the waiting boats or, if there were no boats at hand, into the river itself. As the fire took hold, the pigeons which Londoners kept for food fluttered over their burning homes, hovering at balconies and windows until the flames singed their wings and they fluttered down to their deaths.

As Pepys watched, flames suddenly appeared at the very top of the steeple of St Laurence Pountney, one of the tallest landmarks in this part of the City. The fire 'appearing first at the top discovered itself with so much terror, as if taking a view from that lofty place of what it intended to devour'.[8] Within minutes it had caught hold, and the burning spire toppled over and crashed down into the street.

Pepys decided he had to get to Whitehall. He must see the King.

In a society where most houses were timber-framed, in an age when every home had several open fires and every chamber was lit by naked flame, house-fires were not unusual. Like anyone else, Londoners sometimes set candles under shelves, or left them burning near their beds when they fell asleep, or neglected to fix them securely in their candlesticks; they used rush lights to peer under beds for chamber pots, and aired their clothes by hanging them too close to the fire, and put hot pots and pans

46

on flammable surfaces. Even the King himself was not immune to danger. There was a minor blaze at Whitehall in 1661; another in 1662, when a gale caused the Palace to catch fire four times in a single night; and yet another – this time in the lodgings of the King's mistress, the Countess of Castlemaine – in January 1664.

Nor was it that unusual for a fire to consume streets or even entire districts before it was finally brought under control. Over the course of the seventeenth century, English towns suffered at least twenty major disasters in which fire destroyed more than one hundred houses.[9] In August 1613, for example, around half of Dorchester, the county town of Dorset, was burned to the ground after a chandler accidentally set light to some tallow. The previous year Tiverton in Devon had been laid waste by fire; in 1628 a third of the houses in Banbury, Northamptonshire, were destroyed by flames; in October 1644, 300 houses in Oxford. Like the fire in Farriner's bakery, the disasters at Tiverton, Banbury and Oxford all began on a Sunday, affording Puritan preachers plenty of scope for speculation on wickedness and divine wrath.

The capital, though, had known nothing on this scale since 1212, when fire devastated housing north and south of London Bridge and trapped a large number of people on the bridge itself. (According to one account,* thousands were killed – four centuries later the disaster was still known as 'the Great Fire of London'.) But it had seen its fair share of smaller fires, the most serious of which occurred in February 1633, when a servant left a bucket of hot ashes underneath a staircase in one of the houses at the northern end of London Bridge. The resulting blaze spread up Fish Street Hill and destroyed around eighty buildings in the parish of St Magnus the Martyr.

---

*'Three thousand bodies, some half-burnt, were found in the river Thames: besides those who perished altogether by fire. It broke out on the south side of the Bridge. Multitudes of people rushed to the rescue of the inhabitants of houses on the bridge, and while thus engaged the fire broke out on the north side also, and hemmed them in, making a holocaust of those who were not killed by leaping into the Thames' (John Timbs, *Curiosities of London* [n.d.], 340).

Fatalities were often surprisingly low. An old woman named Cicely Bingham was the only casualty in the 1613 fire that left Jacobean Dorchester 'a heap of ashes for travellers to sigh at'.[10] And when a house in Lothbury – then fast becoming a wealthy merchant quarter of the City – burned to the ground in December 1662, people thought it remarkable that all seven occupants (one of whom was the daughter of the current Lord Mayor) were killed, 'not one thing, dog nor cat, escaping; nor any of the neighbours almost hearing of it till the house was quite down and burnt. How this should come to pass, God knows, but a most strange thing it is!'[11]

There was no fire brigade to call, no police. No emergency services at all, in fact. But there were still procedures for dealing with fires and, if they seemed haphazard, even chaotic, they were usually effective.

So when fire broke out in the City, several things were supposed to happen. The alarm was raised in the street and adjoining homes were evacuated, their occupants grabbing their most precious possessions and bundling them up or, if the fire was moving fast, simply throwing them out of doors and windows. The church bells were 'rung backwards' – that is, with a muffled peal – to call public-spirited citizens to action; and the parish constables and other responsible figures moved quickly to block off both ends of the affected street, 'that the rude people may be kept from doing mischief for sometime they do more harm than fire'.[12]

In theory, all streets and lanes leading to the Thames were to be manned by double rows of firefighters, with one human chain passing empty buckets down to the river, and the other passing full buckets back up to the fire. Anyone on higher ground was supposed to throw down water as quickly as they could in the hope that it would run towards the site of the fire, where those on the front line could sweep it towards the flames.

The supply of water was crucial. There were waterwheels under the northern end of London Bridge, installed in 1581 by a Dutchman, Pieter Morice. When the tide was right they pumped water up to a tower at Cornhill, the highest point in the City;

from there a system of elm pipes and lead quills supplied the houses round about. (Morice apparently demonstrated how effective his system was by shooting a jet of water right over the tower of St Magnus the Martyr.) And in 1609 the New River Company had established a reservoir in Islington, bringing in spring water from Hertfordshire, thirty-eight miles away. The Islington Water House, as it was known, supplied around 30,000 homes in the City through its network of pipes. In the event of a fire it was often possible to open a pipe next to the house that was burning, and either plug a second pipe into it like a hose, to play on the flames, or use it to fill buckets.

The bucket wasn't the only piece of equipment available. Most parishes kept long ladders in their church towers specifically for use in fighting fires. These towers also often housed at least one fire-hook – a heavy pole, perhaps thirty feet long, which needed two or three men to carry and manoeuvre it. (It was sometimes mounted on a wheeled carriage rather like a bier.) There was a sturdy iron hook and ring at one end, and a second ring fixed halfway down. The idea was to use the hook like a grappling iron to grab the timber frame of a burning building or its neighbour downwind; then, using ropes attached to the two rings, firefighters could pull the building down.

Many parishes also carried scoops – iron shovels that were used to scoop water or earth and hurl it over the fire – and squirts. A squirt was shaped like a big syringe with two handles. Made of brass or wood, it held four pints of water, and needed two or three men to work it. (A modern diesel pump supplied from a hydrant delivers more than 33 gallons per second, thus depositing those 4 pints of water onto a fire in 0.015 of a second.) Its nozzle was dunked into a pond, or a tub of water, and the piston was pulled out; then it was pointed at the fire and the piston was pushed in. More sophisticated models were mounted on frames and pivoted, so that they could be dipped into the water and then pointed up at the fire more easily: they were used in London as early as 1584, when, decked with garlands, they led the Lord Mayor's procession to Westminster and squirted water into the crowd, forcing it to give way.[13]

The City authorities advised that 'every parish should have hooks ladders squirts buckets and scoops in readiness on every occasion'.[14] But the most impressive weapon in the Restoration firefighter's armoury was a more elaborate and more recent invention – the carriage-mounted pump, or fire engine.

The fire engine first arrived in England in about 1625, when Roger Jones was granted a patent to produce an 'Engine or Instrument artificiallie wrought with scrues and other devices made of Copper or brasse or other metall for the casting of water'.[15] The idea had surfaced in Nuremberg a decade or so earlier, and the first English engine was much the same as its German counterpart: a single-acting force pump with a vertical cylinder, connected to a short delivery pipe made of brass. (Hoses of canvas or leather didn't appear until 1690.) The pump was worked by long handles at the front and back of the engine, and the whole thing was fixed to a strong enclosed frame – which doubled as a water reservoir – and was mounted on a wheelless sled. The patent claimed that ten men working the engine could quench a fire with more ease and speed than 500 using buckets and ladders, thus saving lives and preserving property which would otherwise have to be pulled down to prevent the spread of the flames.

Roger Jones died of plague within months of the patent being granted, and a Lothbury founder named William Burroughs took up the idea; between the late 1620s and the early 1660s Burroughs made about sixty engines 'for City and Country', at a price of £35 each.[16] They were used at the London Bridge fire of 1633, and again four years later in a blaze at the Earl of Arundel's house on the Strand. As a result the Lord Mayor was urged to see that 'the great parishes should provide themselves with engines and the lesser ones should join together in providing them';[17] and in 1642 he asked each of the major City Companies to supply a fire engine for the public good. At least two – the Goldsmiths and the Ironmongers – obliged. A few years later the lawyers of both the Inner Temple and the Middle Temple had engines of their own, and several were also kept in Scotland Yard, ready to fight a serious fire in the Palace of Whitehall. The best was generally reckoned to be the engine kept in the church of St James Clerken-well, conveniently near to the New River Company's Water House and reservoirs; it was run a close second by a newer engine at St Bride Fleet Street.

So with all this equipment, all these procedures and preparations for managing disaster, what went wrong? Because it was clear by mid-morning on Sunday that things *had* gone wrong, very wrong indeed; a small fire in a baker's shop had already turned into something more frightening. Sir Edward Atkyns, a lawyer living at Lincoln's Inn to the west of the City boundary, was in church when his devotions were interrupted by shouting in the street outside; the story of how the spire of St Laurence Pountney mysteriously caught fire before the flames in Pudding Lane reached it had spread to the Inns of Court, and people were running up and down, screaming that the Dutch and the French 'were in armes, & had fired ye Citty'.[18]

The minister immediately abandoned his service and dismissed the congregation, but Atkyns decided that he was so far from the centre of trouble that there was really nothing to worry about. Further off still, young William Taswell was listening to a sermon in Westminster Abbey when he became aware of a commotion outside. People were running about 'in a seeming disquietude and consternation'. Someone yelled that London was burning; the cry was taken up by others; and Taswell immediately forgot the preacher and dashed out of the Abbey, down to Parliament Steps, where 'I soon perceived four boats crowded with objects of distress. These had escaped from the fire scarce under any covering except that of a blanket.'[19]

The fire engines obviously hadn't helped much in Pudding Lane or down by the wharves on Thames Street. But, judging from contemporary accounts, they were more used to travelling hopefully than arriving. The three engines brought up to combat the London Bridge fire of 1633 had had no impact: 'they were all broken for the tide was very low that they c^d get no water – and the pipes which were cut yielded but little'.[20] And although at the Arundel House fire in 1637 'the good use of the engines for spouting water manifestly appeared', they didn't actually make any difference, because they were so cumbersome and had to come from so far away that none of them arrived until it was too late.

History repeated itself in Pudding Lane. Massively heavy and fixed on sleds, each engine required twenty-eight men or a team of eight horses to move it. Very few streets were paved; most were cobbled, and so narrow that any obstruction – a cart, a crowd – brought progress to an abrupt halt. Even at the best of times, traffic jams were commonplace and entire districts were often brought to a gridlocked standstill for hours at a time. This morning, with panic mounting and hundreds of households on the move all along Thames Street, the task of manoeuvring these leviathans through the lanes and alleys around Fish Street was well-nigh impossible.

By the time the engines *did* arrive, the flames were so fierce that without any delivery hoses they couldn't get close enough to the seat of the fire to be of any use. In fact they couldn't even get into Pudding Lane – it was so narrow that firefighters were unable to maintain a safe distance from the buildings on the western side, where Farriner's bakery lay. Even if they had, the waterwheels under London Bridge were burning, so the water supply for that part of the City had dried up. As gangs of men tried desperately to manoeuvre right up to the river bank so that they could fill their reservoirs, several pumps were lost, including the famous Clerkenwell fire engine, which had been dragged right across the City only to topple into the Thames.

But it wasn't just the engines' failure to perform which allowed the fire to spread so dramatically. The easterly gales of Saturday night were still blowing hard across south-east England: 'the fire gets mastery, and burns dreadfully; and God with his great bellows blows upon it'.[21] Coupled with the effects of the long, tinder-dry summer and the failure of the water supply, the efficiency with which God's bellows fanned the flames took everyone by surprise. And Bludworth's failure of nerve was crucial. As the sun rose on Sunday morning, he could still have authorised the demolition of houses in Fish Street and Pudding Lane. If he had, the history of London would have been quite different.

Fresh from watching the collapse of St Laurence Pountney, Pepys reached Whitehall and went straight to the Chapel Royal, a few yards from his landing place at Whitehall Stairs. Courtiers crowded round him as he told of the chaos he had seen along Thames Street; within minutes the King had been informed and Pepys was brought before him and the Duke. Both men were 'much troubled' by the news. Charles expressly told Pepys to go back to Bludworth and command him to begin pulling down houses; James said that the Life Guards, many of whom were billeted in and around Whitehall, were available to help fight the fire if the Mayor wanted them. Arlington repeated this offer to him as he was leaving, 'as a great secret'.[22] The ordering of troops into the City was a sensitive issue.

Pepys borrowed a coach to take him back into the City. It got as far as St Paul's Cathedral before the crowded streets forced him to walk. Organised attempts to put out the fire had been all but abandoned; everyone was frantic to save themselves and their goods. They carried their possessions on wagons, in handcarts, on their backs. The sick were hauled through the crowded streets, still in their beds. Those of the City's 109 parish churches which were not directly threatened were filling rapidly – not with Sunday worshippers, but with furniture and valuables, as merchants, tradesmen and ordinary householders turned them into warehouses.

Pepys found Bludworth in Cannon Street, between St Paul's and the river. The Mayor was distracted by the effort of trying – and failing – to coordinate the firefighting operation. With a handkerchief round his neck he was close to collapse, 'like a fainting woman'. His response to the King's message was to cry, 'Lord, what can I do? I am spent! People will not obey me. I have been pulling down houses. But the fire overtakes us faster then we can do it.'[23] But anxious to retain some semblance of dignity and civic authority, he was reluctant to take up the Duke of York's offer of soldiers; there was no need for that, he said. And he was exhausted: he needed to go home. So he did.

Pepys also went home. It was now midday, and he got back to Seething Lane to find his dinner guests waiting for him.

All things considered, the meal wasn't quite the disaster it might have been. True, it was interrupted at one point by the arrival of a neighbour looking for news of mutual friends whose Fish Street homes had been destroyed early that morning. But on the positive side, Barbara Sheldon's new husband William seemed a decent enough chap; and if circumstances made it inappropriate for Pepys to show off his new closet to Mr Moone, at least 'we had an extraordinary good dinner, and as merry as at this time we could be'.[24]

But the party quickly broke up; and Pepys walked Moone back to St Paul's. The eastern end of Cannon Street was on fire now, and the rapid spread of the flames was continuing to take people by surprise. Goods were evacuated to 'safe' houses which were streets away from the flames, only to be moved again and again as the fire came closer.

At some point in the afternoon Sir Edward Atkyns wandered out of his Lincoln's Inn lodgings and into the Temple Garden. He wasn't as sanguine as he had been that morning: the distance between the fire and the Inns of Court was noticeably decreased. 'The wind being high,' he wrote to his brother, 'it grew very formidable, and wee began to thinke of its nearer approach.'[25] Great flakes of flame were blowing everywhere, stinging the face and burning the clothes. As far away as Westminster, William Taswell could see them flash up into the air and fly for hundreds of yards before they landed 'and uniting themselves to various dry substances, set on fire houses very remote from each other in point of situation'.[26]

The King sailed down from Whitehall with the Duke in the royal barge to view the destruction. Both men were convinced that demolishing houses to isolate the fire was the only possible way to prevent its spread. And in spite of Bludworth's protestations, that still wasn't happening. They disembarked at Queenhithe, the old quay on Thames Street which was now on the front line of the firefighting operations, and called not for Bludworth but for Alderman Sir Richard Browne. Browne had been both Lord Mayor and an MP for the City in the past; but more importantly, he had a great reputation in London as a military leader, directing trained bands during the Civil War and, during his Mayoralty in 1661, commanding the operation which had put down Thomas Venner's Fifth Monarchist rising.

In a risky move which showed how seriously he viewed the situation, Charles overrode the Lord Mayor's authority as chief magistrate and told Browne to pull down buildings, concentrating on the area below London Bridge towards the Tower, where the presence of large quantities of gunpowder was making everyone nervous. He also ignored Bludworth's refusal to ask for troops. The sixty-year-old Earl of Craven, a Lord Mayor's son and a professional soldier with a string of battle honours stretching back to service with Maurice of Orange in the early 1620s, was ordered into the City with his regiment of Coldstream Guards 'to be more particularly assisting to the Lord Mayor and Magistrates . . . [and] to be helpful by what ways they could in so great a calamity'.[27]

The King and the Duke hoped to contain the fire along the waterfront by halting its slow spread eastward at St Botolph's Wharf, which lay between Pudding Lane and the Tower; and making a stand against its much faster westward movement at Three Cranes Stairs, a public landing stage about 600 yards upriver. But though the wharves and storehouses along Thames Street had initially fuelled the fire, for the most part confining its spread to the waterfront, the wind was now veering erratically both north and south, pushing the flames up into the centre of the City in a broad, bow-shaped arc. They snaked up to the top of Fish Street Hill, through the meat markets of Eastcheap and along into Cannon Street. 'The time of London's fall is come; the fire hath received its commission from God to burn down the city, and therefore all attempts to hinder it are in vain.'[28]

As dusk came on, the moonlit sky over the south-eastern quarter of the City remained bright and yellow, 'in a most horrid malicious bloody flame, not like the fine flame of an ordinary fire'.[29] The blaze seemed to acquire a malevolent life of its own: no matter what men did to extinguish it, it immediately recovered.

'It leaps, and mounts, and makes the more furious onset, drives back its opposers, snatcheth their weapons out of their hands, seizeth upon the water-houses and engines, burns them, spoils them, and makes them unfit for service.'[30]

In the eighteen hours or so since the fire had broken out at Farriner's, it had destroyed twenty-two alleys and wharves, nearly a thousand homes and shops, and six Livery Company Halls, including those of the Vintners, the Watermen and the powerful Fishmongers, whose Hall had been bequeathed to the Company in 1434. Nine churches were in ruins along with the parishes they served: as well as St Margaret Fish Street, St Magnus the Martyr and St Laurence Pountney, St Botolph Billingsgate had gone. So had All Hallows the Great and All Hallows the Less, two medieval churches which stood almost side by side just south of a section of Thames Street known as the Ropery, because ropes were traditionally made and sold in the high street there. They were also just north of one of the City's biggest hay wharves, a fact which ensured their destruction. Other casualties were St Mary Bothaw, where London's first mayor, Henry Fitz Ailwyn, was buried in 1212; St Martin Vintry, 'beautifully glazed' in the fifteenth century, according to Stow; and St Michael Crooked Lane, the last resting place of another famous Lord Mayor – William Walworth, who preferred to stab rebel leader Wat Tyler rather than negotiate with him and thus brought the Peasants' Revolt of 1381 to an abrupt end. Of those nine churches, six were lost for ever: only All Hallows the Great, St Magnus and St Michael would be rebuilt. No one knew it then, of course, but already London was irrevocably changed.

During the evening, the well-to-do whose homes and livelihoods were not directly affected began to gather across the river in Southwark. They listened to the roars and groans as buildings tumbled. They watched the pyrotechnics lighting up the night sky and eating into the metropolis.

Pepys, who had gone back to Whitehall in the afternoon, met up with his wife in St James's Park, and together they took a boat downriver, ending up in an alehouse on Bankside, just across from Three Cranes Stairs. As the darkness grew, through the smoke they could make out burning steeples and rivulets of flame which criss-crossed the City until they met in one massive arch of fire a mile long.

Samuel broke down and cried for his city.

4

A Universal Conclusion

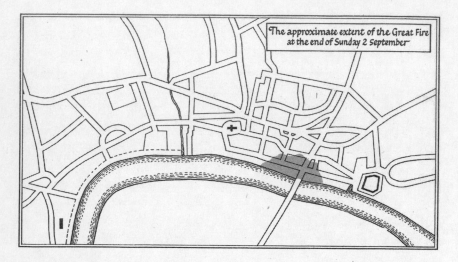

The approximate extent of the Great Fire at the end of Sunday 2 September

*T*he Earl of Clarendon later pinpointed Monday morning as the time when almost everybody began to suspect that the disaster was no accident. The day produced 'first a jealousy,' he wrote, 'and then an universal conclusion, that this fire came not by chance'.[1]

In fact, suspicions had already been roused the previous day. For two or three hours on Sunday afternoon Thomas Middleton, a surgeon living in the parish of St Bride Fleet Street, had stood at the top of a church steeple near the Three Cranes and watched as fire broke out in one house, then another and another some distance away. 'These and such like observations begat in me a persuasion that the fire was maintained by design,' he said;[2] and by that evening the theory that Sir Edward Atkyns had heard in church – that the Dutch had struck back in revenge for Sir Robert Holmes's bonfire – was spreading faster than the flames. The trained bands were out on the streets looking for suspicious characters rather than fighting the fire. The Pudding Lane bakery, it was said, belonged to a Dutch rogue who had fired it deliberately. Now there were rumours that all over London his countrymen had followed his lead, assisted by the French, and that 'fireballs were thrown into houses by several of them, to help on and provoke the too furious flames'.[3] This in itself was enough to provoke a wave of xenophobic violence. William Taswell saw a mob looting the shop of a French painter: the rioters stripped it bare and then levelled it to the ground, on the pretence of foiling any attempt the proprietor might have made to fire it and thus add to the general conflagration. William also watched appalled as a blacksmith walked up to an unsuspecting Frenchman in the street and hit him across the head with an iron bar. More than three decades later he could still remember how the poor man fell, how his blood flowed 'in a plentiful stream down to his ancles'.[4]

There are no reliable estimates for the number of foreigners living in London and its suburbs in 1666, but they certainly ran into thousands. There were various diplomats and ambassadors, of course: a Swedish embassy consisting of 124 people had arrived at the end of June, and its members were currently lodged at various places to the west of the City, including Covent Garden and Lincoln's Inn. But the vast majority of aliens had made London their home. In spite of the war, many were French or Dutch Protestants, asylum seekers who had arrived in England in the wake of religious persecutions in Europe; most were skilled artisans. At the end of the sixteenth century a return of aliens in the City, Southwark and Westminster claimed that there were 5,141. In 1639 the Privy Council ordered another census of foreigners in Westminster and the City; this reported the presence of 1,668 aliens, divided pretty evenly between the two districts. In Westminster there were 641 French and 176 Dutch, along with 15 Italians and 6 Spaniards; they were in the main painters, picture-drawers, engravers, musicians and silver-workers.

One in four of the aliens resident in the City itself was a weaver. There was a large Walloon contingent – 303 out of a total of 830 – and many of these were presumably refugees from the Spanish Netherlands who had settled in London during the Thirty Years War. But there were also 228 French and 221 Dutch, 24 Germans, 11 Italians, 2 Poles and a Bohemian, a Norwegian, a Savoyard, a Venetian, a Bavarian from the Palatinate, a Florentine and a Hamburger.

Periodically during the first half of the seventeenth century the Weavers' Company expressed concern that foreigners were taking work from their own members, so that 'our own people are grown into the most extreme wants, and know not what to do in winter-time when work will fail and be more scant'.[5] And in the months after the Restoration, resentment surfaced in a depressingly familiar way at the 'multitude of French now in town, who eat the bread out of the mouths of natives', with MPs claiming, most improbably, that 35,000 French silk weavers had arrived in London over the previous three years.[6]★

The London weavers weren't the only group to complain about foreign incursions into their territory. Early in 1662, journeymen feltmakers successfully petitioned for a change in local laws which would bar their employers from taking on foreign workers. And at various points in Charles II's reign, London's carpenters, tailors and fishmongers all complained that they were being impoverished by competition from foreign nationals resident in the capital.

A nasty strain of xenophobia already ran deep in the hearts of many Londoners. In Elizabethan times, European guidebooks warned the unwary traveller that the English were very suspicious of foreigners. A century later that attitude was confirmed by John Evelyn. In his *A Character of England* (1659), which purported to be a letter home written by a French visitor, he described how

Arriv'd at the Metropolis of civility, London, . . . we put our

★Around the same time the Lord Mayor and aldermen also complained directly to the King of 'the great increase of the Jews in the City, [and] their interference with the trade of the Citizens', and urged their expulsion from the kingdom (*Index to Remembrancia*, 266). Nothing was done; and, interestingly, there is no record of any anti-Semitic attacks in the aftermath of the Fire.

selves in Coach with some persons of quality, who came to conduct us to our Lodging; but neither was this passage without honours done to us, the kennel dirt, squibs, roots and rams-hornes being favours which were frequently cast at us by the children, and apprentises without reproofe; civilities, that in Paris, a Gentleman as seldome meets withall . . . You would imagine your self amongst a Legion of Devills, and in the suburb of Hell.[7]

Evelyn's view of the reception given to foreign visitors in London is echoed by Pepys, who commented on how his fellow citizens laughed and jeered the arrival in 1662 of an embassy from Russia; and also by Samuel Sorbière, who found the following year that not only were the English haughty towards strangers, but that little boys routinely chased after him in the street crying, 'French dog! French dog!'

Identifiable by their dress, their manners, their accents, their names, foreigners were easy targets for the fear and anger which were spreading from street to street faster than the flames themselves that Monday. The government took steps to prevent terrorists from fleeing the country: Lord Arlington wrote to the governor of the forts at Gravesend, ordering him to prevent all shipping leaving. He also told the authorities at Dover to place an embargo on all vessels and persons attempting to get out of the Cinque Ports.

One of the first foreigners to be arrested was Cornelius Rietvelt, a Dutch baker with a shop in Westminster. The conjunction of Dutchmen and bakeries proved too much for his neighbours. On Sunday evening or early Monday morning he was accused of attempting to fire his premises, stripped of all he possessed and finally committed to Westminster's notorious Gatehouse Prison, of which a previous occupant, Richard Lovelace, had written 'Stone walls do not a prison make / Nor iron bars a cage'. In Rietvelt's case they did.

News and rumour travelled fast. At ten o'clock on Monday morning a distraught Anne Hobart was writing from her home in Chancery Lane to tell her cousin in the country that the fire had begun in a Dutch baker's house in Pudding Lane. Lady Hobart, who was frantically trying to organise the evacuation of her household, was in no doubt as to the cause of the disaster: ''Tis the Duch fire,' she wrote. She also knew of Rietvelt's arrest. 'Thar was one tacken in Westminster seting his outhous on fier & thay have attempted to fier many plases & thar is a bundanc tacken with granades & pouder, Castell yard★ was set on fier, i am all most out of my wits . . . O pray for us . . . O pety me.'[8]

Monday also saw the arrest of a maid, Anne English, who lived in Covent Garden. Five witnesses claimed they had heard Anne say that a group of Frenchmen had recently visited her master's house and advised him to move his goods, 'for within six weeks that house and all the street would be burned down to the ground'. She was taken for interrogation to Whitehall, where she denied saying any such thing. She insisted all she had done was to mention in company that 'she had heard that the French and Dutch had kindled the fire in the city'.[9] Presumably her story was believed, since nothing more is heard of her.

Others weren't so lucky. All through Monday the mob grew more violent – and more irrational. In Newgate Market they beat up a member of the Portuguese Ambassador's household, claiming he had been caught in the act of throwing a fireball into a house which had subsequently burst into flames. He told the justices who interrogated him that he had been walking along the street when he saw a crust of bread on the ground; he put it on a window sill, a common Portuguese custom. The bread was found exactly where he said he had left it – two doors down from the house which was burning – but like many foreigners he was sent to gaol anyway, for his own safety, and quietly released a day or so later. A Frenchman was rescued by four Life Guards, who found him being beaten in the street by a gang that claimed they had caught him in the act of firebombing a house. That afternoon the surgeon Thomas Middleton, who had spent Sunday night at home in St Bride's only to be drawn back to the City,

★Baynard's Castle, on the north bank of the Thames at Blackfriars.

was passing a tobacco merchant's house in Watling Street when a youth was unceremoniously thrown out into the road at his feet. Middleton thought the young man looked suspicious – 'he seemed to be a Frenchman' – so he grabbed hold of him, only to find a powder horn under his coat. Just as sinister, the lad spoke with an accent and carried a book called *The Jewish Government*. He claimed the tobacco merchant knew him, but the merchant flatly denied it; and with the help of a parish constable Middleton dragged him off to the house of correction at Old Bridewell. They only just managed to reach the gaol: angry crowds jeered the 'French rascal' as they passed and, according to the surgeon, were more than ready to kill the hapless suspect. He was placed in solitary confinement until a magistrate could interrogate him.[10]

Bridewell burned down the next day.

Contemporaries agreed that in the course of Monday Londoners lost the will to save their city. 'Now fearfulness and terror doth surprize the citizens of *London*,' wrote the preacher Thomas Vincent; 'confusion and astonishment doth fall upon them at this unheard of, unthought of judgment.'[11] John Evelyn, who that morning came up the four miles from his home in Deptford to Southwark so that he could see the fire at first hand, couldn't believe the strange consternation that seized the people: 'I know not by what despondency or fate, they hardly stirr'd to quench it, so that there was nothing heard or seene but crying out and lamentation, running about like distracted creatures.'[12] On Monday night another observer, John Rushworth, was amazed when the flames began to creep along the eastern end of Cheapside – the most fashionable shopping street in London – and 'not tenn men stood by helping or calling for helpe'. This was neither hearsay nor a one-off incident: 'I have beene an eye witness and cann verify this and 100 tymes more.'[13]

Over in the Temple, Sir Edward Atkyns was of the same opinion as Rushworth: from what he could see, everybody forgot their efforts to halt the spread of the fire and looked to their own goods. Evelyn disagreed; his experience was that no one was even attempting to save their property. But the most interesting analysis comes from the courtier Windham Sandys. Writing to his master Lord Scudamore three days later, he was sure that social class had been the decisive factor in people's behaviour: 'For the first rank, they minded only for their own preservation; the middle sort [were] so distracted and amazed that they did not know what they did; the poorer, they minded nothing but pilfering.'[14]

In the early hours of Monday morning the resident staff began to leave the General Letter Office, a huge building at the lower end of Threadneedle Street, opposite the Stocks Market at the junction of Poultry, Cornhill and Lombard Streets. They followed the not entirely courageous lead of Sir Philip Frowde, a senior official who lived at the Letter Office: he and his wife had fled to safety around midnight, while the flames were still several streets away. James Hickes, the senior clerk, held on for another hour. Post for the entire country passed through the Threadneedle Street office;* and although the last dispatch had gone out on Saturday morning, the next delivery of incoming mail was due on Monday evening for distribution to subsidiary letter offices scattered around the capital. Hickes was dedicated to his job, working closely with Joseph Williamson (whose boss, Lord Arlington, was Postmaster-General as well as Secretary of State); he was crucial both to Williamson's intelligence-gathering network and to his propaganda machine. It was Hickes who routinely opened correspondence, scrutinising it for seditious sentiments and passing it on to Williamson; Hickes, too, who gathered news from correspondents all over the country, sending them Williamson's *Gazette* in return.

But by one o'clock on Monday morning Hickes's wife and children were clamouring to leave; by now the streets were jammed with people and carts. Hickes finally agreed to abandon the office and, grabbing as much of the mail as he could carry, he took his family over to a post house at the Golden Lion in

*There were exceptions: private letters were often delivered by servant, especially if the sender didn't care to have their contents reported to Whitehall.

Red Cross Street, just north of the City wall at Cripplegate. From here he sent a rather desperate note to Williamson by messenger, enclosing the Under-Secretary's post and admitting that he just did not know 'how to dispose of the business'.[15] Then he took his wife and children to Barnet, eleven miles north of the City, where he issued a circular to postmasters between London and Chester, explaining about the disaster and saying official mail should come directly to him, so that he could convey it to Whitehall. 'When the violence of the fire is over,' he wrote, 'some place will be pitched upon for the general correspondence as formerly.'[16]

In peacetime the loss of the post would have been bad enough; but this was not peacetime. The nation was on an invasion alert, and the government was waiting for news of what was expected to be the decisive sea battle of the war. Vague reports had been sent up from the south coast on Sunday, describing the sound of guns out at sea in the night and ships damaged in the storm. But everything was still confused, and the evacuation of the Letter Office could only add to that confusion. The Threadneedle Street bureau burned down, along with large quantities of mail, a few hours after Hickes left.

Williamson managed to get out Monday's issue of the *Gazette*, although it must have been close, since the printer, Thomas Newcomb, was based over by Baynard's Castle at Blackfriars, and his premises went up in flames early that morning. The paper gave news of the virulence of the plague among the Dutch fleet ('where they die in great numbers') and the fact that cannon commissioned by Louis XIV had burst during trials, as well as more pressing social gossip: the young Prince of Saxe was expected any minute to consummate his marriage with the Princess of Denmark, and the Archbishop of Salzburg was busy striking medals, gold chains 'and curiosities of several kinds' to commemorate a reception held in honour of the Holy Roman Empress. Williamson noted Saturday night's storm in the Channel, playing down the English fleet's confusion and announcing with characteristic optimism that 'the next day in all probability we may hear of their Engagement'. Almost as a footnote he announced that a fire had broken out in London at two o'clock on Sunday morning, 'which continues still with great violence'. But for Williamson the fire was an opportunity to praise the King. Referring to Charles's visit to Queenhithe on Sunday afternoon, he said that the sad accident had 'affected His Majesty with that tenderness, and compassion, that he was pleased to go himself in Person with his Royal Highness, to give order that all possible means should be used for quenching the fire, or stopping its further spreading'.[17]

The next edition of the *Gazette* didn't appear and, coupled with the disruption to communications caused by the destruction of the Letter Office, the absence of news fed national fears of conspiracy and terrorist action. By Thursday, it was accepted as fact 200 miles away in York that the Pudding Lane bakery belonged to a Frenchman; that the French, Dutch and Walloons had started the fire; and that the culprits had already been apprehended along with ten baskets of fireballs and grenades.

Samuel and Elizabeth Pepys and their servants spent most of Sunday night taking down hangings and pictures, dragging furniture and other goods out into the garden behind the Navy Office on Seething Lane, and stowing away down in the cellar the things they did not dare to leave out for everyone to see. Then Pepys brought his bags of gold into his office, packed up his accounts and waited. The fire was some distance from Seething Lane and still moving westward, away from it; but Pepys was thrown into a panic by the fact that carts belonging to the Surveyor of the Navy, Sir William Batten, were being loaded up with Batten's goods and driven away through the crowded streets.

Just before dawn, three hours or so after James Hickes evacuated the Letter Office, an empty cart drew up outside the Navy Office. Batten's goods had travelled two miles north-east to Kirby's Castle at Bethnal Green, a big country house belonging to a Baltic merchant and navy contractor named Sir William Rider. Now Batten – or rather his wife – had thoughtfully sent their wagon back so that Pepys could also move his plate and other valuables out to Kirby's Castle. He rode with them in the cart all the way out to Bethnal Green – still wearing his dressing-gown – and then made his way back to Seething Lane. 'Lord, to see how the streets and the highways are crowded with people, running and riding and getting carts at any rate.'[18]

In the chaos, people were looting freely along the wharves, grabbing casks of wine and oil and bowling them along the cobbles towards the nearest City gate. In Bear Lane, William Taswell's father recruited some porters to move his household belongings. They moved them all right; in fact they made off with them, and neither porters nor belongings were seen again. Against this we can set the behaviour of Alderman Samuel Starling, a Seething Lane neighbour of Pepys: when thirty men from the Navy Office saved his goods he gave them a penny each as a reward, and then accused them of trying to rob him when they began clearing debris from the street in front of his house. Sir Richard Browne was more generous when men risked their lives to save a chest of his. He gave them £4 for their efforts; but since the chest was reputed to contain £10,000, perhaps he wasn't being quite so generous after all.

Everyone was trying to get their goods away to safety. The financiers and bankers of Lombard Street evacuated their premises, and, across town, a number of the booksellers and stationers of Paternoster Row struggled to move their stock into the vaults under nearby Christchurch Newgate, or the warehouses in the grounds of Stationers' Hall on Ludgate Hill – although the Clerk to the Company, George Tokefield, was less sanguine, and took all the Company's records out to his house in the suburbs for safe keeping. But the majority of booksellers reckoned that the most sensible place to store highly flammable materials like theirs was in their own parish church of St Faith's, which occupied the western end of St Paul's Cathedral crypt. Securely stowed under ground and protected by massive stone walls that had stood for nearly six hundred years, their books would be as safe there as anywhere.

Later on Monday morning Pepys and his office staff and servants tried to carry the rest of his household possessions down to the Thames, where he had persuaded one of the Navy Office employees to have a lighter waiting. The boat lay at Iron Gate Stairs, just downriver from the Tower and perhaps 300–400 yards from the Navy Office; but Pepys couldn't get through the crowds, and had to take everything home again. Tower Hill was already a vast encampment, covered with refugees and their goods, he noticed. He spent Monday night taking it in turns with Elizabeth to sleep in his empty office under a quilt borrowed from his clerk, Will Hewer – 'we having fed upon the remains of yesterday's dinner, having no fire nor dishes, nor any opportunity of dressing [i.e., preparing] anything'.[19]

When disaster strikes, there will always be those who see an opportunity for making money. Theft is one option; and in a situation as confused as the one developing on Monday 3 September, theft must have been a great temptation, especially since everybody with disposable income kept it in bags and chests in the house. But there were also those who suddenly found their legitimate services in great demand. Nearly one in twenty workers in the City of London were employed in distribution and transport, and maybe twice as many in the suburbs outside the walls. While the citizens closest to the fire struggled to save their possessions, those further afield flocked into the City, eager to offer their wagons and carts and horses and hands – at a price. They added to the confused bottlenecks at the eight City gates, until – according to a Dutch account, at least – the authorities banned carts from entering, not only to ease the gridlock in the streets, but also to persuade citizens to turn their hands to fighting the fire instead of escaping from it. The order was unworkable, and was rescinded the following day.

A few carriers were reluctant to exploit the situation: the Earl of Salisbury's steward, Edward Jolley, hired three wagons to take goods from Salisbury House on the Strand to the Earl's country seat, Hatfield House in Hertfordshire. This was a distance of twenty-five miles – a good day's journey – but two of the carriers charged only a shilling a mile while the third charged a very reasonable fee of 29s for the whole trip.

Most carters were less scrupulous. The carriage of a wagon-load of goods out to Kensington, for instance, cost £4 – nearly

£1 per mile. In Chancery Lane, Lady Hobart's goods were packed and ready to go by ten o'clock in the morning; but she couldn't hire a cart to move them. She was told that £5 was being paid; £10; even £20. 'O i shall los all i have', she wrote poignantly.

In the days and weeks after the fire was over, commentators were united in their condemnation of the way in which carriers had profiteered so shamelessly from the misery of others. Carts 'were not to be had but at most unhumane prices', wrote one.[20] Another railed at rustic greed, in terms which show that metropolitanism has a long and unpleasant pedigree:

But that those Hobnail'd Clowns should be so chubbish,
Whom though we knew much baser than our rubbish:
Those pilfering Country-Coridons, that they
Should come to make of us a second prey;
Ere I'de have answer'd their unjust desire,
I'de first have seen my Goods, and them i' th' Fire.[21]

Thomas Vincent was just as direct:

Now carts, and drays, and coaches, and horses, as many as could have entrance into the city, were loaden, and any money is given for help; five, ten, twenty, and thirty pounds for a cart, to bear forth into the fields some choice things, which were ready to be consumed; and some of the countries had the conscience to accept of the highest price, which the citizens did then offer in their extremity; I am mistaken if such money do not burn worse, than the fire out of which it was *rak'd*.[22]

Heedless of all this unedifying chaos, the fire marched on, roaring and crashing and eating up building after building with astonishing speed and violence. Amazed onlookers watched flames flare out from windows on opposite sides of a street to join together in a terrifying golden wall. '*Rattle, rattle, rattle*, was the noise which the fire struck upon the ear round about, as if there had been a thousand iron chariots beating upon the stones.'[23] The Royal

Exchange caught late in the afternoon or early evening; the flames swept quickly through the galleries and within hours Sir Thomas Gresham's bourse was a smoking shell. The statues of English kings which had looked down on traders for decades crashed into the courtyard, provoking all sorts of moral musings from Republicans and Royalists alike. Simon Ford, in one of his *Three Poems Relating to the Late Dreadful Destruction of the City of London by Fire*, was fairly conventional:

> The *dreadful Wrack* now all together *flings*;
> *Crowns*, *Scepters*, and the *Trunks* of *Kings*.
> And like your *Statues*, *Kings*, said She, you must
> Once *mingled* be with *common Dust*.[24]

Others marvelled that the only statue to survive the destruction of the Exchange was that of its founder:

> That stately Fabrick, and its STATUES rare,
> Spoil'd and consum'd, reduc'd to Ashes are,
> But honouring Reverend GRESHAM'S Effigy,
> Leaves him untoucht, and gently passeth by.[25]

Strangest of all were the thoughts of Joseph Guillim, for whom the burning of spices kept in cellars under the ground-floor shops represented a mystical image of sacrifice and redemption:

> Yet, burn those Statues not like other things,
> Which represent no less than sacred Kings;
> But a perfumed flame doth from them rise,
> Whose smoak sweet Odours sends up to the Skies:
> For th' Aromatick Cavern underneath,
> Doth all the while Sabaean Vapours breathe.
> As flames th' Arabian Spices thus consume,
> They all the circumambient air perfume.
> Soon may we see from this burnt Sacrifice,
> Or spicy bed of flames, a Phoenix rise.[26]

Throughout Monday, sporadic efforts were still being made to halt the spread of the flames. They were often courageous and dogged, but there was little attempt to mount a City-wide operation. Contemporary accounts make no mention of Bludworth, whose responsibility it was to coordinate the firefighting. We can only assume that, like most of his fellow citizens, he decided that discretion and self-interest were the better parts of valour, and ran for cover.

While William Taswell's father was intent on saving his possessions in Bear Lane – and being robbed in the process – the boy himself was more altruistically engaged. Despite the fire, William had gone to lessons as usual on Monday morning. Now John Dolben, the Dean of Westminster, marched the school on foot right into the heart of the City, determined 'to put a stop if possible to the conflagration'.[27] They forced their way through the crowded streets until they reached St Dunstan-in-the-East, 'a fair and large church of an ancient building'[28] which stood between Thames Street and Tower Street, not far from the Custom House. St Dunstan was only a couple of hundred yards away from Pudding Lane but, because the gales continued to push the fire west and north and the eastward creep was much less dramatic, it was still on the boundary of Monday's fire zone. But it had caught nevertheless, and for hours on end the Westminster boys fetched water while young Taswell acted as page to Dolben, running errands and taking messages. They eventually put out the flames; and after this small but significant victory, Dolben duly led his troops back to Westminster.

St Dunstan burned down early the following morning.

Heroic as they were, efforts like that of Dolben and his boys were doomed to fail in the absence of an organised operation. Indeed, where parish-based firefighting was still going on it was so haphazard that it did more harm than good. Buildings may have been pulled down with hooks in the prescribed manner; but no one thought to clear the timbers – indeed, where could they have taken them? – so the flames managed to cross even the widest streets and open spaces, leapfrogging from pyre to pyre.

As 'the spreading Flames now conquer all they meet / And walk in Triumph through the frighted streets',[29] attempts to quell the fire seemed to have ceased entirely. On Monday night Evelyn watched the Thames covered with barges and boats, and straggling caravans of carts and pedestrians making their way out of the City gates towards the open fields to the north and east, where makeshift tents and encampments were springing up everywhere. 'Scarcely a back either of man or woman that hath strength, but had a burden on it in the streets,' wrote Thomas Vincent.[30]

Not one to worry too much about accurate figures, Evelyn reckoned that there were 10,000 houses on fire, beneath a pall of smoke 56 miles long. The true figures weren't quite so dramatic, but they were bad enough. On Monday alone, thirty-nine more parishes had been destroyed as the fire scythed through mansions and hovels alike. The Livery Companies lost another eight Halls, including the brand new Hall in Cloak Lane which the Cutlers had only just finished paying for, and the ancient Hall and chapel of the Mercers at the eastern end of Cheapside, which was destroyed late on Monday night. About 1,500 yards of waterfront were burned: the stairs at Queenhithe, where the King and the Duke of York had surveyed the devastation and consulted with Sir Richard Browne the previous afternoon, had gone; so had Baynard's Castle at Blackfriars, home to Catherine of Aragon and Anne Boleyn, and the place where both Lady Jane Grey and Mary Tudor were proclaimed Queen of England.

Over the past twenty-four hours the great arc of devastation had spread out north and west from the original fire zone until it covered several hundred acres. It snaked through the alleys and roared through the broader streets, moving down Cornhill in the night, burning the Stocks Market and breaking into Cheapside.

There was no darkness: the fire shone with such a bright light that it was as though it was noon. Evelyn thought the City was being engulfed in a firestorm. 'The noise and cracking and thunder of the impetuous flames, the shrieking of women and children, the hurry of people, the fall of Towers, Houses and Churches, was like an hideous storme, and the aire all about so hot and inflam'd that at the last one was not able to approach it.'[31] Worse still, those impetuous flames were creeping eastward, against the prevailing winds – and towards the Tower of London, home of the Ordnance Office and its considerable stores of gunpowder. John, Lord Berkeley, an Ordnance Commissioner and a member of the Duke of York's household, sent a rather desperate note from the Tower to the Navy Office, begging that all available fire engines in the shipyards at Deptford and Woolwich should be sent up as quickly as possible, along with 'all persons, capable either by hand or judgement to assist in the preservation of the Tower'.[32]

Although there was not as yet much evidence of it, organised action to halt the fire was beginning to get under way. At some point on Monday King Charles decided the crisis called for more forceful interference than that which could be provided by the Earl of Craven and his Coldstream Guards. Not only was the fire spreading more or less unchecked, but public order threatened to break down completely, with gridlock and chaos at the gates, and looting, robberies and savage violence on the streets. (Indeed, up to this point Craven's Guards had spent most of their time rescuing innocent foreigners from lynchings and beatings.) If ever a civil emergency called for military rule, this was it.

As Captain-General of the Kingdom, the Duke of Albemarle, George Monck, was the obvious person to lead the operation. He was also Lord Lieutenant of Middlesex, and thus one of the men responsible for mustering the local militias. But Monck was seventy-five miles away on the Isle of Wight, assessing the damage to his tattered fleet, and it would be several days before he could be recalled. Nor was it clear that he *should* be recalled. When news of the fire reached Holland – and it would, very soon – the Dutch might press home their advantage with an attack on the south coast: bringing home one half of the naval high command (and the sensible half, at that) at such a crucial stage in the war was not a good idea. That very day Monck and Rupert were busy dispatching letters to Charles and James explaining why they had failed to engage with the Dutch on Saturday night. Still unaware of what was happening in London, they blithely asked the Duke of York as Lord High Admiral 'to send what fire ships and other ships you can hither for us, and provisions for us

73

at the Buoy of the Nore, and command the Victualler at Portsmouth to furnish us with everything there'.[33]

With Monck unavailable, Charles II placed his brother in charge. The Duke of York was always happiest in a crisis; Sir William Coventry, who in addition to being a Navy Commissioner was his Secretary at the Admiralty, was quite right when he said that James was 'more himself and more of judgement is at hand in him in the middle of a desperate service, than at other times'.[34] He spent most of Monday riding up and down the crowded streets of the City with his Guards in an attempt to maintain public order, rescuing foreigners from the mob and encouraging localised firefighting efforts. He called in at the Navy Office, where Pepys heard he was 'now General, and having the care of all'.[35] And as Monday wore on with no sign of either the flames or the gales subsiding, he began to prepare a coordinated strategy for containing the fire.

James's plan was simple. He decided to set up command posts with teams of firefighters all round the perimeter of the fire. Aside from the Tower, where John, Lord Berkeley was begging for naval workers to come and help, the most strategic points were in the western suburbs, which were now most likely to bear the brunt of the advancing flames. There were five major posts, beginning with Temple Bar at the west end of Fleet Street and arcing north and east to form a cordon which ran through Clifford's Inn Gardens, Fetter Lane and Shoe Lane, before ending with a station in the little thoroughfare of Cow Lane, which lay between Holborn Conduit and West Smithfield. Each was manned by parish constables, who were ordered to bring with them 100 men apiece. Each of the firefighting teams thus formed was supported – or kept at its post – by a troop of thirty foot soldiers under the command of an officer; and rations of bread, cheese and beer to the value of £5 were provided at each position.*

---

*It isn't clear if these provisions were intended just for the night. If they were, it was a generous gesture, since £5 would have allowed each man two loaves, two pounds of ordinary cheese and three gallons of small beer. But then firefighting was thirsty work.

James also installed three courtiers at each station, with orders to reward with a shilling any man who stayed at his post and worked hard throughout the night. Three advance posts were set up closer to the flames, at Aldersgate, Cripplegate and Coleman Street; they were commanded by two gentlemen apiece. The appearance on the front line of so many nobility and gentry was meant to set a good example to the frightened and disorganised citizens; and, no doubt, to provide leadership by men on whom James felt he could rely. But there was another reason for their presence: labourers, constables and aldermen were still reluctant to bring down houses for fear of being held responsible. Perhaps at the Duke's insistence, Charles gave the courtiers manning the fire posts the authority to order demolitions.

Temple Bar had a particular significance. The gatehouse marked not only the junction of Fleet Street and the Strand, but also the point at which the City's jurisdiction in the western suburbs ended, and that of Westminster began. It was up to the men at the Temple Bar fire post to prevent the fire breaking through and moving up the Strand to the gates of Whitehall itself. They were supervised by Lord Belasyse, the absentee Governor of Tangier and one of the Duke's most trusted friends; by Hugh May, the Paymaster of the King's Works, who was currently acting up as Surveyor-General during Sir John Denham's bout of madness; and by Thomas Chicheley, a Commissioner of the Ordnance. May was forty-four; the other two men were both in their early fifties. The Cow Lane station was commanded by Sir Richard Browne; Colonel John Fitzgerald, a Catholic soldier and until 1665 the Deputy-Governor of Tangier, was in charge of Coleman Street. Bludworth was at Cripplegate.

James himself tended to move back and forth between the different posts, but he spent much of his time in and around Fleet Street. He hoped that the Fleet River would form a natural firebreak between Ludgate Hill and the affluent western suburbs leading to Whitehall and Westminster, and decided he and his own men should make a stand of sorts south of the Fleet Bridge, in Bridewell and down to the Thames; while the Earl of Craven would command the firefighting efforts from Holborn Bridge

75

down to the Fleet Bridge – a defensive line more than half a mile long. Holding that line would be hard, but all hope now rested on it.

The exodus of refugees had continued all through Monday, and by nightfall the ground just beyond the Duke of York's cordon was covered with a pathetic forest of makeshift shelters and dotted with little piles of belongings and furniture. Hatton Garden, an open area to the north-west of the City where over the past few years houses had begun to appear, was filled with people's goods; so were Lincoln's Inn Fields and Gray's Inn Fields, and the tracts of open land around the squalid tenements of St Giles's Fields. The Duke and Lord Arlington told the City to call out two companies of militia to patrol these areas in an attempt to prevent looting.

It took some time to put all of these structures in place. John Evelyn, for example, was sent to help at Fetter Lane; but, if his memory served him well, he didn't actually arrive there until some time on Wednesday. And even on Monday night, when the fire posts were all manned to some extent and everyone was preparing like soldiers in the trenches for the flames to reach them, James was still anxious that he hadn't done enough. From his Whitehall lodgings he told Sir William Coventry that justices and deputy lieutenants must summon more workmen and tools to arrive on the front line at dawn; and that surrounding churches and chapels must be searched for fire-hooks, 'which should be brought ready upon the place to-night against the morning'.[36]

Then he waited.

5

Black Towers Mourn

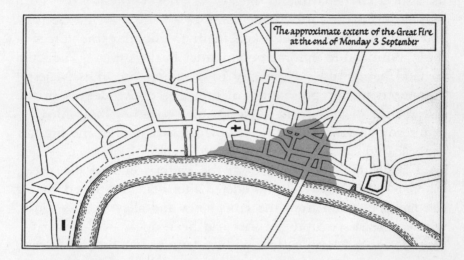

The approximate extent of the Great Fire at the end of Monday 3 September

*T*he fire crossed the Fleet on Tuesday morning. Instead of the expected frontal assault down Ludgate Hill, it launched a surprise attack. Great flakes of flame flew high into the sky over Blackfriars and landed in Salisbury Court, which lay to the west of Bridewell and well behind the Duke of York's position. Parts of the Court were heavily built up, although there was also a substantial mansion there: originally the palace of the Bishops of Salisbury, it had been acquired in the sixteenth century by the Earls of Dorset, who had renamed it Dorset House and leased out parts of the gardens for housing. (Pepys was born in Salisbury Court in 1633 – his father ran a tailor's business in a house backing onto St Bride's Churchyard.) The flying sparks quickly took hold; and by midday the Duke found himself surrounded as the fire moved down to the Thames and began eating into the densely populated area around Bridewell Gaol. Almost stifled by the heat, he and his men were forced to run for it, falling back to Somerset

House in the Strand. A warrant was issued for removing the Exchequer to Nonsuch House. The great Tudor palace near Ewell in Surrey had already served this purpose when the plague was bad the previous summer; now carriages and lighters were hired, and the process of loading up the contents of the Treasury and its associated departments began. Charles wrote to the Lord Lieutenants of the surrounding counties – Kent, Middlesex, Surrey and Hertfordshire – and asked them to mobilise the forces at their command to enforce public order in the capital. 'The hand of God being laid on the city by a raging fire, [His Majesty] enjoins them, for prevention of unhappy consequences in the disturbance of peace and quiet, to draw together the militia.'[1]

Already at dawn it had been obvious that neither the fire nor the gales which drove it were easing. Tracks of flame converged on Cheapside – not only from the eastern end of the street, where Mercers' Hall still smouldered after being destroyed during the night, but also from the cross-lanes and alleys to the south, where at least six more parishes had been devastated during the early hours. St Mary-le-Bow, with its famous bell that tolled each night at nine and which, like the rest of the bells in the City, had been sounding the alarm for two days now, was one of the casualties:

> The Bells before rung backward, did thereby,
> Some accidental Fire still signifie.
> But when the Churches and the Bellfries burn,
> The Bells are dumb, and their black towers mourn.
> What Fire is this, makes the Bells cease to chime?
> Destroyes the Clocks, so triumphs over time . . .[2]

Fires burst through into Cheapside, the City's most important thoroughfare, almost simultaneously at five separate intersections: Soper Lane; Bow Lane; Bread Street; Friday Street; and Old Change, which was right up against the east end of St Paul's Cathedral itself.

By mid-morning the fire had crossed over the broad street, helped by the piles of timber and other combustible debris left lying where they fell as Monday's haphazard efforts to put out isolated fires were abandoned. It kept moving northward, in the process destroying another half-dozen churches and two more Company Halls – the Embroiderers' in Gutter Lane, and the fourteenth-century Saddlers' Hall in Foster Lane.

Further up Foster Lane was Goldsmiths' Hall, a complex of offices and vaults put up in the 1630s by Nicholas Stone, Master Mason to Charles I. The Goldsmiths were arguably the most powerful Company of all: ever since 1478 all gold and silver objects had had to be checked for quality and marked in their Hall before they could be sold (hence the term 'hallmark'). As the flames reached the southern end of Foster Lane the Assayer, John Brattle, who lived on the premises with his wife and family, managed to hire a cart and pile his personal belongings into it. Just as he was about to get his goods safely away, a local alderman and prominent Cheapside goldsmith named Sir Charles Doe arrived on the scene. Doe commandeered the wagon under the hapless Brattle's nose and used it instead to move the Company's records and its considerable collection of plate out to Edmonton, seven miles north of the City. What made matters worse for Brattle was that everything went to the house of a friend of his – presumably the same house where he had intended to take his own possessions. Its owner, a Mr Broadbank, was paid £8 10s for his trouble, and the carter received £5. Later that day Goldsmiths' Hall was gutted – although its walls were left standing – and Brattle lost everything. His employers rewarded his understanding attitude with a gift of £40 when it was all over.

Other Companies were less fortunate than the Goldsmiths. Drapers' Hall stood in Throgmorton Street, right at the north-eastern perimeter of the fire zone. It survived until Tuesday night or Wednesday morning, so that the porter had time to organise impoverished members of the Company to drag the contents of the Hall out into the garden and maintain a watch over them for the rest of the week. The Renter Warden, a man named Burton, had recently taken possession of £446; quite rightly he had locked it up in a secure cupboard in the treasury. Sadly for the Drapers, however, Burton had the only key and he was, as he later said, 'remote from the Hall when the same took fire and engaged in the preservation of [my] own goods and house'.[3] The treasury burned; the money burned with it. And although the Drapers brought in a silversmith to comb through the debris, they recovered only £115 in silver. The porter and his helpers were rewarded for their efforts; Mr Burton was not, although the Company reluctantly agreed that he was not liable for their losses.

By mid-morning on Tuesday the pall of smoke hanging over the city had grown to biblical proportions. It was so great, claimed Thomas Vincent, 'that travellers did ride at noon-day some miles together in the shadow thereof, though there were no other cloud beside to be seen in the sky'.[4] On the rare occasions when the sun did manage to break through the gloom, it was as red as blood.

Teams of workmen under the direction of the Duke of York began to pull down houses in Holborn and around the north-western perimeter of the fire zone, using hooks, picks and whatever came to hand. The Duke himself rode up and down the City with his Guards, urging his men on. 'The Duke of York hath wonn the hearts of the people with his continuall and indefatigable paynes day & night in helpeing to quench the Fire,' wrote an eye-witness a couple of days later.[5] Charles also put in a personal appearance; James was the man in charge, but the King was not content to sit and wait in Whitehall. The official account of the disaster gives him equal credit with the Duke, praising their 'indefatigable and personal pains to apply all possible remedies'.[6] More revealing, perhaps, are the private letters of the time, which marvel over the fact that the two men stood up to their ankles in water and manned pumps for hours on end. Both brothers were admired for their efforts; both were applauded for the fact that 'with incredible magnanimity [they] rode up and down giving orders for blowing up of Houses with Gunpowder to make voyd spaces for the fire to dye in, and standing still to see those orders executed, exposing their persons not only to the multitude but to the very flames themselves, and the Ruines of buildings ready to fall upon them and sometimes labouring with their own hands to give example to others'.[7]

But it was James who received the greatest praise, for his ability to keep his head in a crisis, his determination to stop the fire: 'Next, Princely York, with *sweat* and *dirt* besmear'd / (More *glorious* thus, than in his *Robes*) appear'd'.[8] James was seen 'handing Bucketts of water with as much diligence as the poorest man that did assist'. John Rushworth, a witness who wrote these words, went on to point out that 'if the Lord Maior had donn as much, his Example might have gone Far towards saveing the Citty'. Thomas Bludworth was going to have a lot of explaining to do.[9]

The fire was now approaching the halls, residential courts and gardens of the Temple, on the south side of Fleet Street. The area took its name from its founders, the Knights of the Military Order of the Temple of Solomon in Jerusalem, who had moved their London base here from Holborn in around 1160. The Order had been formed to protect pilgrims to the Holy Land, but when the last Christian enclaves fell to the Mamelukes in the 1290s its power declined and it was dissolved in 1312, after its Knights had been accused of some colourful and improbable improprieties.* The estate was granted to the Knights of the Hospital of St John of Jerusalem, who leased out the two great halls and the dormitories, storehouses, stables and chambers which filled the complex. Most of their tenants were lawyers, drawn to the precinct by its proximity to the river and the central courts at Westminster; and in 1608, nearly seventy years after the Hospitallers in England were disbanded during the dissolution of the monasteries, James I had granted the Temple to the barristers of the two legal societies that were based there, the Inner Temple and the Middle Temple, 'to serve for all time to come for the accommodation and education of the students and practitioners of laws of the realm'.

The Templars' twelfth-century church still stood at the heart of the complex, complete with its famous series of Purbeck marble effigies of medieval Knights Templar. Close by was the medieval Inner Temple Hall, with Middle Temple Hall, which

---

*These included sodomy, idolatry, heresy and spitting at the Cross.

had been rebuilt in the 1560s, standing further west across a warren of both old and new courtyards and lodgings. The whole area was rather like a college at Oxford or Cambridge – or rather two colleges, since there was a clear-cut division between Inner and Middle. The office of the Court of the King's Bench (one of the three courts administering common law, along with the Courts of Common Pleas and Exchequer) was at the eastern edge, a few hundred yards away from Bridewell. It was separated from it by a combustible maze of tightly packed alleys and lanes known as Alsatia, whose volatile and criminally minded inhabitants enjoyed an uneasy relationship with the lawyers, alternately robbing them on the street and appealing to them for help in staying out of gaol.

Salisbury Court and Dorset House were only about 800 feet away from the King's Bench Office; and soon after fire broke out there, the evacuation of the entire area around the Temple was in full spate. The long gap between the end of Trinity term in June and the start of Michaelmas in November meant that many of the lawyers were away in the country on their summer vacations. They were not alone in this – the Earl of Clarendon later blamed the time of year at which the Fire broke out for the destruction of so many household goods and valuables, saying that 'very many of the substantial citizens and other wealthy men were in the country, whereof many had not left a servant in their houses, thinking themselves upon all ordinary accidents more secure in the goodness and kindness of their neighbours, than they could be in the fidelity of a servant'.[10] But the bad timing cost the lawyers particularly dear when the flames arrived in the Temple, since their colleagues had a nice sense of legal proprieties and would neither try to preserve the goods of absentees, or even allow others to do so, 'because . . . it was against the law to break up any man's chamber'.[11]

In spite of the absence of so many lawyers, at two o'clock Williamson and Arlington were informed by one of the Temple residents, John Barker, that 'neither boat, barge, cart, nor coach is to be had. All the streets [are] full of goods, and the fire flaming into the very Temple.'[12] Barker was writing from Covent Garden, having fled to the house of the Swedish Resident, Baron Leijonbergh. But Covent Garden was not considered safe either, and Leijonbergh asked Arlington for a warrant 'to press four wagons to carry his goods, for at this distance, he is desirous to remove'.[13] The Swedish embassy which had arrived in London in June was also lodged in Covent Garden, and after consulting with Leijonbergh the two ambassadors, Count Jöran Fleming and Peter Julius Coyet, agreed that everyone should make for Palace Yard, Westminster, where a house was being made ready for them.

That was easier said than done. Any foreigners stupid enough to walk out on the streets of London that Tuesday were in more danger from the mob than the flames, and refugees from the City were routinely stopped and questioned at unofficial check-points all through the western suburbs. Recalling a few weeks later how frightening this was, an ex-Capuchin monk, Denis de Repas, shed an interesting light on the process: 'I have no reason to complaine of Englishmen for that allarum,' he said, 'but only of English women, who only caused that tumult, having their *corps de gards* in severall streets and did knock downe severall strangers for not speaking good English. Some of them were armed with spitts, some with bread staffs, and the captaine with a broad sword.'[14]

The Swedes decided it would be politic to travel in convoy. Their baggage was sent on ahead, and later in the afternoon a procession – fifty strong and heavily armed – set out from Covent Garden, headed by Fleming and Coyet in their coach.

Even though they were about half a mile from the edge of the fire, the sight that greeted them as they moved out into the Strand was terrifying. The press of people was so great that they could hardly move: young and old, men and women, running, riding, walking, shouting, cursing and praying. 'The burning of Troy came to my mind,' wrote a member of the ambassadors' entourage. 'I fancied that it might have looked just like this.'[15]

The convoy finally arrived at the house in Westminster, where they barricaded themselves in; a guard from the royal household was placed outside the door. The ambassadors ordered that no one should set foot outside, but a nobleman in the group decided he would rather spend the evening with a woman he knew and crept out, accompanied by a single servant. He managed to negotiate the crowds and met with the woman; but on their way home the two men walked round a corner and straight into a mob, who recognised them as foreigners and decided to lynch them from the nearest overhanging shop-board. The servant struggled and yelled and put up such a fight that the crowd decided to hang the nobleman first, but while he was kicking in the air a troop of the Duke of York's Guards rode up. They cut him down, threw him over a horse and carried him off. He was escorted back to Palace Yard the next day, where he was 'dreadfully teased about the blue ring which could be seen around his neck'.[16] History does not record what happened to his servant.

The street violence was getting worse, along with the general paranoia. Over in Soho, a mile from the edge of the fire zone, a man was seen piling all his goods in his garden and then apparently setting fire to his house. A neighbour stopped him, promised to 'run his halbert into his guts' if he tried to escape, and had him arrested.[17] And when curiosity got the better of the Swedish court chaplain, and he ventured out of the Palace Yard house to see how things were in the City, he was beaten up in the street and eventually carried home, his head and face covered in blood, his sleeves and collar ripped in tatters and his cassock turned back to front. Angry that he had disobeyed them, the ambassadors had him brought straight to them and demanded to know why he had left the building after being ordered to stay indoors. He said, 'Your Excellencies, the whole time of the fire I prayed God on my knees that he would keep it away from these rogues: and now what sort of thanks do I get? Oh, may the fires of hell burn them for ever.'[18] They found his lack of Christian charity so funny that they laughed out loud and let him be.

Despite the Duke of York's efforts, the firefighters were losing the battle. In the course of Tuesday the fire broke through the posts at Coleman Street to the north and Shoe Lane to the west. It destroyed the twelfth-century church of St Lawrence Jewry, which stood next door to the Guildhall. Then it reached the Guildhall itself,

> . . . where the grave Senatours still sate,
> When they the City business did debate;
> Whose Purple Robes did such a splendor shed,
> As fill'd those who approacht their Court with dread.
> Yet the rude Fire doth with its Scarlet Train,
> Rush in among them, and their Robes disdain:
> Whose flames a greater awe did with them bring,
> While round about they nought but terrour, fling.[19]

Samuel Sorbière, who saw London's seat of government during his visit to England in 1663, thought it 'an inconsiderable Building and in a narrow Street'. But the Gothic style was particularly unfashionable — the Guildhall was built in the early fifteenth century — and anyway Sorbière wasn't enthusiastic about much of the capital's architecture. It was he, remember, who had dismissed the Palace of Whitehall as 'nothing but a heap of houses'.[20] The Guildhall may have been hemmed in on all sides by civic offices, Company Halls and parish churches but it was nevertheless an imposing building, guarded by huge statues of the legendary giants Gog and Magog★ and with a main hall which at 150 feet by 40 feet 6 inches was one of the largest in England. With a steeply pitched louvred roof it had risen high above most of the surrounding townscape and had been clearly visible from the river, surrounded by a cluster of church towers and steeples.

The buildings all round the Guildhall were burned: not only St Lawrence Jewry, but also St Michael Bassishaw, which was just to the north; Basing Hall, a Tudor mansion which was named

---

★London's tutelary deities Gog and Magog began life as Gogmagog, one of the giants who ruled in Albion before Brute and his band of Trojans settled here, and Corinaeus, a comrade of Brute who slew Gogmagog. They often appeared in City pageants in the seventeenth century, although it isn't clear when Corinaeus was forgotten and Gogmagog turned into twins.

for a prominent medieval family, the Basings, and which adjoined the Guildhall; and the Company Halls of the Coopers, the Weavers, the Masons and the Girdlers. Then the fire swept north-ward until it reached the old City wall.

Miraculously, the stone walls and crypt of the Guildhall had survived. But the interior had been destroyed, along with Gog and Magog and the huge oak trusses of the roof. Thomas Vincent left one of the most memorable images of the entire fire when he described how that night, hours after the flames had moved on, the entire structure was left glowing like a shining coal, 'as if it had been a palace of gold, or a great building of burnished brass'.[21] John Crouch was almost as eloquent, lamenting the fact that 'Chymnies and shatter'd Walls we gaze upon / Our Bodie Politicks sad Skeleton!'[22]

In the east of the City, the men and pumping equipment that John, Lord Berkeley had summoned from the dockyards at Woolwich and Deptford hadn't arrived at the Tower, but the flames were now moving eastward along Tower Street against the prevailing wind – and towards the Tower's magazine. Demolition was the only effective measure, and the teams that James had mustered to man his fire posts simply could not pull down build-ings quickly enough.

They were also hampered, even in such a desperate crisis, by an acute awareness of the legal implications of destroying prop-erty. Only the King, the Duke and the various courtiers who were manning the fire posts had authority for sanctioning demo-litions – and that authority still had to be requested specifically on each occasion. So on Tuesday afternoon, for example, when Samuel Pepys decided that pulling down houses at the south end of Seething Lane was the only way to save the Navy Office from the fire, he actually wrote a letter to James's Secretary, Sir William Coventry, asking for permission. Coventry did not reply.

Pepys had been up since daybreak. Following the previous day's fiasco, he was more than ever determined that his possessions should not burn. He managed to commandeer a lighter just below the Tower; but most of his household servants had left, along with many of the clerks at the Navy Office, so it took him until the afternoon to transport his things between his house and Iron Gate Stairs, from where they were sent downriver to the naval yard at Deptford. There were household goods strewn around the streets, and teams of men frantically working to prevent the flames reaching the Tower. Sir William Batten, who was supposed to be organising dockyard workers to come to the aid of John, Lord Berkeley, was more concerned about what to do with his private wine store. Pepys watched as the Surveyor of the Navy dug a pit in the garden at Seething Lane and filled it with his precious wooden casks.★ Then, seizing his chance, the young Clerk of the Acts hurled bundles of Navy Office papers down into the same hole before it was filled in.

In fact Pepys was so taken with Batten's idea that later in the day he and Sir William Penn dug another pit in the garden and placed their own wine in it, along with one of Pepys's most treasured possessions – 'my parmazan cheese'.[23]

That done, the two men sat down in the garden and waited for the fire to reach them.

Once the fire had crossed both Cheapside and the Fleet, it was only a matter of time before St Paul's Cathedral at the top of Ludgate Hill was threatened. St Paul's was the City's most revered landmark. It was London's own cathedral, at whose altar each Lord Mayor prayed for guidance on the day of his installation. But it was more than this – a godly fortress, a divine bulwark against misfortune, of greater significance at an emotional level than the City churches, the Exchange or the Guildhall or any of the Company Halls. Its destruction was unthinkable.

As it happened, there was a precedent for the fate which was about to befall St Paul's. The cathedral, which had been founded more than a thousand years earlier by St Mellitus, first Bishop of London, was destroyed by fire in 1087. It had been rebuilt by the Normans and extended and enlarged over the next 250 years until it was 585 feet long and 489 feet high. One can gauge the

---

★Seventeenth-century wines were stored in the wood, and only transferred to bottles immediately before drinking.

impact its monumental bulk must have had on Londoners from the fact that it was actually longer than Wren's cathedral, and over 120 feet taller.

It lost height in a dramatic fashion on 4 June 1561, when its steeple was struck by lightning and set on fire. The entire building might have been lost if Londoners hadn't acted quickly to extinguish it. A contemporary pamphleteer noted that 'there were above 500 persons that laboured in carrying and filling water, &c. Divers substantial citizens took pains as if they had been labourers; so did also divers and sundry Gentlemen'.[24]

The spire was never replaced, but in spite of its truncated appearance St Paul's remained the dominant feature of the London skyline, immediately identifiable in every contemporary print, towering over the rest of the City. In *Cooper's Hill*, his topographical poem of 1642, John Denham talked of

> That sacred pile, so vast, so high
> That whether 'tis a part of earth or sky
> Uncertain seems, and may be thought a proud
> Aspiring mountain or descending cloud . . .

– in the process going some way to prove Evelyn's verdict that the Surveyor-General was 'a better poet than architect'.[25] In 1633 William Laud, then Bishop of London, put an end to a series of half-hearted attempts to restore the fabric of the building, which had taken a serious knock in the Elizabethan lightning strike. With the support of Charles I he commissioned an extensive piece of cosmetic work by Inigo Jones, in which the exterior walls of the nave and transepts were classicised with pilasters and bull's-eye windows; and the west front was transformed into a heady concoction of obelisks and scrolls, with a giant colonnade of eight fluted Corinthian columns. Jones also planned to repair the rickety central tower and the roof of the south transept, which was propped up with timbers; but the Civil War intervened, and work halted with the scaffolding still in place. Both Laud and his King found that Parliament had other uses for scaffolding.

The Commonwealth had little time for bishops, and no time

at all for their cathedrals. It was not kind to St Paul's. The New Model Army stabled its horses there on the eve of Charles I's trial. Soldiers baptised a foal in the font, smashed the stained glass and tore out pews and choir stalls to use for firewood. Scaffolding masts and timber props were removed, leading to the collapse of sections of roofing; the churchyard was sold to building speculators, who created a shanty town of lean-to housing against the cathedral walls; and shopkeepers set up their stalls in Jones's portico. Its Corinthian columns were 'most barbarously spoiled, & in some places cut through even almost to ye middle of them'.[26]

The Restoration had brought the re-establishment of the episcopacy and the return of ejected Laudian clergy. Gilbert Sheldon, one of the leaders of the High Church in exile during the 1650s, became Bishop of London in 1660 and Archbishop of Canterbury three years later. His successor on the bishop's throne at St Paul's was Humphrey Henchman, another Laudian who had helped Charles II to escape from England after the Battle of Worcester in 1651. To men like Sheldon and Henchman, St Paul's was a potent symbol of a Church of England which had survived grievous harm at the hands of the fanatics. It was also a potent symbol of monarchy. Charles I had paid for the work at the west end of St Paul's, and his gift was still commemorated in an inscription over the portico. Moreover, he had gone to his death in front of Inigo Jones's Banqueting House at Whitehall; for Royalists, this lent a poignancy to all Jones's work, while the architectural cognoscenti prized Jones's buildings as pearls in a stagnant Gothic sea. 'Amongst the pieces of modern Architecture, I have never observ'd above two, which were remarkable in this vast City,' wrote Evelyn in 1659; 'the Portico of the Church of S. Pauls, and the Banqueting-house at White-hall.'[27] Anyone who reckoned himself a critic of building agreed with him.

So it wasn't surprising that by the mid-1660s the renovation of London's great cathedral had become something of a priority. In 1663 Charles II set up a Royal Commission to explore strategies for 'repairing and upholding that magnificent structure, and restoring the same . . . unto the ancient beauty and glory of it, which hath so much suffered by the iniquity of the late times'.[28]

The shopkeepers were ejected from Jones's portico, and over the next couple of years it was restored to its former glory, a work 'which will much illustrate the Memory of the Royal Founder, and being the most spacious and exposed part of the Building will most strongly excite the Charity of the people as it causes their admiration'.[29]

The problem of how to remedy the structural defects was more difficult and much more expensive. The roof over the south aisle had fallen in, damaging the main vault of the crossing and raising serious questions about the feasibility of repairing that part of the building. Scaffolding was installed to hold it up, and temporary roofing of deal covered with pantiles was put in place to at least protect the exposed sections of walling from the weather. As a temporary measure the entire main body of the cathedral – the crossing, the two transepts and the nave – was partitioned off with boards, and services continued in the choir (now the only stable area) while the Commission and the cathedral authorities considered how best to proceed.

A new Dean was appointed in 1664: he was William Sancroft, chaplain to the King and Master of Emmanuel College, Cambridge.★ An ambitious and dedicated High Church Tory, Sancroft was eager to see the cathedral restored; and in the spring of 1666, after an eighteen-month delay caused chiefly by the plague, three gentlemen 'surveyors' were brought in to advise on what to do next.

One was Hugh May – an obvious choice, since he was currently acting as Surveyor-General of the King's Works while Sir John Denham was ill. Another was Roger Pratt, who lived in the Inner Temple and had trained as a lawyer before spending six years touring through France, Italy, Flanders and Holland in order to avoid the unpleasantness of the Civil War. On his travels he had developed an interest in architecture and – unusually for an Englishman in the mid-seventeenth century – embarked on a systematic study of the Italian masters, including Leon Battista

★Sancroft gave up the Mastership soon after being installed in the Deanery in December 1664.

Alberti, Vincenzo Scamozzi and 'that excellent architect Palladio'.[30] Soon after his return to England in 1649 he had the opportunity to put theory into practice by designing a country house for a cousin. Coleshill in Berkshire was finished in 1662, and led to two more country houses the following year (Kingston Lacy in Dorset and Horseheath Hall near Cambridge) and then in 1664 to his most prestigious commission – Clarendon House, Piccadilly, for the Lord Chancellor, which was begun in 1664 and still unfinished in 1666. Pratt was arguably the most fashionable and advanced architect in the country.

The obvious choice for the third member of this advisory panel was John Webb, who as Inigo Jones's assistant in the 1630s had helped with the pre-war repairs to St Paul's, and who was now working on a remodelling of Greenwich Palace, five miles downriver from the City. But Webb was ignored in favour of a young professor of astronomy at Oxford, Dr Christopher Wren.

Like Pratt, Wren was an architectural amateur, but with rather fewer credentials. He was only thirty-three and had just one finished building to his name. The chapel of Pembroke College, Cambridge, which had been consecrated in September 1665, was impressive for a first attempt at building design, though hardly earth-shattering. But Wren had a considerable reputation as a scientist and an academic; he had an interest in contemporary European architecture, fuelled by a recent trip to France; and he had connections. Wren was not only on good terms with Charles II, but his uncle was Bishop of Ely and Archbishop Sheldon was an ex-Warden of his college, All Souls. Sheldon was also paying for the second building Wren had designed, a theatre which was being put up in Oxford 'for conferring degrees, dissection of bodies, and acting of plays'.[31] The Sheldonian was nowhere near finished, but its patron had seen enough of the design to be convinced of Wren's abilities.

Over the summer Wren, May and Pratt examined the old cathedral and pondered the best way of repairing it. Wren was all for a radical remodelling. The interior should be recased in stone, 'and in doing this,' he told Sancroft, 'it will be easy to perform it after a good Roman Manner as to follow the Gothick

Rudeness of the old Design'. The heavy stone vaulting of the nave roof, which was forcing the walls outward, should be replaced by brick covered with stucco. And the tower over the crossing was in such a precarious state that it must come down to ground level and be replaced by a dome: 'The outward appearance of the Church will seem to swell in the middle by degrees to a large Basis rising into a Rotundo bearing a Cupolo, and then ending in the Lantern: and this with incomparable more Grace in the remote Aspect than it is possible for the Lean Shaft of a Steeple to afford.'[32]

Hugh May's report has not survived, although he seems to have agreed with the main thrust of Wren's proposals. They thought the best way forward was to make a measured survey of the cathedral, draw up detailed plans for the new work and commission a model.

Roger Pratt did not.

Pratt was much more cautious than the pushy young academic. He could see no evidence for a dangerous outward thrust to the walls of the nave, and the idea of taking down the crossing tower and replacing it with a dome was complete folly. 'Mr Jones (who wanted no Abilities in the Art he professed) caused that part to be exactly scaffolded: to no purpose if he intended not rather a Reparation than total Abolition of it?' Nor had Jones needed a model when he repaired the cathedral; 'an ordinary paper Draught' had been enough for him, because he hadn't envisaged any drastic alterations. And if Inigo Jones hadn't seen the need to rebuild the central section of St Paul's, that was good enough for Roger Pratt.[33]

There was a good deal of professional jealousy between Pratt and Wren, who wrote dismissively that 'Mr Pratt's Way will be plausible because it will seeme to aim at great thrift'; and went on to plead for a 'trew latine [style] which the Lawyers say they cannot afford'.[34] The Commission convened a meeting in the cathedral on 27 August, when Pratt, May and Wren put their proposals before a group including Dean Sancroft, Bishop Henchman, John Evelyn, Commissioner of the Ordnance Thomas Chicheley and some expert workmen. The gathering examined the apparent outward thrust of the nave walls, and plumbed the uprights at various points. It was clear that the walls had indeed shifted from the perpendicular, and Pratt did himself no favours by insisting this was a deliberate device on the part of the Norman builders 'for an effect in perspective'. Chicheley supported him. Evelyn said he was being ridiculous, 'and so we entered it' in the minutes.[35]

Everybody moved up the cathedral until they were standing beneath the crossing. Pratt maintained that the tower could be repaired; Chicheley agreed with him. Wren and Evelyn argued hard for 'a noble cupola, a forme of church-building not as yet known in England, but of wonderfull grace'.[36] They offered to produce a plan and an estimate and, after a heated discussion, this was finally agreed, with the proviso that a committee of qualified workmen from the building trades should examine the foundations to establish the stability of the structure.

This was on the Monday. When the fire which broke out in Farriner's bakery the following Sunday began its inexorable move westward and the printers, stationers and booksellers of Paternoster Row rushed to move their stock into the crypt of the cathedral for safe keeping, no one thought that St Paul's would come to any serious harm. Even when the surrounding streets began to burn on Tuesday 4 September – Old Change and Lambeth Hill, Foster Lane and Warwick Lane – the monumental stone edifice rose above the smoke, impervious and immortal. William Taswell later recalled that 'the people who lived contiguous to St Paul's church raised their expectations greatly concerning the absolute security of that place upon account of the immense thickness of its walls and its situation; built in a large piece of ground, on every side remote from houses'.[37] They followed the example of the booksellers and filled the cathedral and its surrounding yard with household goods. Every opening into the book-filled crypt was blocked, so that not even the tiniest spark could enter.

Soon after sunset on Tuesday night William Taswell walked across from his school down to Westminster Stairs, over a mile away from St Paul's, where he looked across Lambeth Marsh towards the City. For more than an hour he stood and watched the fire creep around the cathedral, getting closer all the time, until only the firebreak of Paul's Churchyard stood in its way. At eight o'clock he saw flames appear on the roof.

The demolition work had blocked most of the narrow alleys and lanes round about, making it difficult for firefighters to approach with their ladders and buckets. And what if they did? St Paul's was no row of timber-framed houses to be pulled down with hooks; the nave alone stood about 150 feet high. And within less than half an hour the fire spreading along its roof was melting the lead, so that it dripped and then cascaded down into the body of the cathedral, 'as if it had been snow before the sun'.[38] The stonework split and popped and crashed down with explosive force. The lead ran down Ludgate Hill in a stream, 'the very pavements glowing with fiery rednesse, so as no horse nor man was able to tread on them'.[39] As the mountains of tightly packed books and bundles of paper in the crypt caught, the whole building went up with a huge roar, and by nine o'clock the blaze was so bright that it lit up the entire sky. Still standing on Westminster Stairs, William Taswell could see to read an edition of Terence which he had in his pocket. *Hinc illae lacrimae.**

Londoners had three theories about what had happened. Inevitably, some people thought the cathedral had been firebombed. Another school held that the furniture and bedding which had been dragged out of people's houses and piled up against the walls in Paul's Churchyard had caught fire, and that the flames had broken through the windows of the cathedral, igniting the household goods inside and, eventually, the warehoused books and paper in St Faith's. The fire then spread up the scaffolding poles and deal boards to the roof.

A more likely notion was that the wind carried embers from the burning houses below up to the roof of St Paul's. Once the poles and planking on the temporary sections of the south transept roof had caught, the precarious stone vaulting close by gave way and fell through the floor into the crypt below, followed

*'Hence these tears' (Terence, *Andria*, l. 26).

94

by burning scaffold masts and timbers. Exposed to fire and air, the contents of St Faith's went up like a bomb, gutting the interior of the cathedral in less than an hour. The most plausible explanation of all was a two-pronged attack, with both the roof and the goods in Paul's Yard catching fire at much the same time.

Forty miles away in Oxford, the moon turned blood red that night, and there was a distant sound like the waves of the sea. As St Paul's collapsed in ruins, the fashionable shops of Ludgate Hill burned. So did Ludgate itself. The ancient gatehouse, rebuilt in 1586, had a statue of the mythical King Lud facing towards the City and St Paul's, and another of Queen Elizabeth I looking west. It also housed a prison for petty criminals in its upper storey. Deserted by their gaolers, the prisoners broke out, as did the occupants of Newgate Gaol nearby. Elizabeth turned yellow in the heat but remained in one piece, staring out across Lambeth Marsh to Westminster and Whitehall. The poet John Crouch imagined her mixed emotions as her palace was saved while her capital burned:

> Though fancy makes not Pictures live, or love,
> Yet Pictures fancy'd may the fancy move:
> Me-thinks the Queen on White-hall cast her Eye;
> An Arrow could not more directly flye.
> But when she saw her Palace safe, her fears
> Vanish, one Eye drops smiles, the other tears.[40]

Even while Elizabeth wept and St Paul's burned and cracked in the heat, the Duke of York was struggling to prevent the western spread of the fire. It had now moved into the Temple, and men were pulling down houses around Somerset House in an effort to form a firebreak on the Strand. If that didn't work, there was nothing to stop the fire reaching the Palace of Whitehall itself; and that night work began on demolishing a set of lodgings built for Sir John Denham in Great Scotland Yard. They lay just by Charing Cross, and looked onto the builders' yards and offices that formed part of the Office of the King's Works. They would also be the first part of the Palace to burn should the fire arrive. Workers were told that the stores of timber stacked in the yards were to be thrown into the Thames. As a precaution, Catherine of Braganza, the Duchess of York and their households began to prepare to leave Whitehall for Hampton Court at dawn the following morning. 'Oh, the confusion there was then at that Court!' wrote Evelyn.[41]

While their servants gathered their clothes and jewellery and packed it into chests, there was another sound above the roar of the flames. The eastern sector of the City shook to an explosion. Then another, and another.

After waiting all day for the workmen from the naval dockyards to arrive, John, Lord Berkeley and his men at the Tower had decided to take matters into their own hands. Military engineers from the Office of Ordnance began to set charges in the houses close by on Tower Street. As they lit train after train of powder, the ground shook, and buildings flew apart or rose a few feet into the air before falling with a strangely muted crump. And there was more panic, as word went round that the cannon in the Tower were firing indiscriminately into the streets. 'Nothing can be like unto the distraction we were in,' wrote one of the Duke's helpers, 'but the Day of Judgement.'[42]

Around eleven o'clock that night, the wind veered to the south. Then it began to die.

6

And After Three Days' Toil

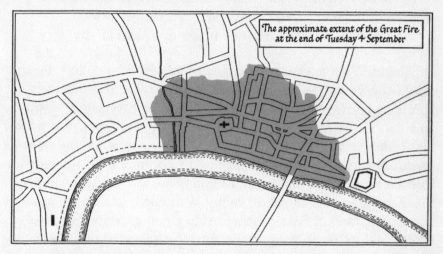

The approximate extent of the Great Fire at the end of Tuesday 4 September

*T*he first signs of hope came a little before midnight on Tuesday. Several messengers appeared before James pleading for men and engines – it looked as if there was a chance of holding the fire before it reached Temple Bar and the Strand. Flames were only yards away from the old church of St Dunstan-in-the-West (so-called to distinguish it from St Dunstan-in-the-East on Tower Street), which stood on the north side of Fleet Street, just past Fetter Lane. But the wind had veered sharply to the south, driving the flames down to Ram Alley between Fleet Street and the Temple, and slowing them down. The stone walls of St Dunstan might provide just enough of a stop to their westward march.

The Duke's Guards had been working for two-and-a-half days without a break, and were by now exhausted; but once ordinary citizens realised that the western suburbs – and hence their own homes – might be saved, they finally joined in the firefighting in earnest. At six on Wednesday morning James arrived on the front line, and found that although the fire zone was still creeping northward, up Fetter Lane and the remains of Shoe Lane, the gales were now definitely subsiding.

> The morning wakes, and with the Morn the Fire,
> Whose whispering voice seems softly to enquire
> For its lost Friend the Wind, who stole away
> By Night i' th' dark, not to be found next day.[1]

Samuel Wiseman's description of the wind as a 'lost Friend' recalls the extent to which it had been driving the fire over the past seventy-two hours. But London had been feeding the flames, and London had more to give. The big houses along the Strand were being evacuated – mostly via the Thames, since the persons of quality who had enough money to command all things were still able to procure barges and lighters. According to Clarendon, the King gave up hope of saving Whitehall, and grew anxious about the fate of Westminster Abbey. James responded to his brother's fears by moving down into the alleys around Chancery Lane and the Court of Rolls and pressing everyone he found there – men, women and children – into service fighting the fire. Those who refused were beaten until they changed their minds.

With the benefit of hindsight, we can marvel at the stupidity and selfishness of Londoners. We can shake our heads in despair at their inability to organise, their reluctance to put themselves at risk, their refusal to fight back against the flames rather than thinking only of their own skins and their own possessions. If they had had more courage, then London might have been saved. Contemporaries certainly shared that view, although, as one noted sensibly in the weeks that followed, 'Thus Chant the people, who are seldom wise / Till things be past, before-hand have no Eyes.'[2] But for the people who were there, things were not so simple. The fire, spreading so quickly, had caused widespread panic, especially in a population jittery with the fear of Dutch invasion. If the authorities had taken a firm hand at the beginning, then things might have been different. But that disastrous lack of leadership was only now being put right.

On Thursday afternoon, for instance, a London physician named William Denton had just moved everything apart from his books and a couple of blankets to the safety of Kensington. He and his wife were facing huge losses from the destruction of property they owned in Salisbury Court, among other places; and they were, he said, 'in such a confused condition that we know not what favor of frends to make use of, though we have need of them all'. He had tried to send a letter to a friend in the country, but he didn't know what had happened to his usual carrier. Two of his servants had been pressed into service by the Duke's men that morning, and another had gone out in search of the carrier and not come back. 'Soe I am goinge myselfe to find him, for I dare not send a man out of doors for feare of being pressed to work att the fier.'[3]

Leave aside the fact that it was only the lower classes who were being press-ganged by the Duke's soldiers, and that respectable middle-aged professionals like Denton had nothing to fear. Put yourself in his place for a moment. You really do not know what is happening. You don't know if you're going to be forced out of your home. Would you leap to the defence of your city and man the buckets and the fire-hooks? Or would your thoughts turn first to your belongings, your wife, your children? It is interesting to note that of all the diarists and correspondents who describe what it was like to be in London during the Fire – and around a dozen have survived – only Windham Sandys, John Evelyn and Samuel Pepys actually took part in the fire-fighting. (And Evelyn didn't show up at his post in Fetter Lane until the flames were nearly out, while Pepys's contribution was confined to accompanying some dockers to extinguish a minor flash-fire in a street close to his home.) Everyone looked to their own goods and complained that no one was doing anything.

Among those who did act, the court seemed to have the edge over the City. That is not so surprising. Courtiers had the confidence which came from being near the top of a society which prized deference and obedience; and unlike the City's aldermen, they did not have to worry too much about offending property-owning citizens. The Earl of Craven was still masterminding the firefighting at Holborn Bridge, and around noon he and his men managed not only to stop the flames from spreading any further, but also to put them out. He immediately rushed over to help at the Cow Lane post, where Sir Richard Browne was struggling – 'but a weak man in this business' said one of the Duke of York's gentlemen.[4] Galvanised into action by the prospect of success, the example of others, or sheer terror, Sir Thomas Bludworth finally began to demolish houses around his station at Cripplegate, where the fire was 'grown to a great head'.[5] And Privy Counsellors rode up and down the streets, urging on the work, authorising demolitions, breaking open pipes and doing their best to ensure that water was available.

At two o'clock on Wednesday morning Elizabeth Pepys had woken her husband, who was spending a second night under Will Hewer's quilt. There were shouts of 'Fire!' in the street outside, and the flames had reached the church of All Hallows Barking at the bottom of the lane. Samuel decided it was time to go. He gathered up all his money – £2,350 in gold – and took Elizabeth, Will Hewer and Jane Birch down to the Thames, where a waterman ferried them eight miles or so downriver to the naval yards at Woolwich.

The gates of the yard were shut, but Pepys was surprised to see that there were no guards posted, in spite of the rumours of imminent invasion. He got them opened, and deposited everyone and everything in the house of William Sheldon, Clerk of the Cheque at the yard. Sheldon had provided the Pepys family with sanctuary once before, when Elizabeth moved there during the previous year's plague. He was a trusted employee of the Navy Office; but Pepys was taking no chances. He locked up his gold and ordered Will and Elizabeth 'never to leave the room without one of them in it night nor day'.[6] Then he went back to Seething Lane, stopping off at the Deptford yard on the way to check on his household goods and make sure they were being watched over.

He was so convinced that the Navy Office had burned that all the way home he couldn't bring himself to ask anyone for news. But when he got back to Seething Lane at seven that morning, he found to his surprise that it was still standing.

Dockyard workers had finally arrived on the scene, and the business of blowing up buildings along Tower Street proceeded with renewed vigour. Several houses at the foot of Mark Lane and a winery and warehouse at the bottom of Seething Lane all went the same way. All Hallows Barking had the narrowest of escapes: its parsonage burned down, and the flames damaged a clock and a dial on the church wall before being brought under control.*

Once it was clear that the rest of Seething Lane was safe, Pepys climbed up to the top of All Hallows' tower, 'and there saw the saddest sight of desolation that I ever saw. Everywhere great fires. Oyle-cellars and brimstone and other things burning.'[7] He took fright and came down again as fast as he could, then walked up to Sir William Penn's lodgings, where he had a breakfast of cold meat.

By Wednesday afternoon it was obvious that the struggle to save what remained of London was being won. The gales, which had been easing all morning, faded away completely by four or five o'clock. There were still fires burning all over the City, particularly in Cripplegate, where Bludworth was now tearing down buildings as fast as he could, and around the western suburbs on the edge of the fire zone. But towards evening the Duke of York decided that the worst was over. He took steps to ensure that the fire posts were still manned, in case of further outbreaks, and then he went back to his lodgings at Whitehall, exhausted. A lot of Londoners were not so lucky: more than 70,000 of them had no homes to go back to.

So where did they go?

There were the unburned suburbs. A certain amount of urban sprawl had occurred around the outskirts of London during the

---

*Pepys claimed that the porch was also scorched, but Walter Bell disputes this in his 1920 book on the Fire, having failed to find any mention of it in the church accounts. All Hallows Barking still stands today, although much restored after being bombed in the Blitz. William Penn, founder of Pennsylvania (and elder son of Pepys's colleague on the Navy Board), was baptised here; President John Quincy Adams was married here; and the headless corpse of Archbishop William Laud was deposited here after his execution. (He was later moved to St John's College, Oxford.)

first half of the seventeenth century. By 1666 ribbon development meant that there was no break between Bishopsgate and Shoreditch, once a little village a mile away on the road north to Ware. Clerkenwell, a rapidly expanding district in which the mansions of the great stood side by side with a workhouse and a gaol, was likewise losing its individual identity as houses crept outward from West Smithfield and the newly developed Hatton Garden, described by Evelyn in 1659 as the beginnings of 'a little towne, lately an ample garden'.[8]

Evelyn – so far ahead of his time in so many of his ideas about urban planning – actually suggested the formation of a green belt around the City. Plantations of trees, wild thyme and entire fields of fragrant flowers should be encouraged, he argued, 'and the farther exorbitant encrease of Tenements, poor and nasty Cottages near the City, be prohibited, which disgrace and take off from the sweetness and amœnity of the Environs of London'.[9]★ A proclamation issued from Whitehall in the summer of 1661 did try to regulate the spread of the suburbs by forbidding any building on new foundations within two miles of the gates of London or Westminster. We can guess how strictly it was adhered to from the fact that the following year the Earl of St Albans leased Pall Mall Field, next door to St James's Palace, and began to lay out an exclusive new housing development, St James's Square. (Ironically, the same proclamation forbade jetties and overhangs, and insisted on brick and stone rather than timber. If Londoners had paid more attention to it, their city might well have been saved.)

Apart from the damage caused along both sides of Fleet Street when the fire broke through Ludgate on Tuesday, the built-up areas outside the walls – Houndsditch, The Charterhouse, West Smithfield, Clerkenwell, over to Hatton Garden and Lincoln's Inn – were still pretty much intact, and the homeless who had friends or relations in those districts might be expected to lodge with them temporarily.

Those with friends further afield, or without ties to keep them

---

★It would be another 270 years before a green belt was established round the capital, by which time 'poor and nasty Cottages' were things of beauty in comparison with the suburban excrescences which passed for housing in the early twentieth century.

near their ruined homes and businesses, might move away from London altogether. The King issued a proclamation on Wednesday which ordered other towns to receive any distressed persons on the run from the fire, and to permit them to exercise their trades. The antiquary Anthony Wood noted in his diary that several refugees were quick to set up shop in Oxford. Closer to home, in Islington and the neighbouring villages, local justices were asked to make sure that a strict watch was kept over any distressed persons and their goods, so that they wouldn't be robbed. The King also requested that 'charitable and Christian reception, lodging, and entertainment' should be given to them.[10]

By and large, the idea of moving out of London was something to think about later. Carriers were still at a premium, and there was still the hope of returning home and salvaging something from the disaster. Anyway, most people were too shocked at the events of the past three days to make serious decisions about their future. They took what they could, moved out of range of the flames, and set up camp while they waited to see what would happen.

'The most in fields like herded beasts lie down', wrote Dryden, 'To dews obnoxious on the grassy floor.'[11] In Restoration London you were never very far away from the countryside, in spite of the spread of the suburbs. There were still open fields between Clerkenwell and Islington, still windmills in Finsbury Fields. You could find wild horse-radish at Hoxton, and orchids in Stepney. Over the river, spaniels were used to hunt duck in the ponds scattered around the marshy ground of St George's Fields in Southwark.

Refugees from the City gathered in St George's Fields; they gathered over by Islington and Clerkenwell; they gathered anywhere they could find shelter, as Anthony Wood recalled with righteous relish: 'Those that had a house today were the next glad of the shelter of an hedge or a pigstie or stable. Those that were this day riding wantonly in coaches, were, the next, glad to ride in dung-carts to save their lives . . . Those that delighted themselves in downe bedds and silken curteynes, are now glad of the shelter of a hedge.'[12]

The main point of assembly was Moorfields, which sounds like a rural idyll, but was in fact one of the City's most notorious centres of vice. Eighteen months later it would be the scene of an unedifying riot when thousands of disgruntled sailors and apprentices attacked the many brothels which lined the fields – not because they disapproved of whores, but because they disapproved of whores who cheated them.★

Moorfields was London's first civic park – an L-shaped piece of fenland of about twenty-two acres, immediately north of the City wall at Moorgate. It was levelled and planted at the beginning of the seventeenth century, and laid out in a series of gravelled walks with tree-lined avenues and benches, which turned the area into 'a garden of this City and a pleasurable place of sweet ayres for Cittizens to walk in'.[13] The New Artillery Ground, where the Honourable Artillery Company practised archery and shooting, and where the trained bands drilled, was just to the north; and Bethlehem Royal Hospital, where Londoners came to while away an afternoon laughing at the caged and chained lunatics, lay to the east.

As the nearest piece of safe open ground beyond the City wall, this was where thousands of burnt-out refugees had gathered by Wednesday. Evelyn, who went to take a look that afternoon, was appalled to find a vast encampment which filled Moorfields and spilled out into the surrounding fields as far as Highgate, almost five miles away. Some people were under tents, others had makeshift sheds and hovels. 'Many [were] without a rag or any necessary utensills, bed or board, who from delicateness, riches, and easy accommodations in stately and well furnish'd houses, were now reduced to extreamest misery and poverty.'[14] Samuel Pepys had also walked up into Moorfields with a couple of friends earlier in the day; he too was shocked to see the park packed with people. More were streaming in by the minute, and everyone was jealously guarding the bundles of possessions they had managed to save.

★The Bawdy House Riots of 1668 actually started in Poplar, at a whorehouse much frequented by sailors. But it soon moved into the main red-light districts – Moorfields, Holborn, Shoreditch and East Smithfield – and after several days it climaxed in Moorfields itself.

There was no hint of trouble as yet, but Charles and the Privy Council which advised him were acutely aware that huge crowds like this were a potential threat to public order. The ideal thing to do would be to disperse them, to send them – where? That was the problem. The proclamation commanding other towns to take in London's homeless was intended to encourage people to move away; but it was not likely to make any difference for several days, at least.

So the government, which had by now taken control of managing the disaster, was faced with two priorities. The same policy that had sent the Life Guards onto the streets of the burning city dictated the need for an armed presence to keep order in the camps; common humanity demanded that those camps be provided with emergency relief as quickly as possible.

Civil policing was virtually non-existent. At the best of times it was carried on by constables, beadles and watchmen – part-timers who reluctantly took their turn at serving their local community or, if they were wealthy enough, paid someone else to stand in for them. They didn't have the strength or the commitment for crowd control – many were themselves victims of the Fire, and they couldn't be depended on to put community interests before their own: in a report submitted the next day on the manning of the eight fire posts, the Earl of Oxford said that only the constables of St Giles-in-the-Fields were in position.

None of the contingents of militia that Charles had called for from Kent, Hertfordshire, Surrey and Middlesex on Tuesday had arrived. (In fact it is not really clear whether they had even been ordered into the City at this stage, or simply told to muster and wait further orders.) Detachments of Guards under the Duke and the Earl of Craven were busy in the streets, coordinating the fire-fighting and supervising those citizens who had been persuaded to help.

This left the trained bands. Theoretically, London's local militia comprised six regiments of around 1,000 men apiece, each commanded by a colonel appointed by the King. (Bludworth had been Colonel of the Orange Regiment in 1660, and Colonel of the Yellow for the past six years.) Like the parish constables, members were part-timers who had their own homes to worry about. But they were relatively well disciplined, and when they were called out early on in the emergency, some, at least, had done their best to fight the fire. The trained bands had also been involved in policing some of the areas where goods were being stockpiled, with companies of militiamen preventing looting and pilfering in Lincoln's Inn Fields, Gray's Inn Fields and Hatton Garden.

Petty theft was a problem, as William Taswell's father had discovered to his cost. One Nathaniel Hubert was gaoled for stealing goods valued at 3s 6d from someone named Serskall, although he insisted that he had only 'detained' them in lieu of a reward for helping Serskall move his belongings during the Fire, and had since returned them. But Hubert was one of the unlucky ones. Even in quieter times, criminals were unlikely to be caught, and the justice system relied mainly on deterrence: the theft of goods worth more than a shilling was punishable by hanging, although it might be commuted to military service or transportation. (Hubert petitioned the King for an order to send him to sea rather than leave him languishing in gaol to await trial.) In the chaos following the Fire, there was little hope of apprehending most of the opportunist thieves, 'men ready enough to fish', as Clarendon put it;[15] and eventually – on 19 September, to be exact – another royal proclamation appeared. With touching optimism it ordered that everyone who had 'wilfully, ignorantly, or of purpose' taken plate, goods or building materials from the ruins should return them to the armoury in Finsbury Fields, where they would be inventoried, stored and eventually returned to their rightful owners.[16] Presumably no action was taken against those who obeyed, but then it was unlikely that any action could be taken against those who didn't.

The most effective way to keep the crowds of dispossessed people under control was to comfort them, to make them feel secure, to keep them fed and watered. Churches, chapels, schools and public buildings on the outskirts of the City were thrown open to accept the goods 'of those who know not how to dispose of them'.[17] But in the days immediately after the Fire, food supply was a bigger problem than pilfering. Huge amounts of corn and other foodstuffs, all the victuals required to service a thriving metropolis, had literally gone up in smoke; and the resulting disruption to food distribution systems within the fire zone was bad enough. But it was worse than that: bakers and brewers in the undamaged parts of the City and its suburbs had taken their families and fled the flames, and, as Clarendon recalled, 'many days passed, before they were enough in their wits and in their houses to fall to their occupations'.[18] This meant that not only were there difficulties in getting food to the people in the fields, but many of those around the perimeter who had stayed put and whose homes had been saved were also facing serious shortages.

Yet another royal proclamation was issued. The King announced that he had taken steps to ensure that supplies of bread were brought in to the capital each day. They would go to three new markets set up around the edges of the fire zone, at Bishopsgate, Tower Hill and Smithfield. Charles also decided that temporary markets should be established in the villages around the City to cater for displaced persons who were unable or unwilling to come back into London. There were five of these: at Mile End Green and Ratcliff, then both small hamlets to the east of the City, close to Stepney, and in the north and north-west at Finsbury Fields, Islington and Clerkenwell. All these markets were just that – places where goods were bought and sold, and not distribution points for emergency aid. The proclamation warned that the King had taken care 'to secure the said markets in safety, and prevent all disturbances by the refusal of payment for goods or otherwise'.[19] The prospect of food riots was very real.

After touring the camps that Wednesday afternoon a miserable Evelyn went home to Deptford, counting his blessings and thanking God that his home and family were safe. The thing that had impressed him most as he wandered through the crowds of homeless people was their pride. 'Tho' ready to perish for hunger and destitution,' he wrote, 'yet not asking one pennie for reliefe, which to me appear'd a stranger sight than any I had yet beheld.'[20] Pepys left Moorfields consoling himself with the thought that at least the weather was fair and not likely to add to the woes of the homeless that night. He picked his way through the ruins of Cheapside, parts of which were still smouldering, and paused at Mercers' Hall. This 'most curious piece of work', as Stow called it, which had once entertained Henry VIII and Jane Seymour, was a burnt-out shell.[21] Its famous chapel was a wreck, and the glass from its windows had flowed into the street, where it lay like parchment. Pepys took up a piece for a souvenir, and carried on eastward. As he passed the Royal Exchange he stopped again to gaze at men working on the ruins. A chimney next to one of the walls of the Exchange was still standing – right across the City, brick chimneys were all that survived of timber buildings – and he watched in horror as a cat was brought out of a hole in the brickwork. It was naked, with all its fur burned off; but it was still alive.

Pepys got back to Seething Lane after dark. The main danger had passed, and everyone was pretty confident that the Navy Office would be safe. But there was still a chance that the Fire would flare up again, and he set about organising the workers from the naval yard, who were still there. Men were set to watch all night; beer, bread and cheese were distributed and makeshift bedding was provided in the offices. An exhausted Pepys finally got to bed around midnight. 'And I had forgot almost the day of the week'.[22]

Out in the open, everyone was tired and scared and hungry:

> And after three days' toil, trouble, and fright,
> Having no ease by day, nor rest by night,
> Nor leisure all this time, due food to eat,
> Now in the fields may sleep, but still want meat:
> Many who late fed on delicious fare,
> Would now skip at a crust, though brown it were . . .[23]

As night fell, it was possible to see that fires still burned all over the City; and the crash of falling timbers, the boom of an occasional explosion rolling across the northern fields, kept nerves on edge.

But to the west, beyond Ludgate Hill, something more substantial than a sporadic outbreak of fire was happening. There was a light in the sky over the Temple and the south side of Fleet

Street; and in the darkness, in the encampments of Islington and Moorfields, a rumour began to spread faster than the flames. The Fire *had* been a terrorist act. It *was* the precursor to an invasion – a softening-up process which would be followed by a rising of all the French and Dutch nationals in the city. Now that rising had started and 50,000 foreigners were on the march, looking to finish what the Fire had begun. A savage army was making for Moorfields, determined to cut men's throats where they lay, to rape defenceless women and to steal the pathetic bundles of goods which these dispossessed Londoners had managed to save from the catastrophe. Within minutes there was general panic in the camps and the surrounding streets – exactly the wholesale break-down of order which the King had been dreading and the Duke had been trying so hard to keep at bay.

The Earl of Clarendon had no time for the mob and its antics. In his version of the events of that night, he dismissed the fright-ened crowds as 'sottish', and described in an exasperated tone how 'the inhabitants of a whole street have ran in a great tumult one way, upon the rumour that the French were marching at the other end of it; so terrified men were with their own appre-hensions'.[24] But then he was writing several years later, after a hostile crowd had cost him his place at court and his reputation and forced him into exile. If he had been burned out of his home, traumatised and disoriented and forced to sleep in a field, he might not have been quite so patronising.

'Who can express the horror of that night,' recalled an anony-mous poet in 1672, 'When people cry'd, Prepare your selves for flight; / The *French* and *Dutch* resolve to take our lives, / And when we are dead, they'll ravish all our Wives'.[25] Crowd psychology is an unpredictable thing. While some people tried to escape, and others simply stayed where they were, many Londoners ran towards the threat. As the story spread, the rising of resident foreigners quickly turned into a landing by a French and Dutch invasion force. The old alarm call, 'Arm! Arm! Arm!', was taken up around the fields and suburbs, and people grabbed staves and knives and whatever weapons came to hand and went out to save their city.

They were wrong, but after all that had happened to them over the past four days, they were brave. 'Fired with rage and fury . . . they begin to stir themselves like lions, or like bears bereaved of their whelps.'[26] They were angry; they were looking for someone to blame; and they were more than ready to make a stand against an enemy they had been fighting for a year and a half. Even at this point the war was uppermost in people's minds. Francisco de Rapicani, an Italian in the service of the Swedish embassy in London, walked out among the burnt-out Londoners and was amazed at their strength of purpose. 'The people's courage was so resilient,' he wrote in his autobiography, '. . . that it was not so much the loss caused by the dreadful fire that they were talking and worrying about, as the war that they were waging on the sea against the Dutch.'[27]

As the crowd surged into the suburbs there was another bout of racial violence: people 'could not be stopp'd from falling on some of those nations whom they casually met, without sense or reason'. The trained bands did their best to push the frightened and angry mob back into the fields. Troops of Life Guards joined them and members of the court arrived to calm things down. 'They did with infinite paines and greate difficulty reduce and appease the people.' So worried were the courtiers that armed guards were mounted for the rest of the night.[28]

The Duke had just returned to his Whitehall lodgings, after a day spent coordinating the firefighting operation around Fleet Street and Chancery Lane, when word of the invasion scare reached him. By now he was dog-tired – according to one of the gentlemen who served with him, he hadn't had more than two or three hours' sleep since Sunday night – but he mounted up and rode out down the Strand once again.

The near riot in Moorfield was under control by the time the Duke set out, but when he and his men reached the ruins of Fleet Street they saw what had caused it. The eastern section of the Temple was on fire again, and although there was a crowd of people gathered at the entrance, the students had barricaded themselves in and were refusing to open the gate. It seemed that another rumour had got about, that the lawyers' chambers were filled with gold and it was there for the taking. 'Unless there was a barrister there,' the students told the Duke, 'they durst not open any door.'²⁹ They opened for him, however. He found that the flames had flared again to the east of Inner Temple and were closing on the Temple Church and the Inner Temple Hall from the south-east. A building called the Paper House stood in the fire's path: the fact that it derived its name from 'paperwork', a seventeenth-century term for timber, lath and plaster construction, is ample demonstration that it was more likely to speed than impede the progress of the blaze.

James decided the only hope of saving the Hall and the Church was to blow up the Paper House. He sent for gunpowder and military engineers; but when the gunpowder arrived and the Duke's intentions became clear to the anxious onlookers, one of the lawyers came to him and pointed out that 'it was against the rules and charter of the Temple that any should blow [up] that house with gunpowder'.³⁰

This was the wrong thing to say to a man who was tired, who was doing his best, and who was the brother of the King of England. James stared in disbelief. Then his Master of Horse, Henry Jermyn – an unprepossessing little debauchee with a big head and skinny legs – stepped forward, grabbed a cudgel and hit the young lawyer with it. No one bothered to ask the lawyer's name, although afterwards the Duke and his household hoped he might have the nerve to bring an action for battery against Jermyn.

They blew up the building.

Even the demolition didn't save the Inner Temple. Large sections were burned, and one end of the roof of the Inner Temple Hall caught fire. It was saved by the prompt action of a sailor named Richard Rowe, who climbed up and beat out the flames. The Templars later awarded him £10 as a thank-you, and a poem which appeared later in the year, 'London's Second Tears mingled with her Ashes', celebrated him as a hero:

> . . . with good Conduct all was slak'd that night
> By one more valiant than a *Templar Knight.*
> Here a brisk Rumour of affrighted Gold
> Sent hundreds in; more Covetous than bold.

But a brave Seaman up the Tyles did skip
As nimbly as the Cordage of a Ship,
Bestrides the sing'd Hall on its highest ridge,
Moving as if he were on *London-Bridge*,
Or on the *Narrow* of a Skullers Keel:
Feels neither head nor heart nor spirits reel.[31]

7

Mighty Merry and Our Fears Over

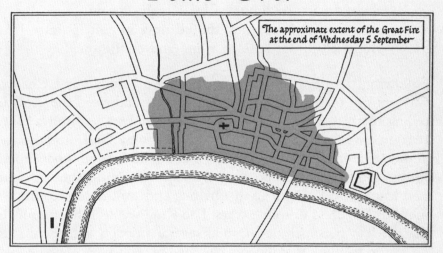

The approximate extent of the Great Fire at the end of Wednesday 5 September

*E*arly on Thursday King Charles went by barge to the Tower, to see just how near to ruin it had come. Without doubt the demolitions in Tower Street and the neighbouring alleys had saved it: 'Stranger Experiment sure ne're hath bin,' wrote John Tabor in 'Seasonable Thoughts in Sad Times', 'thus by a blast to save the Magazin.'[1] Understandably, Sir John Robinson and John, Lord Berkeley had deemed it expedient to move all the gunpowder out of the White Tower. The goldsmiths had brought their coin and bullion here for safekeeping, in much the same way as the stationers had gathered their stocks in the crypt of St Paul's; but when they saw how the fire was approaching, they took steps to have it transferred to the Palace of Whitehall. As it was valued at £1.2 million, that must have been quite a convoy. Precautionary demolitions around the Tower were continuing – in fact several days later the Privy Council would still be issuing orders to

take down houses at Tower Wharf 'for preventing the fire coming
to His Majesty's magazine'.[2]

After watching the workmen and congratulating everyone
concerned, the King rode out into Moorfields. This was the main
object of his trip,

> Lest the rude Rabble in this doleful hour
> Should pass the limits of his Kingly Power;
> And getting head, they should now in conclusion
> Bring all things here to ruine and confusion.[3]

Following the disorder and panic of the previous night Charles
was anxious to reassure his subjects. So he addressed the crowd,
telling them that the Fire had been an accident, and not a plot.
It had come from the Hand of God. Just why God should have
chosen to punish London in such a dramatic fashion he declined
to say, although in the coming weeks and months there would
be plenty who thought it an obvious and well-deserved judgement on Charles's dissolute ways. The King went on to announce
that he had personally examined several suspects and there was
no reason to think that incendiaries had been at work. The people
must not take fright again like they had the previous night. He
had strength enough to defend them from any enemy, and by
the grace of God, he said, he would live and die with them.

It was a good speech, designed to comfort and reassure. And
it seems to have worked. There were no more serious disturbances that day. But just as a precautionary measure, Lord
Arlington, the Secretary of State, wrote to the Lord Lieutenants
of Hertfordshire, Kent, Middlesex and Surrey, reminding them
that on Tuesday the King had commanded that they draw together
their militias in preparation for a march on London. The Fire
was no longer such a serious danger, Arlington told them; but
because the firefighters in the City were so tired, they were still
required to send 200 foot soldiers apiece. The contingents were
told to rendezvous at four points just outside the City: the men
from Hertfordshire should gather at Kingsland, a little hamlet
between Islington and Hackney where there was plenty of pasture

for them to camp; those from Middlesex in the Temple; those from Kent at Southwark; and those from Surrey at Lambeth. They should carry enough food for two days, and bring carts with ropes, buckets and pickaxes – all the equipment they might need 'to prevent the further spreading of the fire'.[4] The Deputy Lieutenants and local justices should also assemble to help with the organisation, and to speed up the movement of bread, cheese and other necessary provisions into the capital.

Although this official request, like the one sent on Tuesday, was addressed to the Lord Lieutenants of the counties concerned, it was forwarded immediately to Deputy Lieutenants. The Lord Lieutenant of Middlesex, for example, was the Duke of Albemarle, who was still with the battered fleet at Spithead and hardly in a position to organise the movement of 200 militiamen complete with firefighting equipment and food. One suspects that the Earl of Southampton, who was Lord Lieutenant of Kent, was likewise out of the picture when it came to mustering local troops, since he was also Lord Treasurer of England.

Arlington's intention was simple. He and his King wanted soldiers in the City. The pretext might be the need to keep watch against further outbreaks of fire, but the real reason was the maintenance of public order. Wednesday night's disturbances could not be allowed to happen again, and the troops in the capital were exhausted. A royal proclamation was also published early on Thursday. It announced that an Exchange was to be set up at Gresham College, an Elizabethan mansion which lay between Bishopsgate Street and Broad Street, in the undamaged north-east quarter. Founded in 1597 under the terms of Sir Thomas Gresham's will as an adult education centre for Londoners, the College was to be a temporary replacement for the Guildhall and, appropriately enough, Gresham's Royal Exchange.

The proclamation also gave more details of the temporary markets which were to be set up to the north and east, adding a site in Leadenhall Street to West Smithfield, Bishopsgate and Tower Hill. Magistrates in the surrounding counties who were coordinating relief supplies should send them to one of these four centres. But the real point of the proclamation was to issue a warning 'forbidding men to disquiet themselves with rumours of tumults' and ordering them not to beat up their fellow citizens on the streets but to 'attend to the business of quenching the fire, troops being provided to keep the peace'.[5]

While the King was calming the crowds in Moorfields, a massive clearing-up operation was slowly getting under way in the City. There were ashes and smouldering timbers everywhere. Many streets were impassable. Where people could manage to pick their way through the debris, they had to move quickly: the ground was hot, almost too hot to walk on. Soon after sunrise William Taswell set out from Westminster School to have a look at the ruins of St Paul's. He got as far as the east end of Fleet Street, where it met Ludgate Hill, and then had to stop. The soles of his shoes were almost scorched and the air was so intensely warm that he began to feel dizzy. 'Unless I had stopped some time upon Fleet Bridge to rest myself,' he wrote, 'I must have fainted under the extreme languor of my spirits.'[6]

After catching his breath for a moment or two Taswell carried on up the hill to the cathedral. It was a dreadful sight. Inigo Jones's portico at the west end had collapsed and broken into pieces, although the inscription carved along the frieze was intact, with not a single letter defaced. This recorded that the portico was the gift of Charles I, and its survival was regarded with superstitious awe, just as the fall of the portico itself was thought to be particularly tragic because of the association with the King's late father. 'When I pass the *sacred Martyrs* West', wrote John Crouch, 'I close my Eyes and smite my troubled Breast; / What shall we now for his dear Mem'ry do/When fire *un-carves*, and *Stones* are mortal too?'[7] At the east end, the high altar was still more or less intact – a fact which also provoked spectators to muse on divine providence – but precious little else had survived. Parts of the building were still burning; the bells had melted; massive lumps of masonry, charred timbers and fragments of Portland stone ornaments were lying all over the place. The nave was open to the sky, smoke still belched from a gaping hole in the floor of the choir where the books and pamphlets of the Paternoster Row stationers smouldered down in St Faith's. Broken monuments were scattered around: marble limbs and dismembered effigies, an alabaster coat of arms, the torso of a knight. John Donne's macabre funerary monument, an upright figure of the poet perched on top of an urn and peering out from behind his shroud, had slipped down into the crypt when the floor gave way.★

There was worse. When the roof fell in, it broke open tombs and exposed coffins – and their contents. Now bones, corpses and other awful souvenirs of mortality were strewn around. Describing an encounter with a skull that he found in the ruins, the poet James Wright was inspired with a Jacobean ghoulishness:

> Gallants, what think you, will this Fashion do?
> A Wig may well supply his loss of hair:
> His Nose is gone, that may be wanting too:
> But here's no Eyes, ah! that is past repair.[8]

There were bodies in various states of decay and putrefaction. 'See there Death's Presence Chamber quite display'd,' said Wright; 'Ha! this doth both the Eye and Nose affright.'[9] Robert Braybrooke, a Bishop of London who had last seen the cathedral back in 1404, fell into St Faith's and out of his coffin on Tuesday night. Neither time nor high temperatures had done him much harm: he was as stiff as a plank, but perfectly intact, with teeth, red hair and beard and skin like leather. When people heard of his miraculous state of preservation some attributed it to his saintly life, others to a quirk of nature – but everybody wanted to see him. Over the following weeks he was hauled out of the crypt along with at least two other mummified corpses, and placed on his feet in Convocation House Yard next door to the ruins, where, having managed one resurrection, he waited for the next. He became quite a celebrity. The Duke of York paid him a visit; so did Pepys; and after a while he grew to be an

---

★Donne's 1631 effigy, carved by Master Mason Nicholas Stone from a painting done during the subject's life, survived its descent into the flames. It was salvaged and placed in the new St Paul's, where it stands today. There are also some fragments of pre-Fire monuments, mostly late Elizabethan, in the Crypt.

accepted fixture, so that in 1675, when the foundation stone of the new St Paul's Cathedral was laid, he was still standing in the yard, still waiting.

Other casualties were accorded less dignity, without even the consolation of posthumous fame. The monument to John Colet, a Renaissance scholar and Dean of St Paul's, broke along with the others and exposed his lead coffin, which was set into the wall a few feet above the level of the floor. Someone poked a hole in it and found it full of fluid, which a couple of enterprising souls actually tasted. According to the antiquary John Aubrey, it was 'of a kind of insipid tast, something of an Ironish tast'.[10] When they prodded the corpse with a stick it felt like boiled brawn.

William Taswell was fourteen years old. So far as he was concerned, the wreck of St Paul's was an adventure playground, not a charnel-house scene from the Last Judgement. He clambered over the rubble, disturbing piles of stones which tumbled down at his feet; he filled his pockets with lumps of melted bell metal as souvenirs. He wasn't even particularly upset when, as he was rooting around by the east end of the cathedral, he stumbled over a corpse – a fresh one. It was the body of 'an old decrepid woman' who had tried to hide here from the flames, imagining St Paul's would keep her safe.[11] Her limbs were reduced to charcoal, her clothes were burned away and her skin was parched and yellow. William picked up a sword and helmet he found in the ruins and put them on to play soldiers. Then he went back to Westminster.

Like so many Londoners, Taswell was struck by how dark the sky had become. 'A black darkness seemed to cover the whole hemisphere,' he wrote in his memoirs many years later, 'and the bewailings of people were great.'[12]* As he made his way back

---

*Taswell also marvelled that half-burned papers from St Faith's were carried on the wind as far as Eton, twenty-six miles away. Lady Carteret, wife of the Navy Treasurer, made much the same comment to Pepys. The Carterets had a house in Windsor Forest, and while the Fire was raging 'abundance of pieces of burnt papers' fell in the grounds. She picked up a fragment, and made out five eerily appropriate words – 'Time is; it is done' (Pepys, *Diary*, 3 February 1667).

through the western suburbs after his adventures, the schoolboy also noticed that fires were still breaking out here and there, and spreading so quickly that the engines brought up to combat them were being abandoned, 'those concerned with them escaping with great eagerness from the flames'.[13] In fact, things really were much quieter, and most people were hopeful that the worst was past; but no one was taking any chances. St James's Palace was stripped and empty. So was Whitehall. So were the houses along the Strand. The trained bands were out on the streets in a show of force.

While Taswell was scrabbling over St Paul's, over on the east side of the City Samuel Pepys was up and in the street outside the Navy Office, anxious to check that there was no more danger. He was horrified to find that there was. The Navy Victualler, Alderman Denis Gauden, was standing at the gate of the Office, looking for the dockyard workers who had slept the night at Seething Lane. They were needed urgently. A blaze had broken out a quarter of a mile away in Bishopsgate, fuelling suspicions that firebombers were at work.

Pepys took the men over to the fire – the only time in the entire week when he played an active part in firefighting – and it was swiftly put out. So swiftly, in fact, that he had an opportunity to cast his appraising eye over the women who were sweeping up the water from the gutters. He enjoyed watching them – Pepys always enjoyed watching women – but he was a little disappointed to realise that they were as drunk as devils and still calling for beer. He was also surprised to see looted barrels of sugar standing open in the street, with people slaking their thirst by grabbing handfuls and throwing it into their beer.

In spite of the scare in Bishopsgate, there was no doubt that the real danger was over. The Strand and most of the Temple were safe; and so, therefore, were Whitehall and Westminster. The Tower was secure, and though there were still sporadic outbreaks of fire, there was little chance of them spreading up into the northern suburbs. Pepys began to relax. He was filthy and covered in dirt, so he did what any Restoration gentleman would do in such circumstances. He went in search of a clean shirt and a pair of gloves; although he took a rather circuitous route – a boat over to Southwark, a walk along the south bank and then another boat up to Westminster. When he arrived at Westminster Hall he was disappointed – the shopkeepers had all taken their merchandise and fled, and the medieval Hall was filled instead with house-hold goods and refugees from the Fire. So he went over to the Swan, an eating-house in New Palace Yard, where he managed to get a shave; then he walked up to Whitehall to hunt for news, but there was no one about, and he returned to Seething Lane. Sir Richard Ford, a merchant, MP and alderman who occupied the other half of the mansion that housed the Navy Office, was holding open house for any gentlemen who cared to join him, and Pepys went in to have dinner – a fried breast of mutton – with a group of neighbours and acquaintances. The company, he said, was 'very merry; and indeed as good a meal, though as ugly a one, as ever I had in my life'. In the afternoon he went down to Deptford to check once again on his belongings, which he moved for safety to the Navy Treasurer's residence by the dock-yard. Then he came back to supper with Ford, Sir William Batten and a couple of others, 'mighty merry and our fears over'.[14] Pepys ended Thursday by trying to get some sleep on his office floor, where the labourers who were crammed into the place disturbed him by talking and wandering about all night.

In the meantime, news of the disaster was spreading across the country. It had reached Harwich on the east coast by Tuesday, when there was 'a report of a great fire in London . . . said to be the doing of the Dutch and French'.[15] It was being talked about in Dover and Norwich by Wednesday, and on the same day there was nearly a riot in Oxford when a butcher driving oxen through the city cried 'Hiup! Hiup!' to move the beasts along. People gathered in St Martin's Church misheard this as 'Fire!' and came rushing into the street 'with the semblance of death in their faces' according to Anthony Wood: 'some saying they smelled smoke, others pitch, and could not be reconciled to their error a great while'.[16]

On Thursday, while Pepys hunted for a clean shirt and Charles addressed the huddled masses in Moorfields, the authorities at

Walmer Castle on the Kent coast were writing to say how much their hearts bled for poor London, and predicting that 'the generation of fanatic vipers will report it God's revenge for Englishmen's valour at Vlie'.[17] No doubt both the King and the Duke of York endorsed the opinion of John Knight, Sergeant-Surgeon to the Fleet, who, when word of the Fire reached him on the same day, wrote that 'a seasonable and good bang to the foe will in some measure gratify this loss'.[18]

Prince Rupert and the Duke of Albemarle, the two men who were best placed to deliver a good bang to the foe, were currently aboard the *Royal Charles* and plotting to do just that. Along with the rest of the English fleet, the flagship of the Generals-at-Sea lay at anchor off Spithead. A council of war had met on Monday 3 September to assess the damage caused by Saturday night's gales, which were still blowing hard and making manoeuvring difficult, even in the relatively sheltered waters between the Isle of Wight and Portsmouth: a third-rater, the 64-gun *Defiance*, damaged its bows that night when it ran straight into the 58-gun *Mary*.

It was also on Monday night that the Generals heard the first news of events in London. Initially, they didn't realise the seriousness of the situation in the capital; or if they did, they didn't allow it to distract them from the main business in hand, which was refitting the fleet as quickly as possible so that they could go back out in search of De Ruijter and the Dutch. They spent the next couple of days sending ship after ship into the naval dockyards at Portsmouth for repairs, and making impossible demands on men and materials in their haste to get the job done.

The Navy Commissioner at Portsmouth was Colonel Thomas Middleton, a man with a straightforward and businesslike approach to his job: he had recently put down a disturbance in his yard by personally laying about him with a cudgel, and believed the way to curb naval desertion was to set up gallows in every town between Portsmouth and London and hang every tenth deserter. But even Middleton was driven to despair by the constant importuning of the Generals. He complained to Sir William Coventry, the Duke of York's Secretary at the Admiralty, that his stores could not supply a quarter of their wants. It was all very well for Rupert and Monck to say – as they did – that he must deliver whatever their commanders asked for; but 'some of the commanders knoweth as well what they demand as a horse, when he hath oysters in his manger, knoweth how to eat them'.[19]

On Wednesday 5 September, in the middle of all these preparations, a messenger arrived from the King. The fact that he was Thomas Clarges, Monck's brother-in-law and one-time political agent, suggested that some delicate diplomacy was needed. And so it was. The previous evening, Charles had decided that in spite of the Duke of York's heroic efforts to prevent the spread of the Fire, Monck was needed in London – not so much to take over command of the firefighting operation as to quell public unrest. As Captain-General, the Duke of Albemarle's place was in the capital.

So, via a carefully phrased letter from Sir William Morice, Secretary of State for the North and a kinsman of Albemarle's, Charles urged the Duke to leave the fleet and come home. He emphasised that this was a request and not a royal command. The Captain-General had it in his power to give Charles his kingdom a second time, and his recall was an honour rather than a demotion. 'The world would see the value the King sets on him,' as Lord Arlington remarked at the time.[20]

For twenty-four hours Monck tried to decide what to do. If he left the fleet under the sole command of Prince Rupert – charismatic, popular with his men and dangerously impulsive – God knew what might happen. With admirals like Sir Robert Holmes ready to rush at the enemy without a thought for the long-term consequences, De Ruijter might just escape from Boulogne harbour and rendezvous with the French, something to be avoided at all costs. The fleet might be drawn into a trap; the war might be lost.

Even worse, Rupert might win.

But Charles had been clever, as he always was in his dealings with his courtiers. Monck most emphatically did *not* think it more of an honour to impose martial law on London than to fight the Dutch. From his vantage point on board the *Royal*

Charles, watching thousands of men desperately trying to re-equip his battle fleet, he had no real idea of the scale of the disaster and he did not believe the situation in the capital warranted his recall. But he couldn't say no. For the Captain-General of the Kingdom to refuse his King's plea was unthinkable.

On Thursday morning there was another council of flag officers aboard the *Royal Charles*. Sir Thomas Allin, Admiral of the White, reported on progress in delivery of stores to the fleet. Rupert discussed the fleet's readiness for battle. Albemarle announced his departure to the assembled commanders. Then Allin returned to his own ship, put on clean linen, and took the Duke ashore in his boat for a last dinner at the Governor's residence in Portsmouth. When the meal was over Albemarle made his goodbyes. As he left, his officers saw him start to cry.

8
Dreams of Fire and Falling

London in flames, by Wenceslaus Hollar.

*O*n Friday morning, Pepys heard that 'the Generall is sent for up to come to advise with the King about business at this juncture, and to keep all quiet.'[1] He discounted the rumour, but he was wrong. George Monck, Duke of Albemarle, arrived in town late on Friday and went straight to his official residence in the old Cockpit on the St James's Park side of the Palace of Whitehall. He was briefed on the situation that night by the King and Lord Arlington; and at first light on Saturday courtiers and officials were queuing to pay their respects.

For all his faults – an awareness of his own importance, a voracious appetite for drink, a somewhat plodding approach to life – the Captain-General of the Kingdom was a good, conscientious public servant, and a popular one. Just about everyone heaved a sigh of relief when they heard of his arrival. 'The Duke of Albemarle came this night to towne,' wrote Anne Hobart's husband Nathaniel to a cousin in the country; 'happily if he had bin heere before the Towne might have bin saved, but God was not pleased, & we must submit to his will.'² Pepys, who was generally exasperated by Monck's lack of flair as a naval commander and defensive over his constant assaults on the Navy Office, produced the most telling contemporary verdict on his character: 'I know not how, that blockhead Albemarle hath strange luck to be beloved, though he be, and every man must know, the heaviest man in the world, but stout and honest to his country.'★

By mid-morning the Duke had heard enough. It was time to see for himself; and he rode out with his retinue along the Strand, where people were huddled with piles of belongings, through the smoking debris of what used to be Fleet Street, and into the ruined City. His destination was Gresham College, the temporary home to the Exchange and the Guildhall.

Six years earlier Monck had taken much the same route. Then – as now – he was greeted with shocked silence from a scared and bewildered population. But that was where the similarities ended. In February 1660 people had stared in awe while his elite Scottish cavalry – forerunners of the Life Guards – arrived in the western suburbs and then rode out of Whitehall and into the history books, swords clanking, carbines by their sides, cases of pistols at the ready. They watched uncertainly while his troops broke down the gates of the City, ended four months of militant Republican rule and took control of the nation.

Monck's march on London had led directly to the restoration of the monarchy; and his pivotal role was acknowledged by a string of honours and the riches to match – a dukedom, the title of Captain-General, a position in the royal household as Master of the Horse and Gentleman of the Bedchamber, and a

★Pepys, *Diary*, 23 October 1667. The context for Pepys's remark was a move to impeach the Earl of Clarendon in the wake of Dutch incursions in the Medway. The House of Commons held Clarendon to blame for the fiasco, while simultaneously giving a vote of thanks to Rupert and Albemarle for their conduct of the war. Hence the Duke's 'strange luck to be beloved'.

pension of £7,000 a year.★ It also turned him into a popular hero: as he accompanied the returning Charles II into Whitehall on 29 May 1660, Londoners cried out 'Hurrah for honest George Monck!'

That popularity – Monck's 'strange luck to be beloved', as Pepys put it – was confirmed when the plague hit London in 1665. As Parliament broke up, court and clergy ran for the safety of Oxford, and the friends of the Good Old Cause muttered that here was a demonstration of God's displeasure upon the nation for 'the ill life the king led, and the viciousness of the whole court',[3] the Captain-General stayed on in his Whitehall lodgings, the only representative of national government left in the capital. He ruled the western suburbs and, together with the Lord Mayor, Sir John Lawrence, he maintained public order and ensured that each night the fires were lit in the streets to ward off the contagion.

Fires were burning now. There was a huge plume of smoke billowing out of St Faith's. The Clothworkers' Hall in Mincing Lane on the north-east edge of the fire zone had also caught light on Tuesday: its cellars were full of oil, and it had been burning for the past three days. Wandering through the City on Friday, John Evelyn had almost been overcome by smoke and fumes as he picked his way over the rubble and struggled past 'the voragos [abysses] of subterranean cellars, wells, and dungeons, formerly warehouses, still burning in stench and dark clowds of smoke.'[4] A thick layer of dust and ash covered everything; every street and alley was wholly or partly blocked by fallen masonry and charred timbers. Alexander Fleming told his brother that the landscape looked like their native Westmorland: 'The houses are laid so flat to the ground that the City looks just like our fells, for there is nothing to be seen but heaps of stones.'[5] You could

---

★Monck's action in occupying London and recalling the Rump Parliament almost brought him a royal palace. Between the occupation and the Restoration the Commons tried to present him with Hampton Court, but he thought it would be tactless to accept a royal estate while the nation waited for its owner to return. His wife Anne was said to be very disappointed.

stand on the site of Cheapside, he said, and see the Thames. This image occurs again and again in contemporary letters: writing on the Saturday, just as Monck was surveying the devastation, Sir Edward Atkyns informed *his* brother that 'there is nothing but stones and rubbish . . . Soe that you may see from one end of the Citty almost to ye other.'[6]

You could also stand on the south bank of the Thames and see right into the heart of London, as the Prague-born topographical artist Wenceslaus Hollar did soon after the Fire was extinguished. Hollar had published a panoramic bird's-eye view of London nearly twenty years earlier, and he returned to his original vantage point, the tower of St Mary Overie a few yards from the southern end of London Bridge, to produce a second view of the City 'as it appeareth now after the sad calamitie and destruction by fire'.[7]

Hollar's engraving is the most accurate surviving picture of London in the immediate aftermath of the Fire; and it comes as a surprise to see a landscape which, at first glance at least, is a far cry from the apocalyptic wasteland described by his contemporaries. In a sweeping view from the Temple Church in the west to the Tower in the east St Paul's Cathedral dominates, as it does in the pre-Fire view. On the river the Custom House is still standing; so is Baynard's Castle. Strangest of all, the skyline is still punctuated with dozens of church towers.

But that's where the resemblance ends. A closer look shows that St Paul's is a roofless shell. The Custom House, Baynard's, the City churches are all in ruins. And the streets and lanes around them have simply vanished, to be replaced by open land, heaps of rubbish and little forests of brick chimney-stacks from the Temple to the Tower.

The bare statistics of loss are terrible. A survey carried out soon after the Fire found that 13,200 houses had been burned down or demolished in 400 streets and courts. That meant that somewhere in the region of 70,000–80,000 people had lost their homes. Of the area within the walls, 373 acres had gone – well over 80 per cent – along with a further 63 acres in the extra-mural parishes to the north and west. Eighty-six churches were either badly damaged or completely destroyed. Thirty-five would never be rebuilt, and it would take more than half a century and well over £360,000 to replace the rest – a colossal amount of money in an age when Pepys paid his cook £5 a year, and 5 shillings would buy a roast beef dinner for four in a tavern.

'Of particular men's losses could never be made any computation,' said Clarendon:[8] and he was right. The stationers were generally held to have suffered the most. Many were bankrupted in the destruction of St Paul's Cathedral, when stock worth between £150,000 and £200,000 burned – a catastrophe for the history of English publishing and, in John Evelyn's words, 'an extraordinary detriment to the whole Republiq of Learning'.[9] The consequences for individual businesses are mentioned here and there, but the overall scale of the financial disaster is well-nigh impossible to calculate, although there were plenty who tried. The figure of £600,000 a year in lost rents was mentioned to Pepys in the week after the Fire, but this was certainly an exaggeration and it was soon revised down to around £330,000. Taking the value of each house as twelve years' purchase (i.e., twelve times its annual rent, an estimate which was thought at the time to be fair but conservative), this would suggest that the 13,200 burned houses alone were worth £3.96 million, without even taking account of their contents. And that figure, of course, excludes the value of London's public buildings. In 1681 Thomas Delaune's *Present State of London* reckoned £3.9 million for lost housing, and £2 million apiece for public buildings destroyed, the cost of moving goods about, and the destruction or looting of goods. This gave a grand total of £9.9 million.

A more detailed estimate appeared in John Strype's 1720 edition of Stow's *Survey of the Cities of London and Westminster*. Strype offered a total figure of £10,788,500, but this is too high: the combined rebuilding costs of St Paul's Cathedral and the City churches, for example, are given as £2,696,000, when the figure was around the £1 million mark. The real sum was perhaps somewhere nearer to £9 million, but one can only agree with the

Earl of Clarendon when he said that 'the value or estimate of what that devouring fire consumed, over and above the houses, could never be computed in any degree'.[10]

With the loss of the Guildhall, the Exchange and St Paul's, the City's political, commercial and religious centres had disappeared. The destruction of the Custom House and the Excise Office severely impaired its ability to bring in fresh revenues; the burning of the General Letter Office disrupted its lines of communication with the rest of the kingdom; and the loss of most of the Company Halls threatened the social and economic structures which underpinned it.

The support networks which the Livery Companies provided for indigent members were also at risk. Most of the Companies owned rental or leasehold property, and its destruction led to a diminution of income for various trusts and pensions. The Vintners lost almost all their property; pensioners in Stoke Newington and St George's Fields who were dependent on the Drapers' Company had their pensions reduced from 6s 8d a month to 4s, 'until it shall please God, by some means, to supply the said loss'.[11]

On the other hand, the Companies that survived the Fire relatively unscathed were quick to see an opportunity to turn the situation to their profit, while helping their fellow liverymen at the same time. The Cooks' Company's Tudor Hall on Aldersgate Street was singed, but otherwise unharmed. On 14 September workmen were summoned 'to putt that parte of the Hall and Gallery which is now defaced by the late fire in good repaire', and £11 was paid out for repairing and reglazing the windows, which had presumably cracked and broken in the heat.[12] On the same day the Cooks decided to let their Hall to any other Company which needed a place to meet. The Haberdashers took them up on their offer. So did the Salters, the Bowyers, the Brewers, the Distillers, the Farriers, the Fruiterers, the Glovers, the Painter-Stainers, the Stationers, the Upholders [upholsterers], the Goldsmiths – and the Society for the Propagation of the Gospel.

The Carpenters, who had had the good fortune to escape with

their Hall and virtually all of their property intact, were just as quick to offer help to Companies which had suffered 'by the late and dredfull fire'. By the beginning of October the Drapers had stumped up £30 a year for the use of certain rooms on a specified number of days, as had the Masons, the Feltmakers, the Weavers and the Haberdashers, who seem to have tired of the Cooks' Hall rather quickly. The Carpenters also managed to rent out most of their Hall and the surrounding garden to Sir Thomas Bludworth, who, with only a few weeks of his Mayoralty left to run, no longer had the use of Vintners' Hall as his official residence. Three of Bludworth's successors as Lord Mayor continued the arrangement at an annual rent of £100.

With accommodation in short supply, those lucky enough to own houses in the unburned parts of the capital were more than willing to make them available – at a price. On Friday, Pepys had heard of an acquaintance accepting £150 for a house he had previously let at £40 a year. The next day people were starting to comment on the demand for property in the western suburbs. 'Houses are now at an excessive rate,' Edward Atkyns told his brother, Sir Robert; '& my Lord Treasurers new buildings are now in great request.'[13] Atkyns was referring to speculative housing put up in fashionable Bloomsbury Square in the early 1660s by Thomas Wriothesley, 4th Earl of Southampton. Five days later the *Gazette* for 13 September announced that 'The Grand Office for the Excise is now kept in Southampton-Fields, near the House of the Right Honourable the Lord High Treasurer of England, and is every day open at the usual hours, for receiving and performing all things relating to that Affair.'[14]

Edward advised Sir Robert to keep his goods in his house, the implication being that if he didn't, he might find that house occupied by someone else when he next came up to town. And there is evidence to suggest that unscrupulous landlords didn't hesitate to turn the situation to their advantage. While the City still smouldered, Sir Nathaniel Hobart and his wife, Anne, found themselves facing eviction from their substantial house in Chancery Lane, in spite of paying a heavy rental of £55 a year. Luckily for the Hobarts, Sir Nathaniel knew the law (he was a

Master in Chancery); and he immediately threatened to slap an injunction on his landlord – 'a person so odious', he said, 'that if his cause were just he would hardly find favour'.[15]★

One point made by a number of writers in the days after the Fire was that it could have been worse. Joseph Williamson's 'short, but true accompt' of the disaster in the *Gazette*, which he managed to get out on Monday 10 September, stressed that the warehouses at the east end of Thames Street were filled with goods that were bulky but not particularly valuable. Their loss was regrettable, but 'the other parts of the Town, where the Commodities were of greater value, took the Alarm so early, that they saved most of their Goods'. Given Williamson's role as government spokesperson, we might dismiss this as propaganda. But he was not the only one determined to find a silver lining in the pall of smoke hanging over London. The anonymous author of a private letter to Viscount Conway, who was absent from his townhouse off Drury Lane, was also at pains to say that 'the greatest part of the wealth is saved, the losse having chiefly fallen upon heavy goods, Wine Tobacco Sugars, etc.'[16] However, even Williamson could not resist a swipe at Londoners' selfishness: 'some think, that if the whole industry of the Inhabitants had been applyed to the stopping of the fire, and not to the saving of their particular goods, the success might have been much better, not only to the publick, but to many of them in their own particulars'.[17]

As silver linings go, the brightest and best was the size of the casualty list. It was tiny. For Bishop Gilbert Burnet, 'the most astonishing circumstance of that dreadful conflagration was that, notwithstanding the great destruction that was made, and the great confusion in the streets, I could never hear of any one

★The housing shortage was still causing problems several years later. In August 1668 Pietro Mocenigo, the new Venetian Ambassador, complained to his masters about the 'grasping habits' of Londoners, the 'severe and exorbitant rents' and the difficulty of finding a suitable residence because the Fire 'has left many convenient houses mere heaps of ruins and rubble' (*CSP Venetian*, XXXV, 240, 260). The Doge and Senate took him seriously enough to raise his allowance.

person that was either burnt or trodden to death. The king was never observed to be so much struck with any thing in his whole life, as with this.'[18] Burnet was writing years after the event, and his memory played him false − but not that false. A contemporary pamphleteer was much nearer the mark when he said he could find no evidence for more than half a dozen deaths.

There *were* fatalities, but considering the cataclysmic scale of the disaster and the densely populated areas that were affected, it seems little short of a miracle that they were so few. There was Farriner's maid, who couldn't bring herself to clamber out of an upstairs window; and the 'old decrepid woman' whose charred corpse William Taswell had stumbled over in the ruins of St Paul's. Sixteen months later Pepys was told by a bookseller that several dogs were found burned in Paul's Churchyard 'and but one man', an old man who had gone into the cathedral to retrieve a blanket and had been overcome by the flames.[19] This sounds very much like Taswell's old woman: since her clothes were all burned and her limbs charred, it must have been difficult to determine her sex.

A deaf old Strasbourg watchmaker named Paul Lawell who lived in Shoe Lane refused point-blank to leave his home, in spite of the advice of his son and his friends; he died when his house collapsed on top of him and crashed down into the cellar, 'where afterwards his Bones, together with his Keys, were found'.[20] A parishioner of St Botolph Aldgate dropped dead from fright on Tower Hill. A few others died when floors gave way as they were searching through the ruins of their homes. And that was it. The third-largest city in the Western world burns to the ground and, if contemporaries are to be believed, the death toll is in single figures.

No doubt some deaths went unrecorded, as the poet John Tabor implied in his 'Seasonable Thoughts in Sad Times':

> How many frighted Parents now miscarry,
> And travail must, at home they may not tarry! . . .
> How many dying persons now expire!
> Breathing their last like Martyrs in the fire . . .
> How many dead have Roman buryal there!

Their Houses funeral piles wherein they were
Now burned, and lie buried underneath
The ruines of the place, where seiz'd by death.[21]

Describing the initial outbreak in Pudding Lane, John Dryden wrote of 'frighted mothers [who] strike their breast too late / For helpless infants left amidst the fire'; and one can't help wondering if he was referring to some now-forgotten tragedy. John Evelyn talked vaguely of 'the stench that came from some poore creatures bodies, beds and other combustible goods' as he walked through the ruins on Friday: although he didn't actually *see* a single corpse.[22] And the Fire continued to kill long after the first week in September. The most pathetic death was that of Richard Yrde, who was overcome by fumes while he sat in a privy in the parish of St Mary Woolnoth. The most poignant was that of the seventy-year-old poet and dramatist James Shirley, who was burned out of his home in Fleet Street and forced to shelter in one of the makeshift refugee camps in St Giles-in-the-Fields; he died there eight weeks later and was buried on 29 October. His wife died on the same day, and they were buried in the same grave.

It is hard to believe that there was not a single casualty among the firefighters – especially when firefighting involved pulling down buildings and blowing up buildings. But all the evidence suggests that the death rate really was negligible. The Earl of Clarendon made no mention at all of fatalities in his account of the Fire, and marvelled that no foreigners were killed in spite of the brutal treatment being meted out by the mob: 'It cannot be enough wondered at, that in this general rage of the people no mischief was done to the strangers, that no one of them was assassinated outright, though many were sorely beaten and bruised.'[23] And Thomas Vincent – who positively revelled in describing his face-to-face encounters with dead and dying plague victims – distinguished clearly between those 'who have fallen by the plague' and those 'whose houses have fallen by the fire', implying that 1665 was characterised by human losses, while in September 1666 property was the chief casualty.[24]

How could that be?

The first thing to bear in mind is that low mortality rates were not unusual in seventeenth-century urban fires. When flames destroyed well over 200 houses in Warwick on 5 September 1694, the only fatalities were a dozen pigs which were burned in their sties. A fire that burned at least twenty-five houses in Dorchester, Dorset, in January 1622 claimed just a single life, and even there it was helped along by an overzealous citizen. The victim, a tile-layer named Edward Benebenewe, was badly burned and ran home in a panic, pursued by friends who were trying to calm him down. Mistaking poor Benebenewe for an escaping criminal, a passer-by who just happened to be carrying a pole 'beat him with it grievously and struck him down, he died within two days'.[25]

The Warwick and Dorchester fires both began in the early afternoon, which helps to explain why damage was largely confined to property. The fact that the Fire of London broke out in the early hours should, in theory, have meant casualties; and a contemporary pamphleteer highlighted as one of the main reasons for the magnitude of the disaster 'the Time wherein it did happen, to wit, about One of the Clock in the Night, when every one is buried in his first Sleep; when some for Weariness, others by Deboistness, have given Leave to their Cares to retire; when Slothfulness and the Heat of the Bed have riveted a Man to his Pillow, and made him almost incapable of waking, much less of acting and helping his Neighbours'.[26] But the alarm was raised very quickly; and the Fire spread very slowly. Between the early hours of Sunday and Wednesday morning, it moved westward from Pudding Lane along the Thames at a remarkably consistent rate – around thirty yards per hour. (It tailed off considerably in the course of Wednesday afternoon when, with the exception of flare-ups in the Temple and around Cripplegate, it had to all intents and purposes been extinguished.) Thirty yards per hour is not only the average rate over the three-and-a-half days; it is also true for each full day – Sunday, Monday and Tuesday. The eastward track of the flames against the prevailing wind was of course much slower – no more than six or seven yards per hour – and the spread to the north was less consistent, varying between nine and sixteen yards per hour.

These figures are crude, and they make little allowance for the realities of the situation: the speed with which the flames could travel down one street before dwindling away almost to nothing in the next; the fact that one house might go up like a bomb while another smouldered for days; the way in which fires could break out without warning hundreds of yards apart, as they did when the Duke of York had such a narrow escape in Salisbury Court.

But the fact remains that most people had plenty of time to evacuate their homes. Even on Fish Street, which backed onto Pudding Lane and was one of the first casualties, the occupants were able to save their personal possessions. In the early stages of the Fire, when people still believed that it was a localised outbreak, those close to the perimeter of the fire zone packed up and moved only a few streets away, a process which they repeated again and again. On Sunday morning, for instance, Pepys had run into a merchant, Isaac Houblon, who was standing at the door of his house in Dowgate, supervising the arrival of his brother's goods. They had been moved twice already that day, and Houblon was quite right when he told Pepys that 'they must in a little time be removed from his house also'.[27] Most of Dowgate Hill was burning by nightfall.

Today, the majority of fire-related fatalities are the result of smoke inhalation. This was not necessarily true in the seventeenth century, when the treatment of surface burns relied on little more than the application of honey and prayers. But death and injury from fire had much the same preconditions in 1666 as they do today; and chief among these were the element of surprise and the lack of an escape route. By dawn on Sunday 2 September most of the City knew there was a serious fire; and many were already taking steps to escape. Even though the flames never reached the Strand, on Wednesday morning its occupants 'fled with their families out of their houses in the streets, that they might not be within when the fire fell upon their houses'.[28]

When Monck arrived at Gresham College shortly before noon on Saturday 'to discourse with the Aldermen' he found a crowd waiting.[29] Some were there just to catch a glimpse of the famous Duke of Albemarle, others to find news of friends, neighbours and relatives, others still simply because they were curious. As news of the Fire carried into the country, a steady stream of sightseers came up to town to find out for themselves just how bad things were.

Amazingly, they were not too bad at all. There were shortages, and some profiteering: penny loaves of bread were going for twopence, and at three shillings each Thames eels were three times their pre-Fire price. The profiteering continued – in mid-October there were reports that merchants in the port of Bristol were raising the prices of those commodities which were in short supply because of the Fire. But on Saturday 8 September the political and commercial structures on which London depended were already being reinstated; order was being maintained; and Monck's presence, although it was welcomed by just about everybody, was nowhere near as vital to the stability of the nation as the King had feared.

Monck found that the merchants from the Royal Exchange, who had begun to set up shop at Gresham on Thursday, were settling in nicely. The Court of Aldermen and the Court of Common Council had established themselves there and, although his name does not appear, no doubt Thomas Bludworth and his Sheriffs were waiting to receive the Duke with a list of requests for aid.

The speed and determination with which London's merchant class began to function again after the Fire astonished contemporaries. Take the case of the goldsmith-banker Sir Robert Vyner, whose Lombard Street premises, the Vine, had burned to the ground on Monday afternoon. Vyner was quite simply one of the best goldsmiths in London. The regalia for Charles II's coronation – two crowns and two sceptres, a jewelled orb and staff, a crown and mace for Garter-King-at-Arms and a whole host of badges, plate and other bits and pieces – had been made at the Vine, which each year turned out about £8,000-worth of plate for the royal household.[30] Sir Robert was also a banker – a comparatively new phenomenon in England. He took money on deposit at one rate of interest and loaned it out at a higher rate, discounted foreign and domestic bills of exchange, and issued negotiable promissory notes which went into general circulation, the forerunners of banknotes. His public and private clients included Joseph Williamson and Samuel Pepys, George Monck and Admiral Sir Thomas Allin, Sir John Robinson and Dean Sancroft.

But his most important client was the Crown, which was constantly in need of cash. Vyner was happy to supply the government's needs, at anything from 10 per cent to 20 per cent interest, depending on the risk. Together with a few other goldsmith-bankers – notably his fellow aldermen and Lombard Street neighbours Francis Meynell and Edward Backwell – Vyner effectively funded Charles II's administration during its early years, advancing the King huge sums of money and in consequence wielding a huge amount of political power for a non-governmental figure. In 1665, for example, he lent £330,000 to finance the navy, the Life Guards and the royal household. This was on top of the £100,000 he had advanced to fund troops in Ireland four years previously, on which the Exchequer was currently paying him interest at £8,632 a year, and a further £15,000 – 'at 10 per cent, and 6 per cent for the exchange' – to pay the same troops when they threatened to mutiny in 1666.[31]

As a result of all this, the 35-year-old Vyner was one of the richest and most powerful men in England. Elected Sheriff of London in June 1666, he had been made a baronet by Charles II, who was grateful for past help and eager to develop their relationship in the future. He had a beautiful if slightly faded new wife, a widow whose marriage portion of £100,000 did a lot to make up for her age. And with that £100,000 dowry he had just bought himself an even more beautiful country house, Swakeleys in Middlesex, where he lived in great state with a black page to whom he was evidently quite attached: the boy died of consumption, 'and being dead, he caused him to be dried in an oven, and lies there entire in a box'.[32]

Vyner had acted promptly when the Pudding Lane fire began to spread. At some time on Sunday afternoon – 'almost twenty four hours before the furious Fire entred Lumbardstreet'[33] – he took steps to make sure that his money, bonds, bullion and business papers were all evacuated from the Vine and carted off to Windsor Castle, twenty-six miles away to the west. Windsor was the obvious choice: Sir Robert's brother Thomas was a prebendary there, and Sir Robert needed the reassurance provided by the family connection, the distance from London and the fact that everything was secure. He obtained a personal warrant from the King to Viscount Mordaunt, Constable of the Castle, commanding Mordaunt to take in his money and jewels and to give strict orders for their safekeeping under guard. He was right, too: his fellow goldsmiths were content to move everything into the Tower, only to lose their nerve and move their bullion again to Whitehall as the flames crept down Tower Street.

Only days after the Fire's end, Sir Robert was trading again, now out of the headquarters of the Royal African Company, 'the Affrican house neer the middle of Broad-street London, where he intends to manage his affairs (as formerly in Lumbardstreet) having by the good providence of God been entirely preserved by a timely and safe removal of all his concerns'.[34] Meynell and Backwell, who had also managed to preserve their estates, were likewise announcing their intention to set up business in the Broad Street area. Backwell moved into the lodgings of Jonathan Goddard, the Professor of Physic at Gresham College. (Meynell may also have moved into Gresham, but he died four weeks later – it took ten years to settle his affairs.)

Vyner, Backwell, Meynell and the other money-men of London were not motivated by altruism. There were profits to be made from loss. People needed to borrow in order to rebuild their homes, their businesses and their lives. The war with Holland meant that the kingdom was still haemorrhaging money. But their motives were not altogether cynical: there was also a desperate desire to get back to normality after the Armageddon of the past few days, to show the world that London was ready to rise from the ashes.

So, James Hickes and the General Letter Office were installed 'at the two Black Pillars in Bridges-street, over against the Fleece

Tavern, Covent garden, till a more convenient place [could] be found'.[35] The following week it was, and the Office moved into Bishopsgate Street. The Custom House was set up in an unburned section of Mark Lane, a couple of hundred yards from the Tower – quite a distance from the wharves and quays on the Thames, to be sure, but nowhere near as far away as the Comptroller of Petty Customs for the Port of London, who announced in the *Gazette* that he had moved to Chancery Lane, well over a mile away. And in a move which really did proclaim to the world just how quickly London was returning to normal, Thomas Warren advertised that he had transferred from burnt-out Bread Street to Leadenhall, where he was appointed, as before the Fire, 'to receive the Charity of well disposed persons for the poor visited people at Cambridge'.[36] Surrounded by makeshift sheds, ragged camps, smouldering ruins and up to 200,000 homeless neighbours, Warren had a touching faith in the generosity of his fellows.

The Fire had some frightening social consequences. Although there were no further mass disturbances, Charles was right to have worried. In the upheavals and mass migrations, law and order suffered. London had always been a dangerous place to walk alone after dark – there were no police, few lights, and the parish constables whose job it was to enforce the law were often as efficient in that department as they were at firefighting – but there is some evidence to suggest that things got worse. In December James Hickes, whose Letter Office was still in Bishopsgate Street, told Joseph Williamson that people had been found murdered in the cellars and ruined alleys. The latest story concerned the link-boys, who made a living from lighting Londoners' way at night with their torches. In the past, the company of these link-boys had been a comfort in the dark lanes. Now, it was said, they were turning to violent crime. When a man alone answered their usual cry of 'Do you want lights?', he might be mugged, stripped and left for dead.

There were other stories, too. Apparently an apothecary's man from south of the river was mugged in Fenchurch Street and knocked into a cellar beneath a ruined house. After his assailants had gone he struck a light and, to his horror, saw he had a woman's corpse for a companion. This has the hallmarks of an urban legend – it was awfully convenient, for example, that the robbers happened to leave behind them a tinder-box so that the hapless victim could discover the body. But, true or not, rumours such as this contributed to a general sense of insecurity which spread in the wake of the Fire. As Hickes wrote, 'For want of good watches, no one dares go in the ruins, after the close of the evening.'[37]

Samuel Pepys had his own encounter with robbery among the ruins. Coming home late one night in April 1668 from an assignation with an actress in the New Spring Garden across the river in Vauxhall, he hired a link-boy. He had just reached the broken walls of St Dunstan-in-the-East when he was met 'by two rogues with clubs, who come towards us'.[38] Thinking discretion the better part of valour, he promptly retreated and retraced his steps round the busy streets by the City wall, arriving home tired but safe.

Pepys's first experience of the emotional aftershock from the disaster came much more quickly. On the night of Friday 7 September 1666, he begged a bed for the night from Sir William Penn, his own lodgings in Seething Lane still being bare of furniture. But 'both sleeping and waking, [I] had a fear of fire in my heart, [so] that I took little rest'.[39] The following night, which he also spent at Penn's, he lay awake in the darkness for some time, frightened by the sounds of looters in the street outside.

On Sunday he went to morning service at St Olave Hart Street, which, like his lodgings round the corner in Seething Lane, had narrowly escaped the flames. Dr Daniel Milles was preaching. Pepys had no high opinion of the rector, or of his pronounced Calvinist views – 'a lazy, fat priest' was his verdict on the man[40] – but today Milles spoke well in a church which was packed to overflowing. Most people were poor and strangers from out of the parish, looking for some spiritual comfort after their own churches had been destroyed.

Milles's sermon was a melancholy one for a melancholy occasion. As the congregation listened, bruised and bewildered, first one person began to cry; then another; until virtually everyone was weeping – weeping for the city they had lost.

This is the figure of the ground taken from the street on the North side containing of Superficiall feet 142 foot

Whortesters   Mrs Whortesters two houses

Ryly   Samuel Ryly one house.

Elmes   Widow Elmes one

Adly   Thomas Adly 3 houses 23-8   4-0
                                      9   1-6
                                     ___
                                     207
                                     ___
                                     312

Keeling Lo: Ch: Justice   The Lord Cheife Justice Keeling at Blackfryers gate measured June the 20th 1668.

166 foot 6 inches

10 ~ 5

Do: This is the figure of the ground taken from the Lord Chief Justice at Ludgate containing to of Superficiall feet 166. 6 inches and more taken away in the Gate side 46 foot in all 212 foot 6 ½ d

The Ticket delivered →   7-6   312
                              166-6   166-6
                                           46

North

This is the figure of the ground taken from Mrs John Fullerton in Creed Marten, & Ground measured the 10th day of June 1668 by Peter Mills

Fullerton

4 - 0

6 - 0

17 foot

4 - 0

6. Page from a contemporary transcript of Peter Mills and John Oliver's survey of the City after the Great Fire. Two of the entries refer to property held by Sir John Kelyng, the Lord Chief Justice.

17. Wenceslaus Hollar's post-Fire map of London, showing the final extent of the damage.

THE CITY OF LONDON FIRST DESCRIBED IN SIX PLATS BY IOHN LEAKE IOHN

...DERMEN AND COMMON COVNCELL OF THE SAID CITY.

Reduced here into one intire plat by Iohn Leake the Citty Wall being added &c. The places where the Hall House are expresst by Coate of Armes, & all the Wards divided by prickes Alphabet &c.

THAMES

Part of Southwarke

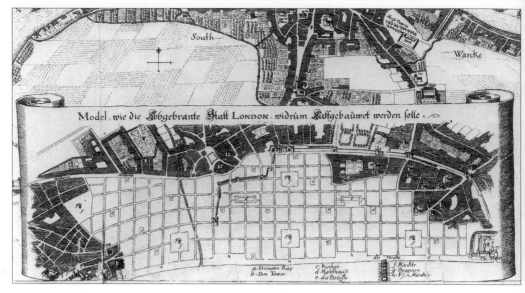

18. Robert Hooke's plan for London (inset from a German map of the city).

19. Valentine Knight's plan for London.

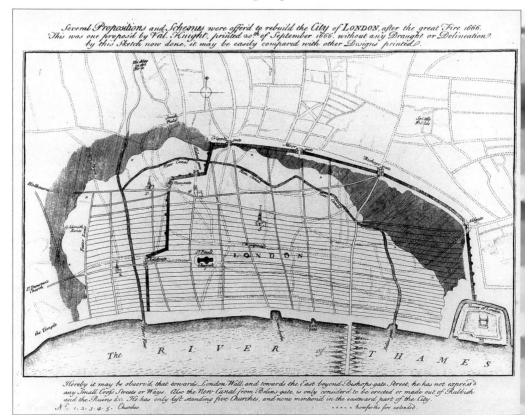

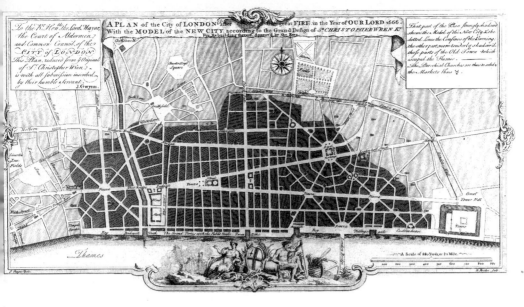

20. Christopher Wren's plan for London.

21. Richard Newcourt's plan for London.

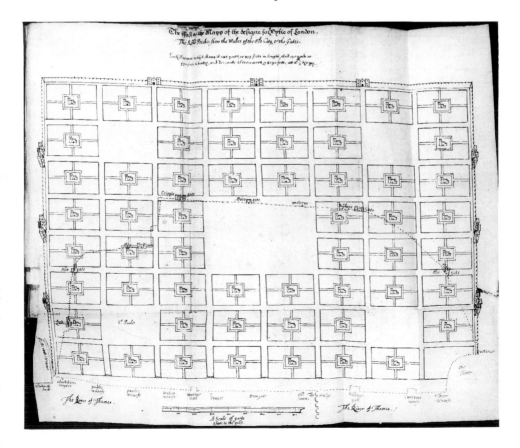

(*Above*) 22. Old St Paul's, modernised in the 1630s by Inigo Jones – 'that magnificent structure', said Charles II. (*Below*) 23. Old St Paul's in ruins, drawn by Thomas Wyck, *c*.1673.

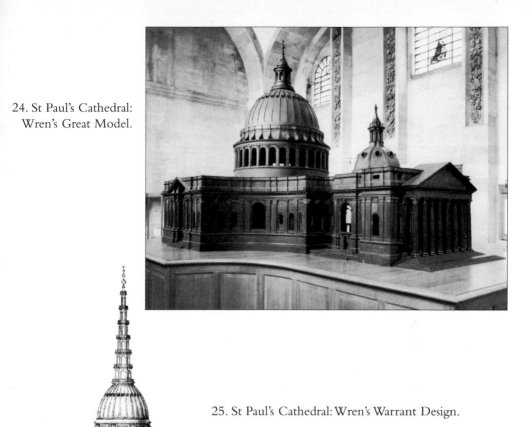

24. St Paul's Cathedral:
Wren's Great Model.

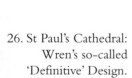

25. St Paul's Cathedral: Wren's Warrant Design.

26. St Paul's Cathedral:
Wren's so-called
'Definitive' Design.

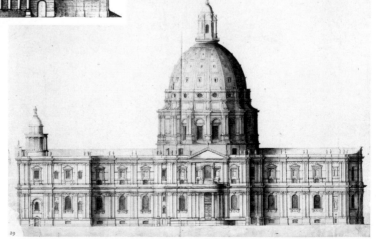

29

27. & 28. Two early designs for the Monument.

29. The Monument, c.1740.

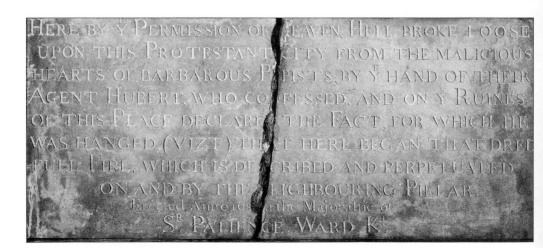

HERE BY $\tilde{y}$ PERMISSION OF HEAVEN, HELL BROKE LOOSE
UPON THIS PROTESTANT CITY FROM THE MALICIOUS
HEARTS OF BARBAROUS PAPISTS, BY $\tilde{y}$ HAND OF THEIR
AGENT HUBERT, WHO CONFESSED, AND ON $\tilde{y}$ RUINES
OF THIS PLACE DECLARED THE FACT, FOR WHICH HE
WAS HANGED (VIZT) THAT HERE BEGAN THAT DREDFULL FIRE, WHICH IS DESCRIBED AND PERPETUATED
ON AND BY THE NEIGHBOURING PILLAR.
Erected Anno 1681 in the Majoraltie of
S.R PATIENCE WARD K.T

30. Commemorative plaque put up on the site of Farriner's bakery in Pudding Lane in 1681.

In fact, many contemporary observers remarked on the robust way in which Londoners coped with the disaster. 'The miracle is,' wrote John Evelyn, 'I have never in my life observ'd a more universal resignation, lesse repining among sufferers.'[41] Henry Oldenburg, the Secretary of the Royal Society, agreed. Writing to Robert Boyle in Oxford on 10 September, he stressed the quiet fortitude of the victims: 'I cannot omit acquainting you, that never a Calamity, and such an one, was so well bourne, as this is. 'Tis incredible, how little the sufferers, though great ones, doe complaine of their Losses.'[42]

Yet the poignant image of St Olave's weeping congregation shows that fortitude was not the only response. And scattered references in journals and letters hint at the confusion and anxiety which follow on from any major disaster. People forgot the day of the month, or the month of the year. According to Anthony Wood, who was struck by the distraction he observed in the victims, some even forgot their own names 'when they with their money or goods under their arms were examined by the watch'.[43] (A cynic might suggest less charitable reasons for this temporary amnesia.) Others suffered more serious mental problems. 'Now she hath had a little time to recollect herselfe, she cryes all day longe,' wrote one London physician about his own wife. 'I shall take what care I can of her, but all in my power cannot make it good to her.'[44]

Pepys's diary gives a few hints of how Londoners reacted to the Fire. Samuel and Elizabeth were not among the worst-affected victims: they didn't lose their home or their possessions; and at no time were they in any real danger. But in the days immediately after the disaster Samuel remarked that Elizabeth was out of temper and moody; so were the couple's friends. When they ate supper with Sir William Penn on Tuesday 11 September Samuel noted that their host was 'in a mad, ridiculous, drunken humour'; apparently Penn and his wife Margaret had been fighting.[45]

Samuel's own initial reaction to the disaster was to throw himself into his work and his extramarital relationships. The morning after the fraught supper with the Penns he went to see

Betty Martin, a Westminster linen-draper and longstanding mistress: while he was there he 'did tout ce que je voudrais avec her'. Later the same day he went to Deptford to visit another regular, the wife of a ship's carpenter named Bagwell, and there 'nudo con lecto con ella did do all that I desired'. He intended to spend the night there, but when he had finished with her he was seized with a fit of self-loathing and went back to Penn's house instead.[46]

By the following Saturday, when Samuel had moved back with Elizabeth into their home in the Navy Office, he was noting in his diary that his sleep was disturbed by nightmares. 'Much terrified in the nights nowadays, with dreams of fire and falling down of houses.'[47] He began to suffer from headaches, and couldn't shake a nagging worry about several of his books, which had gone missing in the evacuation from Seething Lane. He complained of pains in his stomach and bladder. So did Elizabeth, who also suffered a more dramatic reaction to the Fire: her hair began to fall out. Samuel again recorded nightmares about the Fire on 25 September and yet again two days later, when his sleep was disturbed by a furious wind blowing through the City, and 'my mind [was] still mightily perplexed with dreams and burning the rest of the town'.[48]

People were still feeling nervous at the beginning of November. Samuel was at Whitehall with the Duke of York when he heard that there was a French plot to fire the remainder of the capital. A coded message from Paris had been intercepted on 7 November – two days after the anniversary of the Gunpowder Plot. It said that Babel – i.e., London – should be purged by an incendiary, and that 'the most virtuous and great gentlewoman' (presumably Henrietta Maria, who was still in France) was often with the conspirators, 'and gives great assurance of success'.[49] This put everyone on edge; and with some justification, it seemed, since on the afternoon of 9 November a fire broke out in the barracks of the Horse Guards at Whitehall. Pepys was at a party in Covent Garden when the news came, and he and his companions heard and saw the barracks being blown up to prevent the spread of the fire: 'The ladies begun presently to be afeared – one fell into fits. The whole town in an Alarme. Drums beat and trumpets, and the guards everywhere spread – running up and down in the street.'[50]

Samuel began to panic. There were rumours that the Catholics were going to rise up that night and massacre the Protestant population of London, and he had 'mighty apprehensions how things might be at home'. There were stories of a fire in Westminster, and another across the river in Southwark. By ten o'clock he was at his wit's end: he left the party, commandeered a coach, and headed for Seething Lane. There were roadblocks and armed constables on the streets; but he comforted himself by putting his hand up the skirt of Mercer, his wife's nineteen-year-old maid, in the dark of the carriage. 'La fille hath something that is assez joie,' he wrote in his diary.[51]

Everyone has their own coping mechanisms.

Samuel's didn't work. More than three months later he was still suffering from recurring nightmares. 'It is strange to think,' he wrote on 28 February 1667, 'how to this very day I cannot sleep a-night without great terrors of fire, and this very night I could not sleep till almost two in the morning through thoughts of fire.'[52] Those thoughts continued to obsess him into the spring. He was thrown into a panic when his neighbour's chimney caught fire; and into a rage when his cook-maid got drunk, not because she wasn't doing her work, but because it made her careless – 'my only fear is fire'.[53] At the end of March his nights were still troubled with recurring images of the Fire, 'which I cannot get out of my head'.[54]

If Samuel's experiences are anything to go by, then London's brave show of resilience was all the braver because of the fears that hid among the ruins. Its citizens were haunted by demons.

9

Digitus Dei

The Waterhouse, Islington.

'*I*s't still unknowne from whence our ruine came, / Whether from Hell, *France, Rome,* or *Amsterdam*?' asked the anonymous author of *A Poem on the Burning of London*.[1] Reactions among England's European enemies ranged from condolence to unconcealed joy. Hell didn't respond.

News of the Fire didn't reach Louis XIV's court until the morning of Sunday 16 September. Politically, the King regarded it as a great stroke of luck, assuming quite rightly that the English would be too demoralised to attack the French fleet – an action which Louis had been trying to avoid for most of the year, much to the exasperation of his Dutch allies. But even though France and England were at war, Charles II was his cousin, and Henrietta Maria was his aunt. He declared that he would not have any rejoicing over 'a deplorable accident involving injury to so many unhappy people'. He then paid a formal visit to Henrietta Maria to express his sorrow, and offered to send 'provisions of food and whatever else might be needed to relieve the suffering of those unfortunates'.[2]

Marc Antonio Giustinian, Venetian Ambassador to the court of Louis XIV, reported to the Doge that there were several stories about the cause of the Fire: that the French and Dutch had started it deliberately; that it was attributed to 'an accident in the house of a baker'; that a group of merchants, bankrupted by Robert Holmes's burning of so many merchantmen off Terschelling, had sought consolation for their misfortunes 'by a universal ruin'. Giustinian ventured no opinion as to which was the most likely cause; but he did repeat a rumour begun by the Dutch, that two Cistercians on their way to preach the Gospel in the Indies had been captured by the English and brought in triumph to London, where they were abused, insulted and then killed, their limbs being distributed to the four quarters of the city. 'It was on the very day that their quarters were affixed that the fire began, and it may be considered the just punishment of Heaven for such a crime.'[3]

There is no record of these executions in English archives, and the Paris *Gazette*, which published a fair and even-handed account of the disaster, didn't think that they were worth mentioning. The same *Gazette* noted that the people of England blamed either the Dutch, or English fanatics (although, interestingly, not the French), but the paper refused to believe 'that there are citizens so vile or enemies so malignant as to resort to an action of that nature'.[4] It had nothing but praise for Charles II, crediting him with personally organising the firefighting and, through his kindness and courage, earning the lasting tenderness and veneration of his people. A German pamphlet was also accurate and sympathetic, refusing to lay blame and aghast at the plight of tens of thousands of homeless Londoners: 'May God Almighty protect all cities and places from such damage and misfortune.'[5]

Dutch accounts were less kind, although they too mentioned the efforts of the King and the Duke of York. The most vivid comes in the shape of a letter sent by a Dutch eye-witness to a friend in the Hague on Monday 10 September. He gives an accurate description of the spread of the Fire, and says that he hasn't dared to set foot outside his house in days for fear of the mob. The word was that a Dutch baker was to blame, and that French incendiaries had gone about the streets throwing fireballs into houses at random. One story he recounts concerns a woman walking in Moorfields with chickens held in her apron. She was seized by a mob which mistook the hens for fireballs; they beat her with sticks and cut off her breasts.

This wild rage against foreigners was prominent in one of the first Italian descriptions of the Fire, published in Padua towards the end of September. An English merchant in Venice who sent a copy of the pamphlet to Lord Arlington on 24 September claimed it was part of a Dutch misinformation campaign, and repeated the story of the quartered Cistercians – only now the two unfortunate friars described to the Venetian Ambassador in Paris had grown to four. The Italian pamphlet exulted in the destruction of London, comparing the city to Lucifer in its proud arrogance and its spectacular fall. The anonymous author, who claimed to have written his account in London on 14 September, attributed the calamity to the godlessness of its citizens: 'amid all their dire distress, not one person turned to Heaven to ask for mercy'. Like the Hogens' eye-witness, he made a great deal of the atrocities committed against foreigners, stating that their homes were looted and many were murdered. The 'Catholic Ambassador' had saved countless lives by giving refuge to the hunted.[6]

The most lurid of the foreign responses came from Valencia, and turned the disaster into a parable of Protestant wickedness. Claiming a death toll of 8,000, it dwelled in loving detail on the portents which should have turned the ungodly from their evil ways: a pyramid of fire which had appeared over the sea some months before; the recent birth in London of a terribly deformed monster, half red and half yellow, with the breasts of a goat, the tail of a wolf and the ears of a horse. It described how a battered stone had been unearthed from the ruins of a Protestant church, with a barely decipherable Latin inscription: 'When these letters shall be read, woe on London, for they shall be read by the light of a fire.' And it declared that the Fire had started in a black-smith's forge – an appropriate instrument of punishment, since London was itself at one time a forge, which had manufactured many iron tools 'for the sake of torturing glorious martyrs'.[7]

The Spanish author was so keen to point out that heavenly punishment was reserved for Protestants that he didn't let the truth get in his way. The Fire stopped short in its relentless march westward, he said, when it reached the walls of Henrietta Maria's Catholic chapel at St James's Palace. God was showing the heretics that He could make the flames respect those who loved Him. And St Paul's Cathedral was destroyed because 'the great Paul, not satisfied with the worship of the false religion which went on within its walls, preferred to see the magnificent edifice sacrificed to the fire rather than left for the veneration of a heretic cult'.[8]

But the Spanish narrative of events may have been so colourful partly because it was hard to extract information from the English Ambassador to Spain, the Earl of Sandwich. Sandwich was putting an exceptionally brave face on things, claiming that the damage done to London had been wildly exaggerated by England's enemies, and that 'the most ignoble and useless was all buried together beneath the ashes, but what was precious and important had been preserved and was safe'.[9] His optimistic slant on events was repeated elsewhere in Europe: the English Resident in Florence, Sir John Finch, also maintained that fire damage was minimal, that no merchandise had been destroyed and that Charles II was still determined to prosecute the war with France and Holland.

None of these accounts gave any weight to the theory that the Fire was started deliberately by foreign agents. But that didn't quash the rumours. The Dutch statesman Jan de Witt, for instance, had his suspicions. In the aftermath of Holmes's Bonfire, the Dutch Grand Pensionary was approached by a follower of the priest turned Protestant mystic Jean de la Badie, who had recently moved from Geneva to Middleburg. The Labadist brought an offer from persons unknown to set London on fire in revenge for the attack on Terschelling. De Witt was an astute politician. He turned the idea down flat, saying he had no wish to make the breach with England wider, or the quarrel with Charles II irreconcilable. When news of the Fire reached the Hague de Witt began to suspect that the Labadists and their mysterious friends had pressed ahead with their scheme for their own ends, intending to 'lay the odium of it upon the Dutch'.[10] He ordered that they should be brought before him, only to hear that they had vanished without trace.

In England, Charles's Moorfields speech had done little to quiet the conspiracy theorists. Already in a state of high alert because of the expected Dutch invasion, people didn't know what to believe, or what to do for the best. Joseph Williamson's *Gazette* endeavoured to raise their spirits with its own colourful accounts of Dutch morale: a dispatch purportedly sent from the Hague on 3 September recorded that 'Never were our [i.e. Dutch] hearts lower, nor our brags less. We are sensible how far our Fleet is inferiour to that of our Enemies in number, and how much more so in Courage and Vigour.'[11] But English anxieties were real: London was such a huge market that its collapse affected the entire kingdom. In Whitby, Thomas Waade wrote that he 'never saw so many sad faces as in that poor town, which has great trade with London, whence it derived its rise and life';[12] in Coventry, clothiers were distraught at the thought that their businesses had gone up in flames along with the vast stocks of cloth which they had sent down for the big Michaelmas sale at Blackwell Hall, next door to the Guildhall. (When they had time to put a figure to their losses, they reckoned them to be at least £2,000, 'which is a great deal as times go'.[13])

Everyone on the margins of society – Quakers, Roman Catholics, foreigners – became legitimate targets for reprisals or preventive measures. At Pendennis Castle on the south coast of Cornwall, 'all are in distraction about the fire, and think there is more villainy than chance in it'.[14] The word in Devon was that other major cities were now likely to come under attack; up in Newcastle, it was said that the Fire had been started by the Dutch, the French and fanatic Quakers – an eclectic alliance. The mayor of Norwich ordered the town crier into the streets to proclaim that no strangers could lodge in the city's taverns until they had been examined by him; nor were they to leave without his permission. Foreign vessels in Falmouth harbour were interned. A bad-tempered Evesham man was foolish enough to say that the French and Dutch would be there before Christmas, 'and no pity if they be';[15] he was arrested, accused of sedition and thrown into Warwick Gaol.

Trained bands were mobilised across Britain, often with unpredictable results: in the Welsh Marches, the justices suddenly found they had no gunpowder with which to arm their militias, and had to beg supplies from the garrison at Chester Castle; in Edinburgh, a mass march to Holyrood Palace in which 5,000 local men showed their solidarity with the Crown led to a riot when the mechanics' apprentices fell out with the merchants' apprentices, and a man was killed in the ensuing street-fighting.

A telling example of the tension and fear which people felt in the immediate aftermath of the disaster was a series of events that began outside Warwick on Sunday 9 September, a week to the day after the Fire began. A flock of sheep was found butchered in a field; the only thing removed from each carcass was the hard fat, the tallow, which was commonly used for candles. It seemed certain, to the nervous locals at least, that someone in the area was making fireballs.

The mysterious slaughter of sheep continued, and a few days after the first incident a young boy who was out gathering blackberries in Warwick came across a man behaving suspiciously; the man ran off, leaving behind a blackish-brown ball, which the youth took to the local authorities. It was obviously an unfinished fireball, said the mayor, although others insisted it was no such thing; and the townsfolk, already on edge, were gripped with a kind of mass hysteria. 'Hue and cries are sent out every way to apprehend the man, but all in vain; the town is in a tumult all day, every man in arms, besides the militia horse keeping strict guard all night.'[16]

Warwick waited for foreign Papists to arrive and storm the town: but the next day, with everyone still in a state of high anxiety, Sir Henry Pickering rode in with a troop of soldiers and a short temper. Pickering, a veteran of Cromwell's New Model Army and a stern disciplinarian, ordered the local militia to stand down and told everybody to go home. So scared were the townsfolk that they accused him of being in on the plot: 'for aught they knew, he had a design himself to betray the town'.[17] Pickering was exasperated, angry and not at all used to being treated in this way. He told his men to fire into the crowd if it didn't disperse at once. But the people were in no mood to walk away; they dared him to give the order, and cocked their loaded muskets in readiness.

There was a tense stand-off for some moments, with neither side prepared to give way. Then, one by one, the townsmen began to drift away, having thought better of getting into a bloody gunfight at close range with a troop of soldiers.

A week later the Lord Lieutenant of the county, the 3rd Earl of Northampton, rode into Warwick to meet with the local gentry and the trained bands. Ostensibly the Earl had arrived to call a general muster, thus reassuring the locals that everything was being done to combat the Papist menace; four troops of horse and six companies of foot, all armoured and fully equipped, spent two days in and around the town on military manoeuvres. But in reality Northampton was making a show of force and acting to suppress any dissident behaviour. All 'pragmatical praters' found to have spread defeatist reports were made examples of; and he expressly warned the townsfolk about 'the scandalous reports spread against Sir Hen. Pickering, since the late difference between him and the town of Warwick'.[18] Several individuals who had repeated rumours that the Duke of Albemarle had been poisoned, or that the fleet had been beaten, were summarily imprisoned. So was a man who claimed to have seen Sir Henry Pickering taking Mass. The state welcomed vigilance; but it would not tolerate criticism of its representatives.

Warwickshire remained in a state of alert for more than a month, with the authorities continuing to suppress anti-Catholic rumours, only for them to resurface in different guises: if Albemarle hadn't been poisoned, then he had been sacked as Captain-General of the Kingdom; Sir John Robinson had been dismissed from his post as Lord Lieutenant of the Tower, and his place taken by a Papist.

Anxieties in the Midlands were fuelled by a series of mysterious fires. In the last week of September and the first of October there was one at Shipley, near Bromsgrove in Worcestershire; and another at West Haddon in Northamptonshire. Most serious was a blaze at Loughborough in Leicestershire, which destroyed 200 houses and would have done even more damage if the wind hadn't turned. People were particularly worried about a strange comet which skimmed the rooftops of Coventry on the night of Saturday 4 October. It had a bright fiery tail 'which seemed to wriggle and wave as it went, and after it followed a very long stream of blue; its motion was swift but very low, being judged to have been not so high as the spires of our steeples.'[19] The celestial apparition was followed by a mighty thunderstorm which destroyed a barn full of corn belonging to a notorious Nonconformist sympathiser – a divine judgement on Dissenters and troublemakers.

King Charles summoned Parliament to assemble at Westminster on Tuesday 18 September – its first session since the previous October, when it met at Oxford on account of the plague. Only about 150 MPs turned up, much to the disappointment of the King, who adjourned both Houses until Friday, in the hope that the Lords and Commons would overcome their consternation at the Fire and make the journey to London.

The three days' grace made little difference to numbers. (An order subsequently went out that anyone who hadn't put in an appearance by the beginning of October would be fined £20.) Undaunted, the King donned his ceremonial robes and crown as planned and addressed the assembled Parliament under the plain barrel-vaulted ceiling of the House of Lords:

> My Lords and Gentlemen; I am very glad to meet so many of you together again; and God be thanked for our meeting together in this place! Little time hath passed, since we were almost in despair of having this place left us to meet in: you see the dismal ruins the Fire hath made; and nothing but a miracle of God's mercy could have preserved what is left from the same destruction.[20]

But, surprisingly enough, it wasn't the Fire that was uppermost in Charles's mind that Friday. He needed money. Money to refit and rearm the fleet, money for victuals, money to pay his seamen and strengthen coastal defences. When the war broke out at the beginning of 1665, the Commons had voted him the colossal sum of £2.5 million, spread over three years. By October 1665 it was clear that this was not enough, and in the Parliamentary session held at Oxford Charles got another £1.25 million, although it came with a condition – it was only to be used for expenses related to the war.

Now even that had been swallowed up in the summer's naval campaign. (Pepys reckoned the navy's annual running costs amounted to something in the region of £1.6 million, and this was confirmed later when Parliament was told that the whole charge of the navy from September 1664 to September 1666 was £3.22 million.) On the surface, it didn't seem a good time to ask for more, with the ruins of the nation's biggest port and most important centre of commerce still smouldering outside. But Charles was clever. While he never wavered from his stand that the Fire had been a dreadful accident, he told Parliament how insolent their enemies had grown: 'How will they be exalted with this last impoverishment of this city, and contemn all reasonable conditions of peace!' Strength in adversity was vital. 'We have two very great and powerful enemies, who use all the means they can, fair and foul, to make all the world to concur with them.' Now, more than ever, it was time to appear strong.

Both Houses responded by assuring the King that they would set about raising money for carrying on the war. And during the first few days of business, Parliament paid little heed to the plight of the capital. There were bills on importing Irish cattle and the publishing of marriage banns, a motion repealing a statute against the export of raw hides, another bill prohibiting the import of French goods, on the grounds that Louis XIV wouldn't allow English commodities into France. William Prynne, the veteran Parliamentarian who had lost both ears and been branded on both cheeks for his Puritanism, argued that the housing shortage caused by the Fire could be mitigated if all Catholics, Dissenters and foreigners were barred from living within ten miles of the city. He thoughtfully excepted the personal attendants of Catherine of Braganza, but the Commons laid the motion aside.

On Monday 24 September both Houses agreed to get Charles his money, and on Tuesday they attended the King in the Banqueting House at Whitehall to tell him so. Now that the war's finances were out of the way, Parliament could at last turn its attention to the Fire: the same day there was a long and serious debate on the disaster in the Commons, 'whether it was by the hand of God, or by design, and whether a committee should be named for the examination of it'.[21]

The issue was a tricky one. Charles and the Duke of York were both still convinced that the Fire had been a dreadful accident; and there was plenty of support for their view of things. 'Lett us not Lay the Fault upon the French or Dutch,' wrote John Rushworth, 'or our owne people for throwing Fire Balles, &c, for by all I cann observe it was digitus dei.'[22] In the Commons, Sir Heneage Finch, the Solicitor-General and a prominent courtier, argued against a committee of inquiry, and he had plenty of support from MPs who, if they weren't quite as sure as the King that the whole thing had been an accident, were convinced that an inquiry would turn into a witch-hunt without arriving at the truth.

But Finch was unable to get his way. Detailed and persuasive stories of a foreign plot were circulating around Westminster. It was well known that a ten-year-old boy named Edward Taylor had come forward to claim that he had been with his father and his uncle – a Dutchman – when they hurled two fireballs through an open window in Pudding Lane on the night the Fire broke out. Edward, whose parents lived in Covent Garden, also said they had fired Fleet Street and Gresham's Royal Exchange, and that he and his mother had taken part in the burning of a great house at Acton, to the west of London. Apparently Edward's uncle paid his father £7 to undertake the firing; and in a theatrical flourish, the child told the magistrates that his mother wore a black silk suit and black hood, while his father wore a black suit and cloak.

The rage to blame someone for the Fire was strong, and it crossed Parliament's factional boundaries. In the Commons

debate, the pro-court MP for Launceston in Cornwall, Sir Charles
Harbord, and the Parliamentarian lawyer Sir John Maynard both
argued that the nation needed to know the truth; and they eventually carried the day, with the House voting for an inquiry.

The Parliamentary Committee was chaired by Sir Robert
Brooke, MP for Aldeburgh in Suffolk. The evidence which was
brought before Brooke and his colleagues as they sat in the
Speaker's Chamber over the next couple of months – 'many
considerable informations from divers credible persons'[23] – was
quite astounding. Young Edward Taylor's story was lurid enough,
but it was only a beginning. Tales of conspiracy and sinister behaviour poured in. The mildest remark was enough to provoke
Londoners to inform on their neighbours, and they seemed to
possess the most astonishing powers of recall.

Someone came forward to report that back in February he
had been arguing about religion in the Inner Temple with a
Catholic barrister named Richard Langhorne, when the latter
took him by the hand and said, 'You expect great things in 1666,
and think that Rome will be destroyed, but what if it be London?'
Then there was the maid who had rebuffed the advances of a
French manservant the previous spring, only for him to claim:
'You English maids will like the Frenchmen better when there
is not a house left between Temple-Bar and London-Bridge.' He
added that this would happen between June and October. At the
Greyhound Inn in St Martin's, an Irish Catholic had been overheard to say that there would be 'a sad desolation in September';
when asked where this desolation would be, he answered, 'In
London'.[24]

The stories flooded in from all over the country. On the
Thursday before the Fire a local official in Ipswich got into an
argument over taxes with a Roman Catholic named William
Thomson. Thomson said that though times were hard, he would
see that the constable wouldn't go hungry if he changed his religion. Then he asked, 'What will you say, if you should hear that
London is burnt?'[25] William Ducket MP told the Committee of
a report which came from Chippenham in Wiltshire. On 30
August a farmer, Henry Baker, wanted to buy a pair of fat bullocks

at market from a man named John Woodman. When he asked Woodman to keep them for him, Woodman refused, saying that he was leaving the country. He wouldn't say where he was going, but as the two men rode along together he suddenly burst out, 'You are brave blades at Chippenham, you made bonfires lately for beating the Dutch, but since you delight in bonfires, you shall have your bellies full of them ere it be long.' Then he added that if the farmer lived another week, 'he should see London as sad a London as ever it was since the world began'.[26]

There seemed to be no shortage of evidence for a well-planned conspiracy to burn down the metropolis. A justice testified that during the time of the Fire he had seen a man near the Temple with his pockets stuffed full of flax, tow and other combustible materials. A doctor, John Packer, stated that he had watched a man throw something into an apothecary's shop by the Old Bailey, and that immediately there had been a plume of smoke and a smell of brimstone. Several respectable merchants and businessmen – including Sir John Maynard, the MP who had fought for the inquiry – came forward to testify that they had personally seen what they took to be incendiary devices during the Fire.

Some extraordinary evidence was given against Monsieur Belland, the King's French firework-maker, who with his son ran a workshop in Marylebone, to the west of the City. Belland seems to have been guilty of nothing more than a tendency to brag about his trade. He was often heard to boast that he had huge stockpiles of fireworks – thousands of them, which he kept not only in Marylebone but 'elsewhere in three several places, three, four, and five miles off'.[27] He also used to say that he employed an army of men to make them for him.

According to witnesses, on Sunday 26 August Belland turned up at the stationer's shop where he usually bought the pasteboard to make his fireworks. The stationer wasn't there, and the Frenchman found a neighbour and asked him to tell the man 'that he had much wronged him in disappointing him of the four gross of pasteboard which he should have had of him, and said that he should not do his work by the time; and that if he had it not by Tuesday night, it would come too late'.[28] When the neighbour asked if he was putting on a display for the King, Belland blushed and refused to answer; but he did tell him the kind of fireworks he was making. They were of all sorts: some were crackers, others were rockets which 'fly up in a pure body of flame, higher than the top of Paul's, and waver in the air'. The neighbour was impressed and asked if he could come and see the display; at which Belland promised he could, and gave him his hand on it. When the Fire was at its height, the same neighbour was out in his boat on the Thames and saw 'to his great amazement, sundry bodies of fire, burning above the fire of the houses as high again as Paul's wavering in the air, directly according to Belland's description'.

That was more than enough to arouse suspicions. But, in any case, Belland went into hiding with his entire household in the days immediately following the Fire. Hundreds of perfectly innocent foreigners were doing the same, for obvious reasons; and no doubt they echoed the feelings of one Frenchman who declared that 'of all the time I have been in England I did never dislike my being here but five days of last week, wherein I was half dead by the word of killing all French and Dutch'.[29]

A couple of concerned citizens went round to Belland's Marylebone shop to speak to him. They didn't find him there, but in the street they came across his maids and his boy who were carrying some food, rabbits and capons. The servants insisted they didn't know where the Bellands were, but the two citizens were not convinced, and trailed them all the way to the Palace of Whitehall. 'The servants went up stairs, and down stairs, on purpose to have lost them, but could not, for they kept close to them: And at last, one of the maids went to a door, and knocked; crying out, they were dogged by two men, that they could not be rid of.'

Belland's son opened the door, a model of courtesy. 'Sir, your servant,' he said to one of his pursuers. 'How do you do?'

'Both I, and many thousand families more, are the worse for you,' replied the other. 'For you, under pretence of making fireworks for the King, have destroyed a famous city, and ruined a noble people.'

'I make nothing but innocent things, that will do no harm; for which I have a patent from the King.'

'What made you then employ so many men, in so many places?'

Young Belland flatly denied that he employed anyone, or that he even knew of anyone else making fireworks. At this point things descended into farce. Tempers flared, and everyone had started shouting at each other when old Monsieur Belland abruptly popped his head out from behind a wall-hanging, where he had been hiding like Polonius. He begged them to keep their voices down, and said, 'My son doth nothing, but what he hath a patent from the King for; and shall have an order to sue any man that shall accuse him.' Then, filled with righteous indignation, he told them: 'My son is no prisoner, but lodged here, to prevent him from the rage of the common people.'

The two vigilantes didn't know quite what to make of this. So they blustered. One said rather feebly, 'Well, you must give an account for what you have done.' The Bellands shut the door in their faces and left them standing outside. When they asked who was providing father and son with sanctuary, they could learn only that the lodgings belonged to a lady.

Nothing more is heard of the Bellands' fate. But the tale grew in the telling. By Sunday 9 September, when it reached Eton, eight or nine men had been arrested in Marylebone and found in possession of a huge supply of fireworks, including some 'which burned though put into a tub of water'.[30] Aside from the paranoia and absurdity, there are a couple of revealing points about the story. One is the lack of security within the Palace of Whitehall, which reminds us of Pepys's remarks about finding no guards on duty at Woolwich dockyard when he arrived there at the height of the Fire. The thought that two men could walk in off the street and wander round a royal palace when the King was in residence and at a time when England was in a state of alert higher than anyone had known for years is surprising, to say the least.

The other point about the Bellands' tale is the light it sheds on the role of the court in sheltering foreign fugitives from the mob. In spite of the Duke of York's heroism during the Fire, in its aftermath people kept remarking how sinister it was that whenever a Frenchman or a Dutchman was seized and handed over to the Duke or his Guards, nothing more was heard of them. A constable grabbed a Frenchman, whom he insisted he had caught in the act of firing a house, and ran into the Duke on his way to find a magistrate. 'The Duke took him into his custody, and said, I will secure him. But he was heard of no more.' And on the Monday a mob searched another Frenchman and, they insisted, actually found fireballs in his possession; but the Life Guards took him away from them, 'after their usual manner in the whole time of the fire'.[31] Much later, during the Popish Plot and the Exclusion Crisis, this would be trotted out as evidence of James's treasonable pro-Catholic leanings; but in fact from very early in the proceedings he established a lifeline for beleaguered foreign nationals, with his Guards on the streets operating snatch-squads, and the men and women of the court providing short-term safe havens in their own lodgings at the palace.

As more and more evidence was presented to the Parliamentary Committee, a picture of the conspirators began to emerge. 'This devilish Popish Plot', as it was being called by the end of September, was the work of Jesuits and their English sympathisers.[32]

Strange rumours were flying round the City and the court. One, for example, concerned the Catholic statistician Captain John Graunt, who had recently applied to become a trustee of the New River Company, which supplied the Islington Water House. Graunt was successful in his bid for a post. But according to several witnesses, on Saturday 1 September he had arrived unexpectedly at Islington, turned off the water supply and then gone off again, taking the key to the supply house with him. 'So when the fire broke out next morning, they opened the pipes in the streets to find water, but there was none. And some hours were lost in sending to Islington, where the door was to be broke open and the cocks turned.'[33] Graunt later admitted going off with the keys to the place, but swore it was absent-mindedness, and denied that he had turned the cocks.

Then a letter was received from Heidelberg, in which the

writer said that the burning of London was 'constantly expected and discoursed of amongst the Jesuits these fifteen years past, as to happen in this year'.[34] An old Catholic woman in Enfield was reported as saying, on the Friday before the Fire broke out, that there was a plot, and that the capital would be laid to ashes. An Irish Catholic arrived to visit relatives in Essex on the Saturday and, over supper, asked the master of the house if he had heard anything of the firing of London. When the squire looked blank, the man said he would shortly; and the next day he rode up to town, saying, 'I would see London before it be quite burnt; for I shall never see it more.'[35]

One of the strangest incidents took place in a large house near Bridewell. As the flames crept along the street towards it, the owner of the house ran out, begging men to come and help him save his possessions. A man named John Stewart gave evidence that he had gone into the house with several others, breaking windows and throwing trunks, chests, beds and other household goods out into the street, where the owner had two carts waiting. While Stewart was waiting for the wagons to return, he wandered into a library and picked a copy of Ovid's *Metamorphoses* off a shelf; as he did, he noticed a little old man in a white robe standing at his side, staring at the book. Neither spoke. Suddenly a heap of papers on the other side of the room burst into flames; other helpers rushed in and stamped them out, while Stewart grabbed the old man by his collar and said, 'How now, father! It must either be you or I that fired these papers.'

The man opened his mouth for the first time, crying out '*Parce mihi, Domini!*' ('Spare me, Lord!'). Stewart understood him – and was surprised to find that such a humble chap could speak Latin. But the rest of the people in the room assumed he was speaking French, and shouted, 'He is a Frenchman, kill him!' In the ensuing struggle the man's wig fell off, showing his bald skull, and the mob saw he wore black ecclesiastical-looking clothes under his white frock. Stewart saved him from being lynched with some difficulty, and took him to the Duke of York for questioning. He never heard what became of him after that. 'Methought he looked something Jesuit-like,' he told the Parliamentary Committee.[36]

There were around 60,000 Roman Catholics living in Restoration England, making up just over 1 per cent of the population.[37] They were subject to a range of repressive laws dating from the time of Elizabeth I, and strengthened by her successor James I in the aftermath of the Gunpowder Plot. Absence from church was punishable by fines of 1s per week and £20 per month and, ultimately, by excommunication and imprisonment. It was a capital offence for a priest to enter England, a capital offence to harbour him. Catholic schools were forbidden; Catholic marriages were not valid in law; and, in theory, Catholics were forbidden to hold any office, or keep arms, or travel more than five miles from their home, or appear at court.

'In theory', because by 1666 the penal laws were being observed rather loosely. Between 1660 and 1671, for example, the Exchequer took just £147 15s 7d in recusant revenue. And at least one member of the Committee of Inquiry into the causes of the Fire was a Catholic: Sir Solomon Swale had converted in 1660, but presumably no one noticed, since he continued to sit as MP for Aldborough in Yorkshire for another eighteen years.

This is hardly surprising. Charles and his brother were both temperamentally inclined towards Catholicism – so much so that rumours of their conversion to Rome began to fly soon after the Restoration, and in 1661 Parliament passed an act making it a criminal offence to say that the King was a Papist.* Their mother was a Catholic; so was their sister Henrietta, who was married to the Duke of Orleans, Louis XIV's only brother; and Charles's wife, Catherine of Braganza, who ran a chapel at St James's Palace with communities of English Benedictines and Portuguese Franciscans. Moreover, Catholics had served the Crown well in the Civil War and during the years of exile. A strongly Anglican Parliament wouldn't countenance the rehabilitation of their religion, but Charles was happy to tolerate his

---

*Whether or not the rumours had any foundation, Charles converted to Catholicism on his deathbed in 1685, following belatedly in the footsteps of James, Duke of York, who went over to Rome in 1668 or 1669, and allowed his change of faith to be made public in the early 1670s.

Papist subjects so long as they posed no threat to the stability of the kingdom; and no doubt he echoed the thoughts of George Hall, Bishop of Chester: 'I wish the sectaries were but as quiet and yet inoffensive as they are.'[38]

For the most part, individual Papists were viewed with mild exasperation. But Popery itself was not. A tradition of anti-Catholic feeling ran very deep indeed in Restoration society. *Foxe's Book of Martyrs*, which chronicled Mary Tudor's persecutions of Protestants in terrible detail, had been but an early step on the road to an iconography of hate and suspicion that by the 1660s was an accepted part of English culture. Some of its landmarks, like the Gunpowder Plot of 1605, had a basis in reality. Others, such as the Irish 'massacre of 1641', in which innocent and unsuspecting Protestants were raped, horribly mutilated, disembowelled, buried alive or butchered by bigoted and merciless Papists, were at best wildly exaggerated, at worst, the figments of fevered Puritan imaginations.

The English fear of Catholicism was about more than theological differences. As far as most ordinary citizens were concerned, Popery and arbitrary government were natural companions. It went without saying that the dearest wish of Pope Alexander VII was the suppression of ancient English liberties; and that Catholic Europe saw England as a jewel just waiting to be set in the papal crown. Faced with having to explain why in 1649 a Protestant nation had killed its Protestant king, Puritans in the early years of the Restoration began to claim that the New Model Army had been infiltrated by Papists, just as they would later argue that Jesuits were behind Rathbone's plot, and that the foolish Fifth Monarchy Men were the unwitting dupes of Machiavellian Catholics. Although he was writing in 1680, during a particularly virulent epidemic of anti-Catholicism, many citizens in September 1666 would have agreed unquestioningly with the Protestant pamphleteer Henry Care, and his picture of life in a Catholic state:

Yourselves forced to fly destitute of bread and harbour, your wives prostituted to the lust of every savage bog-trotter, your daughters ravished by goatish monks, your smaller children tossed upon pikes, or torn limb from limb, whilst you have your own bowels ripped up . . . or else murdered with some other exquisite tortures and holy candles made of your grease (which was done within our memory in Ireland), your dearest friends flaming in Smithfield, foreigners rendering your poor babes that can escape everlasting slaves, never more to see a Bible, nor hear again the joyful sounds of Liberty and Property. This, this gentlemen is Popery.[39]

And this was the background to the anti-Catholic conspiracy theories that were bouncing around the City in September 1666. But events seemed to show they had some substance, over and above the hearsay of malicious neighbours and the xenophobic paranoia of the mob. In the days immediately following the disaster, a young Frenchman was arrested while trying to leave the country. When questioned, he confessed that he had quite deliberately started the Fire of London.

10

Yes Sir, I am Guilty of It

Ludgate during the Fire.

Robert Hubert was a 26-year-old watchmaker's son from Rouen in Normandy. He was lame and something of a drifter, variously described by contemporaries as a watchmaker like his father and as a common labourer. Caught up in the general exodus of foreigners from the capital, he had been stopped at Romford in Essex while running for the east-coast ports. He was taken in for questioning.

There was nothing unusual in this; it was happening all over the country. But when Hubert was brought before Cary Harvie, the Romford justice, and asked to give an account of his movements during and immediately after the Fire, he blurted out an extraordinary story. He was a member of an organised gang of twenty-four incendiaries, he said, led by a man named Stephen Peidloe. While the city was ablaze he had been landed upriver from London Bridge with instructions to throw a fireball near the Palace of Whitehall, which he duly did.

Harvie sent Hubert back to London under heavy guard.

Newgate and Bridewell were both in ruins, and temporary prisons had been set up in Bishopsgate and Aldgate; but the young man was taken to White Lion Gaol across the river in Southwark. He was indicted on felony charges and sent for trial at the Old Bailey.

By the time Hubert came to trial at the October sessions a few weeks later, his story had changed; and if the original had confirmed the suspicions of the conspiracy theorists, the latest version was a revelation. Now he claimed that there were just four in the gang, including himself and Stephen Peidloe. He had been recruited in Paris the year before, and had come to England during the plague with the aim of firing London, but for some reason he and his accomplices had left again without carrying out their plan. They headed for Stockholm. Towards the end of August, he, Peidloe and a third man sailed for England in a Swedish ship, the *Skipper*. The vessel moored at St Katherine's, just below the Tower of London, an area well known for its floating population of foreigners and seamen. And there they stayed until dusk on Saturday 1 September.

That night Stephen Peidloe took him ashore and led him along the Thames Street wharves and into Pudding Lane. Hubert repeatedly asked where they were going, but Peidloe said nothing until they arrived at Farriner's bakery. Then he said he had brought three fireballs with him; he gave one to Hubert and told him to set fire to the house.

There were many different ways of making fireballs: an Elizabethan recipe advises budding incendiaries to take six ounces of gunpowder, four ounces of saltpetre and half an ounce of resin, half an ounce of sulphur and half an ounce of linseed oil; mix them together; and wrap them in a ball of cotton cloth. They didn't explode like bombs, and one didn't just light the blue touchpaper and throw them; care had to be taken to ensure they ignited properly and remained in contact with other combustible materials.

According to Hubert, he and Peidloe had a brief altercation outside the bakery. The young Frenchman wanted to know why *this* house? What was the point? But Peidloe was impatient to see the deed done, and simply told him to get on with it. 'Then he did the fact, which was, that he put a fireball at the end of a long pole, and lighting it with a piece of match, he put it in at a window, and staid till he saw the house in a flame.'[1]

In spite of London's real need to believe that the Fire was an act of malice rather than an act of God, there was considerable disquiet over Hubert's story. He contradicted himself over the number of fireballs that were used, and the number of accomplices. He claimed he was a Catholic, even though most people who knew him were sure he was a Huguenot and a Protestant. He seemed to have no political motive; when a French merchant named Graves who lived in St Mary Axe in east London, and who knew him well, went to visit him in gaol and told him frankly his confession was nonsense, Hubert replied, 'Yes sir, I am guilty of it, and have been brought to it by the instigation of Monsieur Peidloe; but not out of any malice to the English nation, but from a desire of a reward, which he promised me upon my return into France.'[2] Yet he told the authorities that he had been given a single gold coin, with a paltry promise of five more if his mission was successful. Peidloe had vanished into thin air.

'Nobody present credited any thing he said,' the Earl of Clarendon later recalled. Lord Chief Justice Kelyng, a formidable figure with a reputation for sternness, heard the case at the Old Bailey and told Charles II that Hubert's story made little sense: 'all his discourse was so disjointed that he did not believe him guilty'.[3]*

But although there were no witnesses, Robert Hubert insisted he *was* guilty — *and* that he could prove it. At the request of the

---

*Kelyng was actually accused of 'severity' by the House of Commons in autumn 1667. One of the charges related that a jury brought in a manslaughter verdict with which he disagreed. 'And because they did not find it murder nor would be persuaded to alter their verdict he told [them] that if they would not go out again and find murder he would fine them £2 a man. The jury for fear went out again and found it murder and the man was hanged' (Caroline Robbins (ed.), *The Diary of John Milward* [CUP, 1938], 9 December 1667).

Parliamentary Committee of Inquiry, John Lowman, Keeper of White Lion Gaol, took him across the river to St Katherine-by-the-Tower, and to the place where Hubert said the *Skipper* had moored while he and Peidloe waited to carry out their mission. Sceptical of Hubert's claims, Lowman brought him along Thames Street without saying a word until, as they reached the end of Pudding Lane, Hubert pointed and announced that 'the house was up there'.[4]

In fact, Pudding Lane had ceased to exist. There was nothing left standing. But Lowman and Hubert scrambled over the rubble and debris until the latter called a halt and said that *this* was the spot where he had fired the house. Lowman had no idea if he was telling the truth or not, so he grabbed a local man and asked where Farriner's bakery had stood. It was just where Hubert said it was. First Lowman tried to persuade him he meant somewhere else in Pudding Lane. Then, when Hubert insisted he had the right place, the jailer set him on a horse and led him to several other places. 'No other place would he acknowledge,' Lowman reported to Parliament; 'but rode back again to the baker's house, and said again. "That was the house," pointing at the baker's house.'[5]

Still there was some unease. Doubts about Hubert's guilt were raised by members of the Parliamentary Committee, so Thomas Farriner was called before them and asked if perhaps the fire might have been started by accident? Impossible, he said; he'd gone through every room after midnight to check the state of the hearths, and there was only one fire, and that in a room paved with brick, and anyway he carefully raked up the embers. But considering that a fire in his home had just burned down the third-largest city in the Western world, he would say that, wouldn't he?

No one at the dock could remember having seen the *Skipper*; and its master, Captain Petersen, later testified that although the ship had put in at London, Hubert hadn't gone ashore until Monday or Tuesday. He could easily have been one of the sightseers who flocked to Pudding Lane over the following days to see where the Fire had begun.

When Hubert came to trial at the Old Bailey towards the end of October no one present, not even the Lord Chief Justice, believed he was guilty. No one, that is, except for Hubert himself. He insisted on his confession. Asked if he was sorry for what he had done, he said nothing. Asked if he had intended such catastrophic consequences, he still said nothing. In the face of such determination, the jury had no choice but to return a true bill. They found that Robert Hubert, 'not having the fear of God before his eyes, but moved and led away by the instigation of the devil, on the 2nd day of September, 18 Charles II, about the second hour of the night of that day', kindled and fired a fireball and 'then and there voluntarily, maliciously and feloniously did throw [it] into the mansion house of one Thomas Farriner the elder, baker, set and being in Pudding-lane'.[6]

Assuming that Hubert didn't start the Fire of London – and if Captain Petersen was telling the truth, he couldn't have done it – then the young man's motives for confessing so readily and in so much detail are hard to understand. Rack, boot and thumbscrew, routinely used for extracting information in cases of treason and sedition up to the early seventeenth century, were no longer legal in England;* and although the interrogation of suspects was often quite a physical affair, Hubert's eagerness to confess left his perplexed interrogators with the task of trying to break his story instead of forcing it out of him.

These days, there is quite a body of literature on the phenomenon of false confession. Simple attention-seeking, a desire for celebrity, even an attempt to cast doubt on an earlier, true admission of guilt can all play a part. Emotionally vulnerable or mentally handicapped suspects find it hard to withstand skilful interrogators,

*Strictly speaking, torture had *never* been legal in English law, but in special circumstances torture warrants could be – and were – issued by the Crown or the Privy Council right up until the eve of the Civil War. Many of the Gunpowder Plotters were tortured to force them to name their co-conspirators; it was a 1628 ruling in the case of John Felton, who assassinated the Duke of Buckingham, 'that he ought not by the law to be tortured by the rack, for no such punishment is known or allowed by our law', which heralded the end of the practice. The last torture warrant was issued by the Privy Council in 1640.

and are more likely to be suggestible – a fact which is now so well recognised in English law that if police interrogate a person with a recognised intellectual vulnerability, an 'appropriate adult' must be present during the interview to ensure that questions are fair and not designed to provoke undue anxiety.

There were no such safeguards in 1666. Hubert seems to have been eager for celebrity, but there is also plenty of evidence to suggest that he had mental problems. Apart from Lord Chief Justice Kelyng's remark to the King that the prisoner's narrative was unusually disjointed, Sir Edward Harley MP mentioned in a letter to his wife dated 20 October that during his examination Hubert 'sayd some extravagant things that savored of a distempered mind';[7] Sir Robert Vyner later told Pepys that Hubert may not have been quite mad, but he was certainly 'a mopish, besotted fellow;'[8] and Lord Chancellor Clarendon recalled that he had 'for many years both in Roan [i.e., Rouen] and in London been looked upon as distracted'.[9] Clarendon's own opinion, that Hubert was a 'poor distracted wretch, weary of his life, and chose to part with it this way',[10] was as close as any of his contemporaries came to an explanation of the boy's behaviour.

Robert Hubert was hanged at Tyburn on 29 October 1666. According to one account, he retracted his confession on the gallows. But by then it was too late.

His death didn't put a stop to the conspiracy theories. A story began to circulate that immediately after his conviction, the Parliamentary Committee of Inquiry decided to interrogate him further about his accomplices; and that he was executed the following morning 'and so could tell no farther tales'.[11] However, those who sought evidence of a conspiracy might have noticed that the seven signatories who endorsed the indictment against Hubert included Thomas Farriner, Hanna Farriner and Thomas Farriner junior.

The plea for nighbouring counties to send in food supplies to London's temporary markets worked very well indeed. As a precaution, the Navy Victualler, Alderman Gauden, was ordered to send ships' biscuit from his East Smithfield warehouses: but the feared shortages clearly didn't materialise, since people refused to eat it and it was returned untouched to the Navy stores.

In any case, after the invasion scare on Wednesday 5 September and Charles's speech at Moorfields the next day, people began to drift away from the big encampments. Over the next three or four days they went into the suburbs, or to nearby towns and villages, or back into the City, where they put up sheds and temporary dwellings and took stock of the damage. Those on the outskirts of the fire zone offered homes to the homeless; the King sent tents; some people opened up their cellars, which still survived more or less intact, and roofed them over to make shelters.

A few looked, rather optimistically, to the King for money to help them get back on their feet. Some begged him for what was owed to them. John Gamble, a member of His Majesty's 'wind-instrument concert', had not received his salary for nearly five years; having lost everything in the Fire and run into serious debt, he faced ruin if the arrears – £221 10s 4½d – were not forthcoming. Likewise, the King's jeweller, John Le Roy, had had his house burned down, and asked the King to pay an outstanding debt of £357, the balance due for a diamond ring commissioned for his mistress the Countess of Castlemaine.

Others asked for jobs. A stationer who had lost his business wanted a place in the Custom House; a cook successfully petitioned the King to intercede with the Cooks' Company so that he could set up trade in their Hall on Aldersgate Street. One enterprising individual suggested that in order to prevent mischief from foreigners 'who are suspected to have had a hand in burning the city', he should be granted a patent on the idea that no strangers could stay for a night without providing information on where they came from and their current address.[12] The patent was not granted.

The seventeenth century had procedures for providing emergency relief for local, national and even international disasters. In June 1655, for example, clergy and church wardens across the country made a house-to-house collection in aid of distressed and displaced Protestants in Savoy, Bohemia and

Poland. It raised the considerable sum of £38,232 (although nearly £8,000 of this was siphoned off by Cromwell's Council of State before it could be distributed, and never seen again). Local emergencies – small-scale fires, floods, storm damage and the like – were dealt with by means of local appeals, and donations from gentry and businessmen in neighbouring towns. When Cullompton in Devon was damaged by fire in 1602, justices in the county gave a loan and a donation from a charitable fund they administered; they also encouraged people in the county to contribute to an appeal fund.[13]

The usual response to a major fire was a royal brief, a letter from the Crown which was circulated to officials at every level – diocese, county, town and parish – pressing them to support an appeal fund. The brief which was published after the Great Fire of Warwick in 1694 is typical. After describing the 'wretched and disconsolate Estate' to which the inhabitants of Warwick had been reduced, William and Mary announced that they

> do give and grant unto the said Poor distressed Sufferers, and to their Agents, and other Persons, who shall be lawfully Authorised on their Behalf, full Power, Licence, and Authority, to Ask, Gather, Receive, and Take . . . the Alms and Charitable Benevolence of all Our Loving Subjects, not only Householders, but also Servants, Strangers, and others, within all . . . the Counties, Cities, Boroughs, Towns Corporate, Priviledged Places, Parishes, Chapelries, Towns, Villages, Hamlets, and other Places whatsoever.

Clergy throughout the land were told that they should not only publicise the appeal to their flocks, but 'by powerful Inducements, earnestly perswade, exhort and stir them up, to Contribute freely and chearfully to the Losses of the said poor Sufferers'. All money was to go within twenty days of the collection to one of two designated Fleet Street banks – Childs near Temple Bar or Hoares at the Sign of the Golden Bottle.[14]

The Church of England was the main agency for collecting charitable donations, although heads of university colleges, judges and students of the Inns of Court were often also included in an appeal. On a designated Sunday, suitable sermons were preached from the pulpit and, if the disaster seemed to demand it, passing the plate in church was supplemented by a further house-to-house collection by church wardens, sometimes accompanied by vicars, curates or influential parishioners whose job it was to twist arms.

Money was distributed according to need, but a dispensing authority was not a soft touch. As with the modern insurance claim, suspicions that victims had overestimated their losses would bring in an assessor to reduce them; and anyone fraudulently passing themselves off as a fire victim could expect to be treated harshly. In the aftermath of the Great Fire of Warwick, for instance, the neighbouring counties were plagued with people impersonating inhabitants of Warwick who had been 'ruin'd by the late dreadfull fire'; they also carried passes which apparently entitled them to relief. The justices swiftly issued a statement denouncing these 'lewd and disorderly people', and proclaiming 'that all such testimonials or passes are counterfeit, and the persons producing them [are] to be punished, as vagrants and common cheats'.[15]

The results of such disaster appeals varied wildly. Contributions in a typical parish might range from £10 given by the local squire down to a widow's mite of a few pence. The Warwick appeal yielded around £11,000; a similar appeal after a fire at Marlborough in Wiltshire in 1653 produced £18,000; and when Northampton was burned down in 1675, the nation stumped up an impressive £25,000.

In comparison, the appeal to help victims of the Fire of London was not a great success. There were impromptu gifts, and suggestions for gifts, in the weeks immediately after the Fire. The people of Lyme in Dorset, for instance, managed to raise £100 through a 'large and liberal collection'.[16] Joseph Williamson received a touching letter from Southwold, which had been badly damaged by fire seven years previously. His correspondent, William Waynflet, wrote that he knew from experience how the poor would want for food. Cheese prices were low in the county, and if Williamson were to contact some of the local gentry, Waynflet was sure they could be persuaded to load a small vessel and send it to London, to be distributed among the poor.

The main appeal followed a more conventional pattern. Wednesday 10 October was appointed as the day for a national fast, the ostensible purpose of which was, as Evelyn wrote, 'to humble us on the late dreadfull conflagration, added to the plague and warr, the most dismall judgments that could be inflicted, but which indeed we highly deserv'd for our prodigious ingratitude, burning lusts, dissolute Court, profane and abominable lives'.[17] (Evelyn managed to combine a Protestant line in hellfire rhetoric with a Catholic sense of guilt.) But a more practical reason for the fast day was to provide a nationwide focus for the appeal fund.

In Coventry there was a house-to-house collection. In Truro, they were proud that around £20 was collected, 'a very liberal contribution considering the meanness of the place'.[18] The vicar of Falmouth, Francis Bedford, preached such a stirring sermon that the people stumped up £7 – not much, perhaps, but considering that previous charitable appeals in Falmouth had yielded no more than 15s, not a bad effort.

Other parts of the country did their bit. Derby contributed £32, Berwick-on-Tweed £48. Devon subscribed £1,480 and Yorkshire gave £1,184. All in all, the collection raised £12,794. Individual gifts and a second appeal in 1668 took the final total up to £16,201. This seems quite a lot, but it was pretty paltry in comparison to the appeals for Marlborough and Northampton. There was a simple reason for this: throughout the seventeenth century London had been a major donor whenever national disaster appeals were launched. Now, although some unburned London parishes were generous, others were in no state to offer aid.

Another reason for the poor response was what the twenty-first century would call compassion fatigue. In July 1665 a series of solemn fast days – with their attendant collections – had been instituted for the first Wednesday of every month, to provide relief for sufferers from the plague. Uninfected areas were asked to send their contributions direct to the Bishop of London, Humphrey Henchman. By February 1666 the country had given

£1,397, including substantial donations of £205 from Bristol, £170 from Exeter and £190 from Chester. Derby managed £151 10s, nearly five times as much as its Fire donation the following year.

In the autumn of 1666 many English towns were still suffering from the plague, and this also played a part in reducing the giving. Cities like Cambridge and Norwich, Canterbury and the south-coast ports were all looking for relief themselves. (One thinks of how swiftly Thomas Warren had resumed his fund-raising efforts in London on behalf of the plague victims of Cambridge.) But the idea that charity begins at home was also dear to the hearts of a number of prosperous Londoners. In December the Pewterers, who had lost their Hall in Lime Street, were asked to contribute to the appeal fund. They declined to help: 'in consid-eration of the late calamities by fire in which the Company hath been very great sufferers, and the generality of the poorer sort of people hath been in some measure gainers, it was concluded nothing should be given'.[19]

The Restoration was very much alive to the politics of aid. On 29 September the Duke of Ormond, a powerful Anglo-Irish politician who had been appointed Lord Lieutenant of Ireland at the Restoration, wrote to Sir Thomas Bludworth to express his condolences and those of the entire Council of Ireland. The country was poor, but still wanted to help in some way – perhaps by sending over some cattle? Ormond himself would give 300 head; the Earl of Cork, who was Lord Treasurer of Ireland, would give 100; and other Irish nobles would give whatever they could. As W. G. Bell wrote in the 1920s, 'In the troubled history of the relations of Ireland and England there is no incident it is more pleasant to recall than the offer of help voluntarily made by the warm-hearted Irish to distressed London.'[20]

Perhaps. And perhaps it was a coincidence that Ormond's offer came just one week after a bill to prevent the import of Irish cattle into England was introduced into the House of Commons. Irish landowners, it was argued, could breed cattle for nothing and transport them for very little; they undersold English farmers, brought down the price of beef and, as a result, kept agricultural rents low. 'And this was a principal cause of the want of money in the country [i.e., in England]'.[21] There was a good deal of opposition to the bill in the Commons, chiefly from East Anglian MPs whose counties made a good living from bringing in lean Irish cattle and fattening them up to sell on. In fact more Parliamentary time was spent on it than on any other issue, including the Fire and the war.

After several fierce debates the Irish Cattle Bill went up to the House of Lords on 15 October, where it provoked even more controversy. The wild and wicked Duke of Buckingham led support for it, much to everyone's surprise – he usually stayed in bed until eleven and rarely spent more than fifteen minutes in the House all day, but now he was one of the first peers to arrive in the morning, and one of the last to leave in the afternoon. No one could work out quite why he was so enthusiastic for the bill, until it emerged he was convinced that rents would rise dramatically in Ireland if it failed, and he couldn't stand the thought that the Duke of Ormond – whom he hated as much as Ormond hated him – would be the richer for it. The bill almost led to a duel, when Buckingham said that whoever was against it 'had either an Irish interest or an Irish understanding'.[22] Ormond's son, the Earl of Ossory, who was present during this particular debate, took exception and called him out. The duel failed to take place only because Buckingham didn't turn up, claiming – not altogether convincingly – that there had been a misunderstanding about the venue.

Ormond's offer of aid on the hoof for distressed Londoners appears rather less altruistic in the context of the Irish Cattle Bill. But there is no denying that it was a very clever move, and the question of how to respond came to dominate discussion during the final stages of the bill. The offer was publicised in England, and the numbers of cattle involved rose from 2,000 or 3,000 head at the beginning of October to 15,000 and, by November, to 20,000. The Lords moved an amendment to the bill suggesting that these 20,000 cattle should be exempted from the ban on Irish imports, but killed and salted in Irish ports and sent to England in barrels. The amendment was passed back for discussion in the Commons on 27 November, when London MPs argued that this would be no use at all – apart from anything else, the Lords had suggested that the Lord Mayor and the Court of Aldermen should pay for the beef to be salted, barrelled and transported. The beasts must arrive in England alive. Then they could be sold, and 'the money that was taken for them would be serviceable for the poor people'.[23]

Most MPs believed that Ormond's gift was 'a device and project to cross the whole bill, and under the colour of 20,000 to bring in many 20,000's'.[24] It was, but the suggestion was still hurtful. 'Whoever expected it should have been said in an English Parliament that our charity to the city of London was an abominable cheat, a piece of hypocrisy, a mischievous design to ruin the kingdom?' one Anglo-Irish nobleman asked.[25] That was putting it a little strongly, but the Commons was faced with a dilemma. If Parliament threw the gift back in Ireland's face, it would look as if it didn't care about the plight of burnt-out Londoners. If it allowed the cattle to come in, there was no way of monitoring just how many would arrive, and the whole purpose of the bill was undermined. Some MPs tried to get over this by proposing that strict conditions must be imposed on the aid – the cattle could only arrive during a certain time period, for example – but in the end the whole matter was referred to a Committee, only for its recommendation, that the cattle be imported live, to be rejected.

The House eventually decided that the Irish aid should not be exempt from the embargo, and that 'the English should advance as great a supply to the city as this would be'.[26] That was fine, as far as it went – but no Englishman had actually *offered* cattle as a gift to relieve the fire victims. And no Englishman did. The Bill against the Importation of Irish cattle was given the royal assent on 18 January 1667. Ireland and the Duke of Ormond had lost, but so had London.

In spite of Robert Hubert's confession and execution, the arguments about his role in the Fire rumbled on. He was obviously mad, said one faction. So what if he was? asked another, citing the Catholic barrister Richard Langhorne who, it was said, was in the habit of employing halfwits on dangerous business, 'for if they should change their minds, and turn informers instead of agents, it would be easy to discredit them'.[27] Langhorne, who himself had been the target of accusations, was convinced the Fire was an act of God rather than an act of terrorism, writing to his friend and fellow Catholic William Blundell that 'all the discourse of a mad distracted multitude which would fain have called it a plot of the French or Dutch or Papists or anything but what it was, are vanished'.[28] (He was being optimistic. Thirteen years later the mad distracted multitude was to be the death of him when he was caught up in the Popish Plot and hanged at Tyburn.)

The Frenchman's conviction had one intriguing result. According to a strict interpretation of English property law, tenants rather than landlords were responsible for making good any damage to the property they leased. But the courts ruled that although tenants should bear the loss of damage caused by fire beginning in their own premises or those of a neighbour, 'where it is done by an Enemy, they are not to do it'.[29] As far as the law was concerned, the guilty verdict in Hubert's trial made the Fire of London an act of war, and, since the majority of citizens were tenants or under-tenants, this meant that landlords had to foot the bill for rebuilding the city. Needless to say, this state of things did not last for long.

Throughout the autumn, as Hubert went to his death, the Parliamentary Committee of Inquiry – and the nation as a whole – continued to wrestle with the cause of the Fire. Had London been burned as part of a great Catholic conspiracy or was the calamity a simple but dreadful accident? Joseph Williamson noted in a private memo at the end of September that 'after many careful examinations by Council and His Majesty's ministers, nothing has been found to argue the fire in London to have been caused by other than the hand of God, a great wind, and a very dry season'.[30] Sir Thomas Osborne, who served on the Committee, agreed; he wrote on 2 October that 'all the allegations are very frivolous, and people are generally satisfied that the fire was accidentall'.[31] And it was certainly true that with the single sad exception of Robert Hubert, not one prosecution resulted from the plethora of accusations made before the Committee. No little old ladies or mysterious Jesuitical old men were brought to trial; no knowing Irishmen or French firework-makers or Wiltshire cattle dealers. When Sir Robert Brooke presented his report to Parliament in January 1667, it was clear that in spite of the 'many wicked and desperate expressions' it contained, there was not enough hard evidence to indict anyone or to prove conclusively that Papists or Frenchmen had burned the city. 'I cannot conceive that the House can make anything of the report,' wrote John Milward MP in his diary.[32]

. Yet on 5 November 1666 – a public holiday – Sir Thomas Crewe MP was still telling Samuel Pepys 'that it was done by plot – it being proved by many witnesses that endeavours were made in several places to encrease the fire, and that both in city and country it was bragged by several papists that upon such a day or in such a time we should find the hottest weather that ever was in England, and words of plainer sense'. (And Pepys noticed, with that attention to detail which makes his account of the Fire so poignant, that there were no bonfires in the streets that Bonfire Night – 'which is strange, and speaks the melancholy disposition of the City at present, while never more was said of and feared of and done against the Papists then just at this time'.[33] John Tillotson, a future Archbishop of Canterbury, was always convinced that the Fire had been started deliberately; so were a number of MPs, including the poet Andrew Marvell. The cause had become and would remain a political shuttlecock, batted back and forth from Protestant to Papist whenever anti-Catholic feelings ran high.

The astrologers of England found themselves in an awkward position. Not only had they signally failed to predict the most dramatic catastrophe to befall the nation for centuries, but since their prophecies and tables went to press in October in order to reach the booksellers and street-vendors by November, the deadline for their copy was fast approaching. Many of them had already written their 1667 almanacs – without, of course, even a passing mention of the destruction of London.

There was a rumour that the almanac-writers had indeed been expecting the Fire, but that their warnings had been suppressed by the government to avoid the inevitable panic. It was reported as fact by the Reverend John Ward, vicar of Stratford-upon-Avon, that Sir Roger L'Estrange, who as Surveyor of the Press was effectively the state censor, had 'confest that most of them did foretell the fire of London . . . but hee caused itt to bee put out'.[34] But few really believed that, and even the astrologers didn't dare to suggest such a thing in print. Instead, they opted for a variety of strategies which ranged from embarrassed silence to implausible excuse.

For sheer nerve, Richard Saunders is hard to beat. He reminded his readers that in 1666, and 'from good and rational grounds', he had predicted that London would enjoy a great year 'which Gods goodness hath ratified to her, above many other places': and then went on to predict another great year in 1667, 'which promiseth much prosperity to come to (formerly) afflicted London, and her Governors, in her Re-edification'.[35] And that was that.

John Tanner, whose postscript to his *Angelus Britannicus* was written on 9 September, is rather more endearing. The only hint he gives that London has just burned down (and that it came as a complete surprise to him) is a single sentence: 'For my own part, I never durst be positive in Predictions.'[36] Others sought to deflect the blame. John Booker, who had apologised the previous year for the attack of dysentery which had prevented him from making detailed observations of the comets of 1664 and 1665, now criticised fellow astrologer Vincent Wing for having led him astray by claiming that in the partial solar eclipse of summer 1666 the moon would have south latitude and darken the lower part of the sun; in fact it had covered the upper part. (He was plain wrong in this, incidentally, and Wing was correct: the moon passed across the *lower* half of the sun between 5.42 a.m. and 7.37 a.m. on 22 June 1666.)

William Lilly adopted a similar line to Booker in his *Merlini*

Anglici Ephemeris. In his preface he tried to brazen things out, proclaiming triumphantly how right he had been to pour scorn on the Millenarians and Fifth Monarchists who were expecting the Apocalypse: 'What miraculous Thing or Change hath hitherto happened, in 1666, in Rome or Italy, either by fire or other casualty? There is no particular Antichrist, no Man of Sin revealed or discovered, more than in many foregoing years . . . Christ is not come down from Heaven to rule as a Temporal Prince upon Earth.'

He then attributed his failure to predict the actual Fire to a misreading of the comet of December 1664. He had thought that it first appeared in the constellation of Taurus; but now he came to think of it, he remembered his servant saying that he had first seen it in Gemini, the sign usually associated with London. If he had realised this at the time, he would have taken the hint 'given of a great fire to be in *London*'.

As well as apologising in advance for any mistakes in his monthly tables for 1667 – 'the Materials for Impression of a Work of this nature being for the most part consumed by the late prodigious Fire' – Lilly also claimed that he and his fellows *had* predicted the disaster. Only not recently. He referred darkly to the cryptic emblems he had published fifteen years previously showing the Gemini twins falling into a bonfire and a city in flames, 'the Hieroglyphick which we printed in 1651, of which we say no more at this time . . .'.[37]

This was a line taken by other astrologers. In *Newes from the Starres* William Andrews recalled how *he* had predicted the Fire back in 1660, when he noted that the malign influence of a 1652 comet was still operating and might affect the capital. And John Gadbury reminded his readers that in 1663 he had foretold how a conjunction of Saturn and Jupiter would affect London in some way: 'But considering with my self, that as great bodies move slowly, so are they tardous in their operations; I durst not presume to affix the stupendious effects of so unusual Congress, upon, or limit them to a particular year.'[38]

Much was made of the planetary conjunction mentioned by Gadbury. With the benefit of hindsight, William Lilly was sure that it had pointed the way to the many misfortunes which subsequently befell London. Booker agreed. Although he hadn't actually managed to foresee the Fire, he directed sceptics to a work published two years earlier, Richard Edlyn's *Prae-Nuncius Sydereus: An Astrological Treatise Of the Effects of the Great Conjunction of the two Superiour Planets, Saturn and Jupiter, October the Xth 1663*. Edlyn, he said, had warned his contemporaries of great destruction by fire, and had specifically prayed God 'to preserve the Citie of *London* from Fire and Plague in the year 1666'.[39] Booker even gave page and verse for Edlyn's predictions.

This was clever. It relied on the reluctance of unbelievers to check his claims. (Of course, Booker was preaching to the converted: sceptics were hardly likely to be reading his almanac in the first place.) But the astrologically-inclined who did turn to *Prae-Nuncius Sydereus* would find enough to reassure them. Discussing the effects of another conjunction, this time of Saturn and Mars, Edlyn had predicted 'Conflagrations, or sudden and vehement Desolations by Fire, hot and pestilent Diseases in the bodies of Men, strange Meteors, or fiery Apparitions in the Air; some say or conjecture, in the year 1664. I fear a great Plague in sixty five or sixty six.' And in a passage which was crucial to Booker's vindication of astrology, Edlyn had specifically prayed God to 'preserve the City of *London* from Fire and Plague, from Combustion and Tumults'.[40] He believed that the combustion and tumults would arrive in 1667; but no doubt that was close enough for the credulous.

One did not need to be an astrologer in the autumn of 1666 to predict that if the Fire hadn't been a deliberate act of terrorism (indeed, even if it was), it must ultimately have come from the hand of God – a just God who chastised His children when they strayed from the paths of righteousness.

Making sense of senseless acts – and handing over the burden of moral responsibility – was something the Church of England was particularly good at. Wednesday 10 October was the national 'day of humiliation and fasting'. Parliament was adjourned, and the Commons gathered in the medieval church of St Margaret Westminster to hear not one, but two sermons on recent events.

The first was given by the young Dr Edward Stillingfleet, a popular London preacher who was generally thought of as intellectual, astute, yet with an 'unconcerned and easy' manner.[41] People packed into St Margaret's, and there was standing room only; Samuel Pepys couldn't even get into the church, so he opted for a meal of herrings at the Dog tavern close by in New Palace Yard. Stillingfleet took for his text Amos 4:11: 'I have overthrown *some* of you, as God overthrew Sodom and Gomorrah, and ye were as a firebrand plucked out of the burning: yet have ye not returned unto me, saith the LORD.' Given the text and the circumstances, the thrust of Stillingfleet's argument was predictable. The Fire was God's judgement on London; His mercy was mixed with his terrible wrath; He had given Londoners another chance to make amends.

The second sermon was by Dr Robert Frampton, a High Church Royalist of whom Pepys later wrote, 'The truth is he preaches the most like an Apostle that ever I heard.'[42] Frampton preached this day on 3 Jeremiah 3:21–2: 'A voice was heard upon the high places, weeping *and* supplications of the Children of Israel: for they have perverted their way, *and* they have forgotten the LORD their God. Return, ye backsliding children, *and* I will heal your backslidings. Behold, we come unto thee; for thou *art* the LORD our God.' Pepys made another foray into St Margaret's to hear him, but gave up again and went to another pub in New Palace Yard, where he 'basai la fille and drank' instead.[43]

Like Stillingfleet, Frampton took an orthodox line, working through each phrase in his text, glossing it and relating it to contemporary circumstances. Londoners have forgotten the Lord their God. They have become backsliders, but they can still be healed if they turn to God with tears, supplications and true repentance.

This mild, 'could do better' approach to the Fire was typical of the Establishment response, which tended on the whole to be quite level-headed. (It was also effective as a fund-raising tactic: the congregation at St Margaret's donated a more than respectable £135 1s 3d to the appeal.) In *Observations both Historical and Moral upon the Burning of London*, a pamphlet written at the end of

September,[44] its pseudonymous author 'Rege Sincera' made the usual references to the Fire as a divine punishment for Londoners' pride, drunkenness, whoring, swearing and false dealing, before going on to discuss with commendable common sense the *real* causes of the disaster. First and foremost, he said, was the irresponsible behaviour of Thomas Farriner in going to bed with his oven still glowing, and 'leaving his Providence with his Slippers'.[45] But the pamphleteer also noted the dry summer and the easterly gales, the time of night and the tightly packed wooden buildings, the lack of water and the fact that 'the Quantity of combustible and bituminous Matter hath given the greatest Encouragement to this devouring Fire'.[46] No conspiracy, no fire-bombers; just an unfortunate set of circumstances which came together at the wrong moment.

It was the Dissenters who had the best tunes, or at least the best line in rhetoric. They were more comfortable with the God of the Old Testament, with sin and retribution, with anger and righteous indignation, than with Frampton's comfortable pieties. For sheer apocalyptic frenzy, it is hard to beat James Janeway, a popular Nonconformist divine with a meeting house in Rotherhithe:

The voice of the Sword was not heard; the Language of the Plague was not understood; therefore the dreadful *Jehovah* speaks louder and louder still. He hath now spoke as he did once from mount *Sinai*, in Fire, Flames, and Smoak; and in the thundring crackings of falling Houses, Churches, Halls, and in stately Buildings; in the howlings, skreekings, and doleful outcries of poor creatures, that were almost at their wits end. He rode upon the wings of the wind, he rode in a Chariot of flaming Fire; neither Bricks nor Stones can hinder his course, but the fury of the Lord drives over them all . . .[47]

Like Thomas Vincent, Janeway was one of those Dissenting ministers who had earned the respect of Londoners by ministering to the sick during the plague. Dissenters of all persuasions – Independents, Presbyterians, Baptists, Quakers and plain non-sectarian

Puritans – had had a rough time of it since 1660. In spite of Charles II's declaration at Breda, while he was waiting to be restored to the English throne, that 'no man shall be disquieted or called in question for differences of opinion in matters of religion',[48] the Anglican Establishment clamped down quickly on nonconformity, and well over 2,000 clergy and university lecturers and fellows were ejected from their livings and deprived of their posts between 1660 and 1662. Those who insisted on preaching God's word in their own way were beaten up, fined, imprisoned and transported.

Yet when so many Anglican clergy deserted their flocks at the height of the plague, ejected ministers came out of the shadows, resolving to stay with the people, 'and to go into the forsaken pulpits, though prohibited, and to preach to the poor people before they died'.[49] Suspicious of such dedication – and even more suspicious of the Dissenters' links with subversive elements like the Fifth Monarchists – Parliament had responded with the Five Mile Act. Nonconformist ministers were forbidden to come within five miles of any parish in which they had previously preached, or any city, town or parliamentary borough at all.

For a time, this had done the trick, and Dissenters had returned back to the shadows of their suburban conventicles and meeting houses. But the Fire gave them another chance to bear witness: 'while the terrors occasioned by this conflagration remained on the minds of men, the persecuting bishops and magistrates suspended their rage against the Protestants who had not conformed, and many of their ministers preached in the midst of the burning ruins, to a willing attentive people'.[50] And, one might add, to a people who desperately needed to make sense of disaster. Why had this thing happened? And why had it happened to them?

James Janeway was in no doubt. Most Dissenters were certain that the Fire had been started by Catholics, with the approval of the Pope: 'This doth smell of a popish design,' said Thomas Vincent, 'hatcht in the same place were the Gunpowder-plot was contriv'd, only that this was more successful.'[51] But, as Janeway noted, even though it *was* the work of foreign Papists, 'had not our wickedness made our City more combustible than Briers and Thorns, the Jesuite should with more ease have set the Sea on fire, and dried up the vast Ocean, or pull'd the Sun out of the Firmament, then have laid *London* in the dust.' The true adversary and enemy was the people's own wicked hearts.

The anonymous author of *Pyrotechnica Loyolana, Ignatian fireworks; or the fiery Jesuits' temper and behaviour exposed to publick view* (1667) told his readers how the Jesuits had two colleges – one in Madrid and another at Thonon on the shores of Lake Geneva – where they kept stores of gunpowder and designed fireworks, with the aim of subduing Protestants by advancing the 'the *Art* of making and casting about *Fire-balls* and *Wild-fire* to burn *Houses* and *Cities*'.[52] They had certainly been responsible for starting the Fire, he said; but they were used by God as instruments when He tired of our incorrigible and heinous transgressions and was provoked to anger. It was God who ensured the Jesuits' success:

> [He] break forth into his *fury*, very conspicuous in the raging *fiercenesse* of the *burning*, through the violence of the *wind*, which he commanded to go forth, when he could have held it in his *fist*, or turn'd it another way; or have given our *Magistrates* wisdome, and our *people* strength, or many other ways have prevented our ruines, by the *devouring flames*. But it seemed good to his Majesty to humble us for our iniquities . . .[53]

Janeway, too, was depressingly sure of what London – and England – had done to deserve the spectacular display of divine censure which was the Fire of London. There was a general lack of enthusiasm for God, he argued, and a fragmentation of the Protestant ideal, so that true Christians were divided one against the other. Instead of uniting to fight the common enemy of Popery, the different sects had devoted their energies to attacking each other.

At the top of his list of faults were lust and uncleanness. London was crawling with whores, he said, 'whole Streets standing in the Attire of Harlots'. He also bewailed the fashion for homosexuality among affluent metropolitan gentry: 'Have not some of our young Absaloms, even, as it were, spread their Tents to commit folly in the face of the whole City, as if Fornication alone were too little to sink them into Hell, except joyned with Sodomy and horrible Blasphemy?'[54]

Not everyone shared Janeway's view that homosexuality was on the increase and hence attracting the wrath of God. Vincent, for example, merely said he hoped the unnatural uncleanness for which Sodom was notorious was 'little known and practised in the city'. But he, too, was in no doubt that sexual impropriety had played a part in London's downfall: 'O the boiling, burning lusts that have been in *London*! O the wanton eyes and looks! the speculative uncleanness, and secret self-pollutions! the obscene and filthy speeches! the toying and lustful dalliances! and the gross actual uncleanness which God hath been witness to every day in *London*!'[55]

Vincent's list of London's sins was more comprehensive than Janeway's. In *God's Terrible Voice in the City*, his own analysis of the disaster, he gives a formidable total of twenty-five moral failings, beginning conventionally enough with 'slighting of the Gospel', hypocrisy, 'formality and lukewarmness in the worship of God' and division among different sects; and moving on to pride, idleness and the endearingly familiar 'profaneness, and a loose and frothy spirit, especially in the youth and springing generation'. (Vincent was only thirty-two himself.) Uncleanness was ranked fourteenth, and sandwiched between unmercifulness – a lack of charity towards others – and drunkenness, which in a highly imaginative metaphor was exemplified by the flames in the heart of the city and the tumbling-down of its houses, a reproof 'of such persons as had inflamed and distempered themselves with excessive drinking'. The last on the list was something the preacher called 'carnal security', by which he seems to have meant smugness. Londoners had been so sure that 1666 would see the fall of Babylon; and that was one more reason why their city had fallen instead.[56]

Anglicans and Dissenters alike were keen to stress that even if the English were suffering for being as sinful as Sodom, this was nothing compared to what was coming to their enemies.

England was still at war, and despite appearances to the contrary, God was still on her side. In churches and meeting houses all over the country the faithful took heart from 1 Peter 4:17: 'For the time *is come* that judgment must begin at the house of God: and if *it* first *begin* at us, what shall the end *be* of them that obey not the gospel of God?' And divines were quick to remind their shell-shocked congregations that things might have been worse:

> If bloody Papists had come into our houses in the dead of the night, with such of knives in their hands as were found after the fire in barrels; and having set watch at every street's end, had suffered none to escape, but cruelly slaughtered the husband with the wife, the parents and the children together, ripping up women with child, and not sparing either the silver hair, or the sucking babe; if there had been a cry at midnight, *They are come*, but no possibility of flying from them, or making resistance against them; if instead of heaps of stones and brick-ings in the top of every street, there had been heaps of dead bodies, and the kennels [gutters] had been made to run down with gore and blood; sure this judgment would have been more dreadful than the plague or fire, which have been among us.[57]

So Londoners should realise how lucky they had been.

The hellfire rhetoric of the Nonconformists and the more moderate reactions of the Anglican Establishment were both driven by ideology. The King, his ministers and his church were anxious to portray the Fire as an unfortunate accident – not only because that was just what it was, but also because a government which couldn't protect its people against such a devastating act of terrorism had obviously forfeited Most Favoured Nation status with God; indeed, it was well on the way to forfeiting the right to govern. Many of the Dissenters, on the other hand, were temperamentally inclined towards the Good Old Cause and against the monarchy, which had after all ejected them from their livings, restored the Anglican hierarchy and introduced Papists into the royal household. Laying the blame directly at the feet of Charles II would have been foolhardy, to say the least; but men like Janeway and Vincent had a vested interest in not only playing on anti-Catholic sentiments, but also talking up the scale of the disaster and the moral culpability of the nation. Over the past two years, God had visited War and Pestilence on His people. Now there was Fire. Didn't that suggest something about His attitude to the restoration of the monarchy?

> And in the places where God hath been served, and his servants have lived, now nettles are growing; owls are screeching; thieves and cut-throats are lurking: a sad face there is now in the ruinous part of *London*: and terrible hath the voice of the Lord been, which hath been crying, yea, roaring in the city by these dreadful judgments . . .[58]

Meanwhile, the hapless Bludworth was doing his level best to convince anyone who would listen that it hadn't been his fault. In the official account which had appeared the Monday after the Fire, Joseph Williamson's *Gazette* had hinted at negligence, saying that the flames had spread so quickly 'that care was not taken for the timely preventing the further diffusion of it by pulling down houses, as ought to have been'.[59] The Lord Mayor felt that this was a dig at his conduct of the early firefighting operations, and he was quite right. Pepys had commented as soon as the flames were out that 'people do all the world over cry out of the simplicity of my Lord Mayor in general, and more particularly in this business of the fire, laying it all upon him'.[60]

On 29 September, Bludworth wrote a rather pathetic letter of complaint to Williamson. His year in office was coming to an end, and at the election of his successor, which had taken place that day, he had felt impelled – he told Williamson – to devote most of his customary speech to vindicating himself. He had 'had the misfortune to serve in the severest year that ever man did', and now he needed some support from the government. Perhaps when Williamson published the name of his successor (who was Alderman Sir William Bolton), he might also devote some space to saying how close Williamson and Bludworth were, 'so as to assure distant friends, that he is not out of favour till something is made out against him'?[61]

Williamson didn't oblige. It was more politic to allow an outgoing Lord Mayor to take the blame for the Fire than it was to give credence to a mythical army of fanatics, Papists and foreign terrorists. The swearing-in of the new Mayor on 29 October was a muted affair. All the City Companies were excused, except for those of the two Mayors and the Sheriffs, who went to and from Westminster by coach rather than making the usual state progress by barge. 'Lord,' said Pepys, 'to see how meanely they now look, who upon this day used to be all little lords, is a sad sight and worthy consideration.'[62] A month later he bumped into Bludworth on the way to Whitehall. The man was still whining.

Pepys was not being very fair. He wasn't alone: everyone heaped scorn on Bludworth's lack of leadership, and within weeks of the Fire the street balladeers were poking fun at him:

> Theires nothing fixt beneath the skyes
> London late fyred in ashes lyes
> All though a strong man and a stoute
> Did say at first hee'd pisse it out
> Yet did to such a Blazing grow
> With London twas in five dayes spase
> Touch and goe.[63]

But Bludworth's detractors failed to understand that his powers were circumscribed by the men of property, the merchant class which had spawned him, elected him and supported him in office. These were the people – the Vyners and Starlings and Fords and Brownes and Backwells – to whom he had to answer if he carried out demolitions without proper authority. He was certainly at fault; but like Robert Hubert, he became a scapegoat. In truth, he could no more act against the laws of property than he could have pissed out the Fire.

As things turned out, his successor was worse. One can argue over whether Bludworth was weak and ineffectual or a victim of circumstance: Sir William Bolton was a crook. He enjoyed the trappings of mayoral power. He enjoyed meeting with the King and discussing how to measure up the new streets of the City. He also took the opportunity to line his own pockets, something of which Bludworth was never accused. A month after he left office a story began to circulate that he had embezzled £1,800 from the relief fund set up after the Fire. In an effort to deflect attention, he accused the Bishop of London of misappropriating £50 from the fund, and then withdrew his complaint. He was suspended and then forced to resign from the Court of Aldermen in 1668, and eventually convicted of 'misimploying the great sume of Money hee received of the Collections for the releife of the poore distressed by the late dismall fire'.[64] That ruined him: he ended his days in penury, supported by a pension from the City.

11

A More Glorious Phoenix

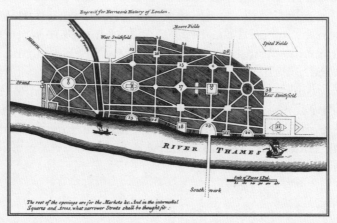

One of Evelyn's plans for rebuilding the City.

'Twas yesterday in many meetings of ye principal Citizens, whose houses are laid in ashes,' wrote Henry Oldenburg on the Monday after the Fire, 'who in stead of complaining, discoursed almost of nothing, but of a survey of London, and a dessein for rebuilding, and that in such a manner (with Bricks, and large Streets, leaving great Intervalls and partitions in severall places) that for the future they may not be so easily subject to the like destruction.'[1]

For all the turmoil of the past few days, most educated Londoners believed that the Fire offered an incredible opportunity to create a modern, convenient capital. The Lord Mayor and the Court of Aldermen approached the King and asked him to consider a completely new ground plan. He agreed, and a rumour circulated that Charles and Parliament were going to buy up the entire City to facilitate the process. 'Truly there was never a more glorious phoenix upon earth,' wrote Evelyn, 'if it do at last emerge out of the cinders.'[2]

But effective urban planning requires a degree of centralised control which was quite unknown in the laissez-faire climate of Restoration England. Londoners were about to find that out. As the poor began to drift back to what remained of their homes, and 'with more expedition than can be conceived, set up little sheds of brick and timber upon the ruins of their own houses',[3] the first step towards a coordinated rebuilding plan was taken. After receiving approval at a meeting of the Privy Council on Wednesday 12 September, a royal proclamation was published on Thursday. It was, as Joseph Williamson declared in the next issue of the *Gazette*, 'full of that Princely tenderness and affection, which [the King] is pleased on all occasions to express for that His beloved City'.[4] No one had suffered a loss comparable to his own, said Charles; but he hoped to live to see a more beautiful (and also more fire-proof) city rise from the ashes.

The main thrust of the 13 September proclamation was to establish some basic rules for the new capital. London was going to learn from experience. During the Fire, for instance, everyone remarked that timber-framed buildings had burned far too easily, while structures of brick or stone – even garden walls – had been much more resistant to the flames. No one should be allowed to rebuild unless they used brick or stone, and they were to be 'encouraged to practise the good Husbandry of strongly arching their Cellars, by which divers persons have received notable benefit in the late Fire'.[5]

Having dealt with the general principles of rebuilding, the proclamation made a start on tackling the practicalities. First, Bludworth and the Court of Aldermen were to initiate an exact survey of the ruins, to establish who owned what, who rented what and on what terms, so that no one's rights should be sacrificed to the public good without proper acknowledgement. And some people's rights would have to be sacrificed: it was obvious that London's streets needed to be widened. The most important, such as Fleet Street, Cornhill and Cheapside, would be made of a sufficient breadth 'to prevent the mischief one side may receive from the other by fire'.[6] But all streets, and especially those which led up from the wharves and warehouses on the river, were to be wide enough that passing along them would be easy and convenient.

The proclamation forbade the creation of alleys or lanes unless they were absolutely necessary. And even then, the authorities intended to draw up rules and orders governing their dimensions and materials. The nomenclature probably meant rather more to Restoration Londoners than it does to us: around a third of them actually lived on a 'street', by which was meant a major thoroughfare; another third lived on lanes, which were narrower and less important; and the last third (last in more ways than one) lived in alleys, yards and courts. An alley was an extremely narrow way, roofed over with the jettied upper storeys of buildings on either side; a yard or court was enclosed, and reached via a turning off a street or lane.[7] 'Wide' and 'narrow' are relative terms, of course: even the most ambitious rebuilding schemes would not go beyond widths of ninety feet for the City's major thoroughfares.

The King and the City authorities were not yet in a position to give detailed rules and directions for the rebuilding – it was still far too soon – but while these were being discussed and developed 'by those persons who have most concernment as well as experience',[8] there was an embargo on all building work. And if anyone should obstinately erect such buildings, on the grounds that it was up to them to decide what to do with their own property, then Bludworth and the Court of Aldermen had the King's authority to pull them down again, and to pass on the names of the guilty parties to the King and Council, 'to be proceeded against according to their Deserts'.[9]

There was a let-out clause. Anyone who was really desperate to get on with rebuilding their homes or business premises could submit their ideas to the Court of Aldermen; if they passed muster, the seventeenth-century equivalent of planning permission would be given. (Only one person made use of this facility: at the end of October Sir George More appealed directly to the Privy Council on behalf of eight tenants in Fleet Street and was authorised to go ahead with rebuilding their houses.)

Exactly how all this work would be paid for was a question

which the proclamation didn't really address. King Charles urged the wealthy to fund the rebuilding of some of the burned churches, and rather vaguely announced that he would assist and direct them, 'and by his bounty encourage, all other ways that shall be desired'. He also committed himself to financing the rebuilding of the Custom House, 'to encourage the work by his example', and he promised a seven-year holiday from Hearth Tax to everyone who put up approved new buildings.[10] (In the draft of the proclamation, this clause on tax was added in Clarendon's own hand, suggesting that it was the Lord Chancellor's idea. If so, it was a good one: the half-yearly payment of 1s for each hearth in houses worth more than 20s a year was deeply unpopular.)

The 13 September proclamation was arguably the most important single document in the entire history of London. It set out the scale of the Crown's ambition for the new city, and by establishing the principle that national and civic government intended to regulate individual efforts within a just framework, it launched England on a course which would involve executive, legislature and judiciary in half a century of activity. There were two general Rebuilding Acts, and three further Acts relating exclusively to funding. The Privy Council and the City both set up their own Rebuilding Committees. Nobles and bishops and merchants sat on a bewildering number of Royal Commissions – six devoted to St Paul's Cathedral alone. There were public proclamations from the King, public proclamations from the Lord Mayor. The most distinguished judges in the land worked for close on a decade to disentangle the property rights of Fire victims and their landlords. By the time that one of the last pieces of reconstruction, the tower of St Michael Cornhill, was finished in 1722, it was a full fifty-six years since the Fire. Charles II was long dead. So were four other monarchs: James, Duke of York, his brother and successor; James's usurping daughter Mary, and her husband, William of Orange; and James's second daughter, Anne. George I, the Hanoverian great-grandson of James I, was on the throne. The world was a very different place: people were listening to Handel and reading

Robinson Crusoe, Palladianism was the architecture of choice, and you could insure your home against fire.

As Joseph Williamson reported in the *Gazette*, the 13 September proclamation included plans to prevent the rebuilding of all houses by the Thames, leaving a strip of open space forming 'a fair Key and Wharfe'. The proclamation explained why:

> The irreparable damage and loss by the late fire being, next to the hand of God in the terrible wind, to be imputed to the place in which it first broke out, amongst small timber houses standing so close together, that as no remedy could be applied from the river for the quenching thereof, to the contiguousness of the buildings hindering and keeping all possible relief from the land-side, we do resolve and declare, that there shall be a fair key or wharf on all the river-side; that no house shall be erected within so many feet of the river, as shall be within a few days declared in the rules . . .[11]

In a considered response to the problems of a modern urban environment that went far beyond knee-jerk reactions to the Fire, certain trades were to be moved away from the river altogether. Brewers, dyers and sugar bakers, whose continual smoke contributed to the general unhealthiness of the Thames Street area, were to be moved, with the Lord Mayor and aldermen proposing 'such a place as may be fit for all those trades which are carried on by smoke to inhabit together'.[12]

This last suggests the influence of John Evelyn, who was a member of the Privy Council and had the King's ear in such matters. Since the publication in 1661 of *Fumifugium*, his tract on pollution and 'the Inconveniencie of the Aer and Smoak of London', Evelyn had been agitating for legislation to move particularly noisome trades away from the City. Charles had actually commanded him to prepare a Parliamentary bill on the matter after reading *Fumifugium*, but nothing had come of it.

As well as deporting the brewers and dyers, Evelyn suggested the removal of butchers, chandlers, fishmongers – any tradesman whose premises smelled, in fact. And the space thus freed up could be put to good use:

> The Places and Houses deserted (which commonly take up a great space of Ground) might be converted into Tenements, and some of them into Noble Houses for use and pleasure, respecting the Thames to their no small advantage. Add to this, that it would be a means to prevent the danger of Fireing, those sad Calamities, for the most part, proceeding from some Accident or other, which takes beginning from places, where such great and exorbitant Fires are perpetually kept going.[13]

Evelyn had always been interested in cities. Among the conventional tourist platitudes he set down during his travels in Europe in the 1640s were comments on the even and uniform streets in Amsterdam, the high standard of paving in Siena, the straight and noble streets in Rome. Over the past five years his concern for environmental issues in London had been subsumed into a more general curiosity about the problems of urban planning. For eighteen months in 1662–3 he had been a commissioner 'for the Repairing the High-Wayes and Sewers, and for Keeping Clean of the Streets, in, and about the City of London and Westminster'. The subject was close to his heart. In the dedication to his translation of the French architect Fréart de Chambray's *Parallèle de l'architecture antique et de la moderne*, which appeared in 1664, he praised Sir John Denham for his work as Surveyor-General – a triumph of hope over experience – and congratulated him on introducing paving to the western suburbs of the capital. This, he said, would prove a great public advantage

> for the saving Wheels and Carriages, the cure of noysom Gutters, the de-obstruction of Encounters, the dispatch of Business, the cleanness of the Way, the beauty of the Object, the ease of the Infirme, and the preserving of both the Mother and the Babe; so many of the fair-Sex and their Off-spring having perish'd by mischances (as I am credibly inform'd) from the ruggedness of the unequal Streets.[14]

In the Fire's aftermath, Evelyn's thoughts were turning to something more ambitious than pavements and pollution. On 13 September, the day the royal proclamation on the future of London was published, he was at Whitehall, presenting the King with a design for an entirely new capital. Charles was intrigued, and after dinner he sent for Evelyn to come to the Queen's bedchamber, where Charles, Catherine and the Duke of York examined the plans for almost an hour, 'seeming to be extreamely pleas'd with what I had so early thought on'.[15]

Evelyn was operating here within a tradition of designing urban utopias which stretched back to ancient Rome. Vitruvius, whose first-century-BC treatise was the only ancient text on architecture to survive, described a street plan which consisted of an octagon with a central octagonal piazza and eight radiating streets – an idea which was picked up and developed in loving detail during the Renaissance. In his *Trattato d'Architettura* (*c*.1457–64), for example, Antonio Filarete set out his ideal city of Sforzinda, which was dedicated to Francesco Sforza, the powerful Duke of Milan. Filarete's Sforzinda, which was never built, was a regular eight-pointed star contained within a circle, with sixteen radial streets (actually fifteen and an aqueduct) running from the centre to the perimeter. The central area contained a main square for the cathedral and the Sforza palazzo, with two smaller squares for the exchange and the markets.

The symmetrical stellate city plan, almost always based on circles and regular polygons, became a feature of the model urban design during the sixteenth and seventeenth centuries. The simplicity of a geometrical pattern exerted a powerful visual appeal, while the projecting angular bastions, designed to combat the increasing power of artillery, were in line with the latest theories in fortification. Pietro Cataneo's ideal city – a grid-iron layout within a heptagon, surrounded by a perimeter wall in the form of a seven-pointed star – was published in 1554. Palladio's pupil, Vincenzo Scamozzi, designed a twelve-pointed star enclosing a grid-iron in the shape of a twelve-sided polygon; it appeared in his *L'Idea dell'Architettura Universale* of 1615. Leonardo da Vinci and Albrecht Dürer both experimented with regular urban design.

Sir Thomas More, who coined the term 'Utopia' in 1516, boasted that the towns of his imaginary country were indistinguishable one from another; they had 'streets which are very convenient for all carriage, and are well sheltered from the winds. Their buildings are good, and are so uniform that a whole side of a street looks like one house.'[16]

A rare example of a stellate town which was actually built is at Palma Nova, a military outpost of Venice which was put up in the 1590s as a nonagon within a nine-pointed star. Tentatively attributed to Scamozzi, it seems to owe rather more to the Sforzinda tradition, since it consists of a radial plan rather than a grid-iron. In France, Jacques Perret's *Des fortifications et artifices* (1601) contained schemes for geometrical and stellate fortified towns; and a series of planned new towns were constructed in the later sixteenth and early seventeenth centuries, such as Vitry-le-François (1545 onwards), Nancy (1588 onwards) and Charleville (1608). All these three were defined by central squares, a grid-iron plan and a stellate perimeter wall.

However, so far as most seventeenth-century Englishmen were concerned, the most admired piece of town planning was the Rome of Pope Sixtus V. In many ways a rather puritanical and repressive man – he sent Sabbath-breakers to the galleys, made incest and abortion capital offences and insisted that his cardinals shouldn't have children – Sixtus instituted a major programme of urban renewal during the five years of his pontificate. Between 1585 and 1590 he put the dome on St Peter's, rebuilt St John Lateran, and rehoused the Vatican's collection of books and manuscripts in a new library. More than 120 streets were paved or repaved, and some 6 miles or so of entirely new roads were laid out, including a network of straight thoroughfares linking various focal points. Only death prevented Sixtus from extending this network until wide roads linked all the major churches and many of Rome's classical monuments. When the troubles of the 1640s led numbers of English gentlemen – including John Evelyn – to seek solace on the Continent, Rome was the obvious destination. Besides being the cradle of culture in an age which thought there was no style but classicism, it represented the acme of architectural excellence, the urban peak of perfection to which every other city in the civilised world aspired.

Evelyn's experience of European town planning and his long-cherished dream of a better London meant that he was well-equipped to respond quickly to the Fire. But he wasn't quick enough. When he went to present his scheme to the King on 13 September, he found that it 'was the second that was seene . . . Dr Wren had got the start of me.'[17]

Christopher Wren presented his own plan to King Charles at Whitehall on Tuesday 11 September. He was eager to be first in the queue. When the Secretary of the Royal Society, Henry Oldenburg, wrote to Wren rather ruefully a couple of days later to say that the Society, less than six years old and still struggling to establish itself as a reputable scientific institution, might have benefited if a model by such a distinguished founder-member had been 'reviewed and approved by ye R Society, or a Committee thereoff, before it had come to the view of his Majesty',[18] he replied that he had been so pressed to complete it before any other designs were submitted that he simply hadn't had time. Evelyn also belonged to the Royal Society, but no one seemed to care that he too had bypassed them with his plans.

A third member of the Royal Society *did* do the right thing, however. Robert Hooke was Professor of Geometry at Gresham College, where until the Fire the Society had held its weekly meetings. He presented his plan to them on 19 September, and it was duly approved and passed on – not to the King but, in a move which suggests some political manoeuvring, to Thomas Bludworth and the Court of Aldermen. They were currently considering yet another scheme. This one came from Peter Mills, ex-Bricklayer to the City, and a surveyor and architect with a considerable reputation. Even so, Sir John Lawrence recalled that everyone preferred Hooke's plan; they recorded their 'good Acceptance & Approbacion of the Same' and asked that it should be shown to Charles.[19]

At least four more 'models' of the new City were produced. One was devised by Sir William Petty, a physician and anatomist, statistician and cartographer – and yet another founder-member of the Royal Society. Another was by the map-maker Richard Newcourt. And on 20 September a Captain Valentine Knight published 'Proposals of a new modell for rebuilding the City of London, with houses, streets and wharfes, to be forthwith set out by his Majesties and the city surveyors, etc.' He claimed the proposals would earn the King a lump sum of £372,670 and bring in additional annual revenue of £223,517 10s.

Charles was particularly sensitive to any suggestion that he might gain any advantage from London's loss. He was extremely upset, for example, when one of his courtiers said that the Fire

was the greatest blessing that God had ever conferred upon him, his restoration only excepted: for the walls and gates being now burned and thrown down of that rebellious city, which was always an enemy to the crown, his majesty would never suffer them to repair and build them up again, to be a bit in his mouth and a bridle upon his neck, but would keep all open, that his troops might enter upon them whenever he thought necessary for his service, there being no other way to govern that rude multitude but by force.[20]

Now he took steps to punish Knight for his presumption: the man was gaoled, and Williamson wrote a critical piece in the *Gazette* declaring in a high moral tone that the King would never dream of drawing any benefit from so public a calamity.

Without any doubt, there were dozens of other plans. 'Everybody brings in his idea,' wrote John Evelyn. 'Divers others have also made desseins and explain'd them by discourses,' noted Oldenburg in February 1668.[21] *The Sullen Lovers*, a popular comedy by Thomas Shadwell which was first performed in the same year, boasted a character named Sir Positive At-all, a knight with an extraordinarily high opinion of his own abilities – 'I will give dogs leave to piss upon me, if any man understands mankind better than myself'. When Sir Positive declared that 'I have seventeen models of the city of London of my own making, and the worst of 'em makes London an other-guess London than 'tis like to be', King Charles and the Duke of York, both of whom were present when Shadwell's play was premiered at the Lincoln's Inn Fields Theatre, must have laughed a little wryly at the memory of half the courtiers and experimental philosophers in the kingdom arriving at Whitehall after the Fire with big ideas for rebuilding the capital.

Of the seven big ideas that we know about, that of Peter Mills – the only contender with a background in the building trades – has disappeared without trace, and all there is to say is that the City liked Hooke's proposal better. William Petty's ideas were never fully worked out or submitted to either the King or the City; they were, in fact, little more than headings and notes produced immediately after the Fire and returned to over a twenty-year period. But Petty was an interesting character, and, as a pioneering economist and statistician, he had a particularly innovative perspective on the rebuilding.

After a colourful academic career which included standing in at dissections for the Regius Professor of Medicine in Oxford, because the latter 'could not endure the sight of a bloody body',[22] and a spell as Professor of Music at Gresham College, Petty had gone to Ireland in 1652 as Physician-General to Cromwell's Army. He stayed on to carry out the first detailed survey of the country, and made £18,000 in 'commissions' from allocating forfeited lands to Parliamentarian soldiers. A hefty chunk of this ill-gotten fortune went towards the purchase of a mansion and garden in Lothbury, which he developed as investment housing, only to lose it all during the Fire.

Unlike the others, Petty did not draw up a plan for the new City, but the questions he asked were eminently sensible. First, he attempted to work out the ill effects of the Fire: the loss of buildings and rentals; the migration of trades away from the capital; the inconvenience which would arise 'from nonconformity of men to the methods and order propounded for repair of such calamities'; the delays 'and other mischeifes of dealinge or treatinge with multitudes'.[23] Then he pondered some of the political considerations. Everything else being equal, was London really the best site for a metropolis? And, if it was, how big should it be, and how could the authorities best prepare for the changes that would inevitably occur in population size and density over the coming centuries?

Petty's answers to these questions looked towards radical political and administrative reform rather than architecture and urban planning. He recommended the establishment of a Greater London, covering an area of 7,500 acres and accommodating half a million people. (In his later writings this rose to 20,000 acres and 720,000 citizens.) The city thus formed would also be a county, with its own general and admiral, its own surveyor-general and banker. There would be 400 parishes of 300 families; and each parish would have its own JP, who along with his fellows would elect 40 aldermen to govern and represent the city. Petty also advocated the creation of a vast new wall to serve as both a defensive and an administrative boundary, and suggested a second river crossing – at Lambeth, where there was already a horse-ferry in operation. (It had sunk at least twice in the seventeenth century – once under the weight of Archbishop Laud's possessions when he was moving to Lambeth Palace in 1633; and again in 1656, as it ferried Oliver Cromwell's coach and horses across.)★

Newcourt, Knight and Hooke all produced variations on the simple grid-iron plan. It was the oldest and most obvious form of urban planning, far pre-dating the sophisticated variations seen in the work of Renaissance designers. It occurred in ancient Greece: famous examples include Miletus, destroyed by the Persians in 494 BC and rebuilt to a regular grid pattern by Hippodamus, described by Aristotle as the man 'who invented the art of planning cities'.[24] The provincial towns of the Roman empire were built to standard rectangular grids, with two main

★Petty also itemised the advantages of having a city like London. They included ethnic diversity, the variety of food and drink, and the fact that in no other city 'is greater liberty at the Court, in St James & Hide parks, in Churches, at Theaters & elsewhere, to see beautifull Women with & without Impunity' ('The Uses of London', *The Petty Papers* I [Constable, 1927], 42).

cross streets dividing the settlement into quarters: Caerwent in South Wales is one example. Ta-tu, the great walled capital from which Kublai Khan ruled over China in the thirteenth century, was a square with a sixteen-mile perimeter, its streets laid out in regular blocks. Latin American towns put up by Spanish colonists in the sixteenth century were planned as grids; so were ancient Japanese cities. As a plan form, the regular grid was a global phenomenon, although only for new settlements – with good reason, as London's aspiring town-planners were soon to discover.

Richard Newcourt adopted a rigid but radical approach to rebuilding London. He swept away the old boundaries and created a checkerboard twice the size of the pre-Fire City. An eight-by-eight grid of blocks and streets stretched from the Tower across to the Fleet River, but extended much further than the old London Wall which formed the existing northern boundary. A new rectangular wall was punctuated at regular intervals by nine gates – three to the west, three to the east and three to the north, with the Thames forming the southern boundary as before – and there was a huge central square, well over a quarter of a mile long and 380 yards wide. (That's about four times the size of Red Square in Moscow.) Newcourt gave no indication of what was to go on in this space. He placed smaller open spaces in the centre of quarters to the north-east, south-east, south-west and north-west; the south-west square corresponds to the site of St Paul's Cathedral, and St Paul's is marked on his plan, suggesting that Newcourt regarded it as a fixed point, like the Tower and the Fleet. The rest of his new city consisted of 55 uniform blocks 570 feet wide and 855 feet long. Each block was divided into four, with a little square containing a church in its centre. It was a drawing-board dream which would have involved the demolition of the remaining sections of the City and all the northern suburbs.

Valentine Knight's proposals were more vague. He suggested a main thoroughfare running more or less parallel with the river from St Dunstan-in-the-West to St Paul's and on to the Tower, and a second east–west street a few hundred yards to the north. Ten north–south streets ran up from the Thames, beginning at Fetter Lane and ending at Fish Street; but they didn't reach as far as the old northern perimeter. One of the features of Knight's scheme was the way in which his grid extended east, through the unburned parts of the City around Leadenhall and Bishopsgate, but stopped short of the burned parts to the north. He did not specify what he had in mind for the ruins of Lothbury, Aldersgate and Newgate. His really big idea was the creation of a canal which was to run in a great arc from Billingsgate, between London Bridge and the Tower, until it joined the Fleet River. The advantages of the scheme were that the city would be built 'with large streets, the houses not in danger of fire, and the ground all put to the best profit', while the canal meant that 'the people will walk easy and dry, the houses of office and streets kept sweet and clean, and goods delivered much cheaper'.[25]

Robert Hooke confined himself to laying out the burned area of the City, although his fascination with a regular grid meant that unconsciously or otherwise he managed to straighten the line of Leadenhall Street. He would have had the main streets 'to lie in an exact strait Line, and all the other cross Streets turning out of them at right Angles';[26] the grid broke through the old City wall at Ludgate and extended westward into fire-damaged Fleet Street. But, with the exception of the rebuilt Royal Exchange, which was more or less on its original site, there were no concessions to the pre-Fire street plan. The new Guildhall was to stand in Newgate; there were four big markets distributed equally around the city; and a broad new quay ran the entire length of the river bank, so that buildings were set a long way back from the water.

Hooke allowed for fifteen churches to serve the reborn community of Londoners. Newcourt allowed for fifty-five. Eighty-six had been either totally destroyed or badly damaged. Just how many churches did it take to attend to the spiritual needs of the capital? A 1667 broadsheet, 'The Citizens Joy for the Rebuilding of London', put it in a nutshell:

> We must have fewer *Churches*, but more Zeal.
> Before we had so many, one in ten
> Could scarce on *Sundays* count so many men.[27]

The anomalies caused by the unequal distribution of London's population had been a talking point for years. The pioneering demographer John Graunt had taken up the issue in 1662, when he argued that the boundaries of the City's parishes should be re-drawn: 'We encline therefore to think the Parishes should be equal, or near, because, in the *Reformed Religions*, the principal use of *Churches* is to Preach in: now the bigness of such a *Church* ought to be no greater, then that, unto which the voice of a *Preacher* of middling Lungs will easily extend; I say, easily, because they speak an hour, or more together.'*

John Evelyn agreed. In his proposals for the rebuilding he applauded Graunt's remarks – 'for 'tis prodigiously true, that there are some parishes no less than two hundred times larger than others'[28] – and suggested that the number of churches in the burned area of the City should be reduced to a mere twenty-five. He didn't intend to resite them, but then he didn't really need to: by weeding out sixty-one, he could easily achieve a regular distribution while still building on the old foundations.

However, Evelyn did propose that the new churches should stand either at major intersections in open piazzas, 'as some of the Roman obelisks are', or provide the termination of new vistas. He also thought that the City's churchyards should be relocated to an area just inside the northern wall; the custom of burying people in churchyards set in densely populated streets – or worse, within the churches themselves – seemed to him offensive and indecent. The monuments and inscriptions which were such an important part of the ritual of death could be set into the City wall, 'affording a useful diversion to the contemplative passenger of his mortality, and human frailty'.[29]

Evelyn's scheme for London was much more sophisticated than those of Knight, Newcourt and Hooke. To be fair, he revised the

---

Natural and Political Observations . . . upon the Bills of Mortality, 57–8. This was the same John Graunt who was accused by the Countess of Clarendon of shutting down the water from the New River Company's supply house in Islington at a crucial moment during the Fire. He was also, incidentally, a friend and collaborator of William Petty's.

original discourse and sketch-plan that he showed to the King
at least twice: once in December 1666, after he saw a detailed
'Map or Ground Plott of the Citty of London', a post–Fire survey
of streets which had been engraved by Wenceslaus Hollar; and
again in February 1668.[30] The existence of three sketches can be
quite confusing. In the surviving version of the discourse, for
example, he suggests a good site for the Royal Exchange would
be on the quay between Queenhithe and London Bridge, where
it can be an ornament to the riverscape and 'where the traffic,
and business is most vigorous'.[31] So it stands in one of his schemes;
in a second there is no legend to indicate which buildings are
which; and in the third and most developed plan, the Exchange
is back on its original site between Cornhill and Threadneedle
Street. There are also any number of variations in Evelyn's street
layouts. At one stage he envisaged the entire area between Temple
Bar and a newly canalised Fleet Ditch being developed into a
huge octagon of streets with the Fleet Conduit at its centre.

But Evelyn never deviated from his basic premiss, which
combined a grid-iron layout with radial vistas and piazzas at major
intersections. All three variant designs proposed a broad Thameside
quay, running from the Tower to the Temple; and four completely
straight east–west thoroughfares. A new Thames Street running
from the Fleet to the walls of the Tower gave access to the storehouses and wharves by the river; then came 'Charlesgate', which
began at Temple Bar and terminated at the eastern edge of the
City in a triumphal arch 'in honour of our illustrious Monarch'.[32]
The third went from Newgate to Aldgate, and the fourth and
northernmost from Aldersgate to Bishopsgate. A fifth, which more
or less followed the route of the old Watling Street, makes an
appearance in the third and last design. Cross-streets completed
the grid; but its unbending geometry was relieved by eleven trans-
verse avenues. Four radiated out from the northern entrance to
London Bridge, for instance, and two others broke out beyond
the east end of St Paul's, running north-east and south-east:

In the disposure of the streets due consideration should be
had, what are competent breadths for commerce and inter-

course, cheerfulness and state; and therefore not to pass through the city all in one tenor without varieties, useful breakings, and enlargements into piazzas at competent distances, which ought to be built exactly uniform, strong, and with beautiful fronts. Nor should these be all of them square, but some of them oblong, circular, and oval figures, for their better grace and capacity.[33]

This was all rather impressive, and betrayed more than an ordinary gentleman-amateur's feel for urban planning. Yet Evelyn's London really came to life in the detail. He recommended an official residence for the Lord Mayor, and a Guildhall modelled on the Town Hall in Amsterdam, built in 1647–55 by Jacob van Campen. He wanted to sweep away 'those deformed buildings on London-bridge' and replace them with raised pavements for pedestrians and substantial iron balustrades punctuated at regular intervals by statues. He advocated the establishment of firebreaks around all magazines, places of public record and churches – open zones where no housing could ever be erected. He insisted yet again that noxious trades – brewhouses, bakehouses, dyers, salt-, soap- and sugar-boilers, chandlers, slaughterhouses and fishmongers – must be moved out of the City en masse. (Islington and Wandsworth were the preferred sites for their relocation.) And he would provide fountains in public spaces, a common sight on the Continent but not in England. 'An officer for a small stipend, might protect them from injury and pollution, till custom has civilised us.'[34]

Evelyn's plans were good. Christopher Wren's were better.

Of all the surviving schemes for rebuilding London, Wren's has attracted the most attention, and aroused the strongest emotions.[35] This is scarcely surprising, considering his reputation as being one of the greatest architects England has ever produced. By the eighteenth century his vision for the capital had already become a lost opportunity of mythic proportions. It would have been 'the Wonder of the World', as one critic lamented in the 1730s.[36] A few years later Wren's son condemned 'the obstinate Averseness of great part of the Citizens to alter their old Properties, and to recede from building their Houses again on the old Ground and Foundations; as also, the Distrust in many, and Unwillingness to give up their Properties, tho' for a time only, into the Hands of publick Trustees'. Because of this obstinacy and distrust the chance was lost of making London 'the most magnificent, as well as commodious for Health and Trade of any upon Earth'.[37]

As town-planning evolved into a recognised science in the course of the late-nineteenth and twentieth centuries, historians tended to adopt a much more critical line. The very idea that Wren's London could ever have been built was seen as a dangerous distortion of the truth. It was, in any case, no more than a dream-scape hastily put together by someone who at that stage in his career was no more than a well-meaning amateur. According to Professor T. F. Reddaway in his *The Rebuilding of London after the Great Fire*, Wren completely failed to appreciate the financial and social implications of a wholesale remodelling: 'Divorced from circumstances, a new plan may seem simple, Wren's magnificent: to contemporaries, anxious examination showed that both were Utopian.'[38] To another observer, Wren's design was 'totally irrel-evant to the needs of the City . . . It is surely not possible to see Wren's plan as more than an overnight exercise based on a super-ficial use of continental Renaissance plan-motifs.'[39]

So what was all the fuss about? The first thing one notices is that Wren's scheme bears a striking resemblance to Evelyn's. They both proposed that the area between Temple Bar and the Fleet should be given over to a piazza which formed the intersection of eight streets radiating out on the points of the compass. They both enclosed the buildings which fronted onto this piazza within an octagon of connecting streets. They both made the entrance to the northern end of London Bridge a focal point of their plan, and created a semicircular piazza as a grand introduction to it. They both sent main thoroughfares in from the east to converge at St Paul's. (Wren was still determined to get his own way over the cathedral, evidently, since he depicted it with a circular domed choir at the east end.)

A passing reference in Evelyn's discourse confirms some sort of collaboration and suggests that he adopted some of Wren's ideas. He implies that the two men discussed their respective schemes on or immediately before 11 September – the day on which Wren showed his to the King – and says that the 'street from St Pauls may be divaricated like a Pythagorian Y, as the most accurately ingenious Dr Wren has designed it, and I willingly follow in my second thoughts'.[40]

Significant differences remain between the two schemes, however, and they show that while Evelyn was a gifted amateur with a cosmopolitan knowledge of European urban planning, Wren added a flair and a more deeply thought-out sense of how a modern city should function. So, as we have seen, Evelyn originally placed his new Exchange on the Thames a few hundred yards upstream from London Bridge. He may have argued that this was 'where the traffic, and business is most vigorous', but in reality he conceived it as no more than a visual element in his reconstructed quayside.[41] Wren kept *his* Exchange on the site of Thomas Gresham's original building; but he gave it a massive double portico, set it in the centre of a magnificent piazza at the intersection of ten streets and avenues, and encircled it with the city's major commercial buildings – premises for the Excise Office, the Mint, the General Letter Office, banks, goldsmiths and 'ensurances'. This new commercial district, a tremendously imposing focus for the heart of a major trading nation, was linked directly to the Custom House, which was also left on its existing site between London Bridge and the Tower. It was also linked to the Bridge itself; to St Paul's Cathedral; to all the main routes into the City; and to Wren's new quayside, which was much more straight and regular than Evelyn's, forming a 'Grand Terrace' which was lined with the Halls of the major City Companies. And he made a much more effective show of St Paul's. Whereas Evelyn's main thoroughfares diverged *behind* the east end of the cathedral, as if their parting were something to be ashamed of, Wren split them in front of its entrance portico, creating a triangular piazza which would have been a spectacular termination to the vista from Fleet Street and Whitehall.

The overall effect of Wren's plan was to divide the new London into zones which were functionally independent but visually and physically connected, to bring the labyrinthine medieval metropolis into the seventeenth century. Twentieth-century critics have pointed out that he seems unaware of the undulating topography of London: the City is built on two hills with a valley between them, so that the long, straight, east–west vistas which he and Evelyn valued so highly would not have worked. However, Evelyn understood this – and considering the collaboration between the two, it is impossible to believe that Wren didn't. Evelyn's solution was to use the rubbish left over from the ruins of the Fire to level the City, 'for the more ease of commerce, carriages, coaches, and people in the streets, and not a little for the more handsome ranging of the buildings'.[42]

The residential suburbs to the west of Wren's Fleet Ditch (which, like Evelyn, he converted into a canal) were structured around the octagonal geometry radiating from the site of the Fleet Conduit, a stone tower decorated with saints and angels which had been an important Fleet Street landmark before the Fire. The central section was a grid, broken by the two broad avenues which ran either side of St Paul's to the Exchange and the Tower; and the eastern district showed a more complicated arrangement of radial streets and asymmetrical polygons. God was given His due and His cathedral continued to preside over the City, although St Paul's was actually reduced in size slightly and the number of rebuilt churches dropped from eighty-six to nineteen – even fewer than Evelyn, although not as few as Hooke's paltry fifteen. But the real pride of place went to the Exchange piazza with its radial vistas and its surrounding complex of commercial buildings. The absolutist ideology underlying the planning of Sixtine Rome, which Louis XIV and André Le Nôtre were currently putting to such good use in the laying out of Versailles, was here called into service to pay homage to mercantilism. Trade was to be the new religion.

Whether all this could ever have seen the light of day is a question which has to be asked of all the surviving schemes for rebuilding London; and the answer, as we shall see, is 'Probably not'. Another couple of questions are also relevant. Would any of the schemes have resulted in a capital which was both practical and an improvement on what was there before the Fire? Would any of them be preferable to what was actually built *after* the Fire? Only the proposals of Evelyn and Wren have the sophistication and variety that allows us to answer 'Yes' to both; and only Wren's proposal has that dynamic quality which makes us genuinely regret what might have been.

Whatever subsequent generations have thought of Wren and his plans, in September 1666 he swiftly emerged as the front runner in the race to design a new city. King Charles was enthusiastic: he produced Wren's proposal at a meeting of the Privy Council within days of receiving it, and 'manifested much approbation of it'.[43] This effectively put an end to Evelyn's dreams, although he was quite sanguine about the matter. Bludworth and the Court of Aldermen initially championed Hooke, but they were happy to give way to the King as long as something was done, and done quickly.

But, even in the seventeenth century, cities weren't built by individuals with vision. They were built by bureaucracies and administrators and lawyers, by financiers and tax gatherers and ordinary working people. The mechanics of rebuilding were starting to loom large in everyone's minds: questions of finance, the supply of labour, exactly *how* the detailed survey of the ruins was to be carried out.

The House of Commons spent two days debating the rebuilding, on Thursday 27 and Friday 28 September. It wasn't a very satisfactory business. One faction was keen on Wren's model, but in the end the House rejected the idea. A second proposal, that everybody should have leave to put up their houses as they were before, was also thrown out. A third was that two large streets should be created, one from Temple Bar in the west to Leadenhall in the east, and the other from Bishopsgate down to the Thames; then 'all other streets should be orderly fallen upon and where of necessity they must be enlarged, every man's property should be considered'.[44] This was the favoured option, but when it was referred to a Parliamentary Committee, the

Committee promptly passed it back. The House took its cue from this and moved that the issue should be presented to the King, but the whole matter was left unresolved because, quite sensibly, a sizeable number of MPs were unhappy about abdicating their responsibilities so swiftly without at least coming up with a few ideas to speed up the rebuilding. They never did, and by Friday afternoon they had given up and moved on to debating weightier matters, such as raising a tax on wine of a farthing a half-pint. But the general opinion of the House was that 'if some speedy way of rebuilding the City was not agreed upon that the City would be in danger never to be built, for if the citizens found a difficulty in it, and that things were not speedily provided for, the merchants and wealthiest of the citizens would alter their course of life and trade and remove themselves and their estates into other countries and so the City would remain miserable for ever'.[45]

The following Tuesday, 2 October, members of the King's Council and other interested noblemen met with representatives of the City to discuss how they were going to move things forward before the population of London dispersed to such an extent that it would never come back. All the time, the war with the Dutch was lurking in the background. 'The great stresse will be,' Oldenburg told Robert Boyle, 'how to raise mony for carrying on the warre, and to rebuild ye Citty, at ye same time.'[46] The upshot of this meeting was that the King decided to refer the entire matter to a group of specialists. He announced that the three gentlemen-surveyors brought in to advise on the pre-Fire repairs to St Paul's were to be 'Commissioners for Rebuilding'. Roger Pratt, Hugh May and Christopher Wren were to supervise a survey of interests — to establish ownership and property rights among the ruins, in other words — and to devise some detailed proposals for making improvements to the City. Charles's idea was that the civic authorities would match his Commissioners with three surveyors of their own, and so they did. Two days later they announced their own triumvirate: Robert Hooke, whose scheme had obviously impressed the aldermen; Peter Mills, whose role as City Surveyor made his inclusion a foregone conclusion;

and Edward Jerman, a City carpenter with an interest in archi-tecture and 'an experienced man in building', according to Pratt.[47] These six men were handed one of the most challenging and exciting opportunities in the history of urban design. Exactly thirty-two days after Farriner's bakery burst into flames and destroyed a city, they were asked to rebuild London.

12

Grief Cramps My Heart

Plague engraving, used in a street ballad about the Fire.

One of the more surprising cultural consequences of the Fire was the way it spawned an entire literature of loss. The wild rhetoric of Dissenters like Vincent and Janeway certainly had its readership, although their self-satisfied blend of high drama and hellfire was always intended to appeal to the converted. The sophistry of the almanac-writers went unnoticed among those sections of the population that believed in astrology, while providing amusement for the sceptics. But the diatribes of Dissenters and the excuses of astrologers were only two aspects of Fire literature. The poets also made a contribution.

Poetic responses to current affairs were not uncommon in Restoration England. Charles II's restoration had produced plenty of fawning panegyrics in 1660, with Edmund Waller's effort, 'On His Majesty's Happy Return', being pretty typical of the genre: 'Faith, law, and piety (that banished train) / Justice and truth, with you return again'. Just as typical were Waller's elastic principles –

his oeuvre also included a 'Panegyrick to my Lord Protector' which he prayed would be forgotten as easily as he had forgotten his commitment to the Commonwealth.

The arrival of the King's Portuguese bride two years later also brought forth a few verses, such as the jobbing elegist John Crouch's 'Flowers strowed by the Muses, against the Coming of the most illustrious Infanta of Portugal, Catharina Queen of England'. And the plague had recently been yielding up verse meditations on the Divine Will, a few satires on the speed with which London's clergy had rushed to save themselves, and some straightforward and poignant narratives:

> Here a man brings his shovell and his spade,
> In the churchyard he digs a pit,
> But dyes as soone as he has finisht it
> And falls into the grave he for another made.[1]

The burning of London offered rather more possibilities in the way of drama and spectacle, and over the twelve months or so following the Fire, at least twenty-three poems were published. (These are only the ones we know of, survivors of a literary genre which was profoundly ephemeral.) Ballads with titles such as 'The Londoners' Lamentation' and 'London Mourning in Ashes' began to appear on the blackened streets within weeks. They were direct and eloquent in their simplicity:

> Old *London* that,
> Hath stood in State,
>   above six hundred years,
> In six days space
> Woe and alas!
>   is burn'd and drown'd in tears.[2]

But simplicity was not the defining characteristic of Restoration poetry. The Fire also produced heroic couplets and Pindaric odes and Latin verses. There were outrageously mannered compositions: 'And still the surly flame doth fiercer

hiss / By an Antiperistasis'.★ There were conceits of metaphys-
ical weirdness: the makeshift camps of Moorfields, for example,
were so full of sleeping refugees that the area was 'the Counterfeit
of the *Great Bed of Ware*'.³ The most bizarre metaphor is perhaps
stanza 281 of John Dryden's *Annus Mirabilis*, a long meditation
on the progress of the Dutch War which ends with a description of the Fire. Ascribing the way in which the wind dropped
at the crucial moment to the mercy of God, Dryden explains
it thus:

> An hollow crystal pyramid He takes,
> In firmamental waters dipped above;
> Of it a broad extinguisher He makes,
> And hoods the flames that to their quarry strove.

This so astonished one early reader of the poem, which was
composed in the summer and autumn of 1666 and published the
following January, that he wrote a parody on the endpaper of his
copy:

> An Hollow far-fetcht Metaphor he takes
>   In non-sense dipt of his fantastick braine
> Of which a broad extinguisher he makes
>   Which hoods his witt & stifles all his flame.⁴

Then there were dubious displays of wit, like this account of
the burning of booksellers' stocks in St Faith's:

> Th' imperious Flames about each Arch did hover,
> Till every Book had got on a red cover;
> And so continued in that furious rage,
> That it writ Finis in the Title Page.⁵

★Antiperistasis: resistance or reaction roused against any action (*OED*); the poet
was explaining how the Fire responded with renewed vigour to the play of water
by the engines (John Allison, 'Upon the Late Lamentable Accident of Fire in the
Famous City of London' [1667], ll. 165–6).

There were even literary puzzles, anagrams and acrostics:

> *Lo!* now confused Heaps only stand
> *On* what did bear the Glory of the Land.
> *No* Stately Places, no Edefices,
> *Do* now appear: No, here's now none of these,
> *Oh* Cruel Fates! Can ye be so unkind?
> *Not* to leave, scarce a Mansion behind . . .⁶

(This is just the first verse. In nine stanzas the full acrostic spells out '*LONDON LATELY ENGLANDS GLORY NOW BECOM A TRAGICK STORY*'.)

The authors of these poems were as diverse as their literary output. Some were hack journalists, printers, impoverished academics; and of the twenty-three known poems, seven came from anonymous hands. Others were the work of dedicated amateurs, like Simon Ford, the Royalist vicar of All Saints Northampton. Ford, whose *Three Poems Relating to the Late Dreadful Destruction of the City of London by Fire* have already figured in these pages, was from 1670 chaplain to the rebuilt House of Correction at Bridewell, and a prolific poet. He produced no fewer than eight poems on the Fire and its aftermath – four in Latin and four English translations. He also published verses on fishing; an elegy on 'The Fall and Funeral of Northampton', another fire poem, which described the burning of Northampton in 1675; and a host of sermons and dialogues, including a memorable discourse on Psalm 9:16 which accompanied a true story of 'the man whose hands and legs lately rotted off in the parish of Kings-Swinford in Staffordshire'.⁷ Singularly inappropriate, one feels, since the relevant verse in the psalm declares that 'the wicked is snared in the work of his own hands'.

In contrast to Ford, others were commendably hesitant at setting pen to paper. Joseph Guillim, a Fellow of Brasenose College, Oxford, whose 'Dreadful Burning of London' came out in May 1667, published nothing else. John Tabor, who was probably but not certainly a Cambridge graduate and a Hampshire rector, also confined himself to a single meditation, 'Seasonable

Thoughts in Sad Times, Being some Reflections on the Warre, the Pestilence, and the Burning of London'. Tabor's poem is not without a certain charm, and in his preface he gives a glimpse of the confusion and anxiety which the whole country felt when reports of the Fire began to circulate:

> The startling and astonishing news of the Cities Conflagration, hurried my Muse to a new wrack of tormenting griefs . . . till at length occurring the joyful report of the miraculous extinguishing of the Flames, and unexpected Preservation of the unconsumed part of the City and Suburbs, my mind became more sedate and quiet, and my Muse set her self to reflect on this woe . . .[8]

But even the most generous assessment of 'Seasonable Thoughts' falters on meeting lines like the following:

> Upon *September's* second day i' th' year
> Much talkt of Sixty six, did there appear
> By two i' th' morning these consuming Flames,
> *Which did break out first in the Street of* Thames . . .[9]

In fact one can't deny that there is a McGonagallish quality to much Fire poetry; my favourite is perhaps Samuel Wiseman's couplet, 'Now all turn Porters, poor, and wealthy men, / Slow Age, strong Youth, and little Childeren'.[10] Notwithstanding its 'Hollow far-fetcht Metaphor', the only really fine poem to emerge from the flames was Dryden's *Annus Mirabilis*. But the genre's importance doesn't lie in its literary quality. Nor does it really depend on its value as historical evidence, since although there is plenty of corroborative detail in these poems, they weren't intended as history. One might as well rely on *Slaughterhouse Five* for a clear and accurate account of the bombing of Dresden.

No, the real value of these Fire poems is what they unwittingly say about contemporary attitudes to the disaster – the assumptions and expectations and hopes. One or two recall, rather nervously, the bout of English triumphalism which followed Sir Robert

Holmes's firing of Terschelling: Guillim evokes the passage in the *Aeneid* where the Trojans lay waste to the Greek navy at anchor with Phrygian fire, calling Holmes 'our English Hector', but still pointing out that his exploit foreshadowed 'a more fatal Fire'.[11]

Classical images abound, as one might expect: London has fallen like Troy; it burns like another Rome. The obvious biblical cities also put in an appearance. Jerusalem is laid in the dust once more, Babylon is conquered. And of course, parallels are drawn with the notorious Old Testament city which was overthrown by brimstone and fire from heaven – although with one important difference, as far as the Dissenting preacher Thomas Gilbert was concerned:

> London and Sodom may sit down together,
> And now condole the Ashes of each other.
> For sin they perisht both, and both by Fire,
> But here's the odds; Efficients did conspire
> In different methods, that from Heaven came,
> This from beneath: a black and hellish flame . . .[12]

A high moral tone and a certain remoteness characterise most Fire poetry. And perhaps we shouldn't look for emotion from an age which excelled in cold conceits, although it can be found anyway, here and there: 'Grief cramps my heart,' writes Simon Ford; and the anonymous author of 'The Londoners' Lamentation' ends with a childlike yet tender plea for reconciliation: 'If we still hate each other thus, / God never will be friends with us.'[13]

Many of the poems were written over the autumn of 1666, when Sir Robert Brooke's Parliamentary Committee of Inquiry had yet to report, and they naturally speculate on the causes of the disaster. Simon Ford reflects the suspicion and uncertainty felt by many when he talks of how England's enemies deny any involvement:

> We, (sith we wish 'em *innocent*) not *dare*
> To *charge* 'em with a Guilt they thus *disclaim*.
> And yet, if *Time* shall *hidden fraud* proclaim,
> Resolve to *lash* 'em.[14]

The author of 'The Londoners' Lamentation' is more cautious, suspecting that although many French and Dutch have been arrested, 'Our sinful hearts more guilty are'.[15] And John Crouch, in a glorious mixture of classical, biblical and historical references, puts the blame fairly and squarely on England for daring to kill the King's father:

> Had *Tyber* swell'd his monstrous *Waves*, and come
> Over the seven Hills of our flaming *Rome*,
> 'T had been in vain: no less than *Noah's* flood
> Can quench flames kindled by a *Martyr's* blood.[16]

The most remarkable thing about this literature of loss is that almost as soon as it saw the light of day it began to evolve into a literature of renewal. Guillim, for example, ends his 'Dreadful Burning' with the hope that 'from our Ruin'd City may arise / Another, whose high Towers may urge the Skies'.[17] Dryden in *Annus Mirabilis* dreams of a city of gold whose streets will be paved with silver. Crouch looks for the rise of 'a fairer *Phoenix* after Death'. The anonymous author of 'London Undone' waits for a clearer day when Peace will 'make *rude Stones* into a *City Dance*'.[18]

And poems which looked with anticipation towards a new London instead of lamenting the loss of the old were already appearing within weeks of the Fire. 'Vox Civitatis', a broadside published in September 1666, has the subtitle of 'Londons Call to her Natural and Adopted Children; Exciting them to Her speedy Reedification'. It portrays the city's destruction as part of a natural cycle of growth, decay and rebirth. After a fruitful summer and a scorching autumn London will lie dormant over the winter, to burst into new life when spring rolls round again. Another broadside, 'The Citizens Joy For the Rebuilding of London', suggests how excited the more optimistic citizens were at the opportunity to create a new capital:

> The streets shall be dilated, and our wealth;
> More room to breath; better injoy our health.

Old things shall be converted into *new*,
Antiquity shall bid the World *adieu*.[19]

Jeremiah Wells expressed similar ideas in 'On the Rebuilding of London'. The streets will be wider and more stately; the buildings will be more sumptuous and uniform, the courts and tenements more graceful, the churches bigger and the mansions more magnificent. Merchants who wept when the Exchange was destroyed will grow richer:

So shall the City thank her cruel fate,
    And bless those flames that did their help afford:
Counting even Desolation no dear rate,
    Glad to be Ruin'd So to be Restord.[20]

Unfortunately, the road from ruin to restoration did not run quite so true.

The Commissioners for Rebuilding – Pratt, May and Wren for the King, and Mills, Jerman and Hooke for the City – met on Thursday 4 October, again on the following Monday and again on Thursday 11 October, after which some members of the Council of State resolved to sit every Tuesday afternoon to hear how they were getting along. Their first meeting was taken up with the most basic issue of all – was it really going to be possible to measure the burned area? It had to be. The proclamation of 13 September which set out the King's wishes for the City was absolutely clear on that point. No matter what changes took place for the betterment of the community, Charles was determined to secure everyone's property rights and compensate them – not for losses suffered in the Fire, but for street-widening schemes, the uprooting and zoning of particular trades and, of course, for the massive relocation which would be necessary if Wren's scheme for rebuilding was implemented. That meant establishing 'to whom all the houses and ground did in truth belong, what term the several occupiers were possessed of, and at what rents, and to whom, either corporations, companies, or single persons, the reversion and inheritance appertained'.[21] A ground plan of each and every building was required, with a schedule of owners, tenants and other relevant information attached.

After some debate the Commissioners agreed that a survey *was* possible; and at their second meeting they asked for the appointment of surveyors at a fixed fee of a shilling a house, and suggested that the City authorities should order each householder to clear away all debris within the next fourteen days, so that foundations would be exposed and the surveyors could get to work. In fact Bludworth and the aldermen had already tried to speed up the clearance work right after the Fire – and in advance of the royal proclamation forbidding unauthorised building – by telling citizens to move debris from the streets in front of their ruined houses before starting work on the buildings themselves. But the order had been ignored.

The City had also taken steps to facilitate the survey. The *Gazette* of Monday 24 September announced that as of the previous Saturday, each 'last occupier' of fire-damaged properties had fourteen days to produce a perfect survey of 'the Ground, whereon his House, Shop, or Warehouse stood'.[22] They should present them at booths which would be set up in every ward in the City, and clerks would be on hand each working day from eight in the morning until twelve, and from two till four in the afternoon, to record all claims.

This also was ignored, which was hardly surprising in the circumstances. A fair number of 'last occupiers' had left London to stay with friends and relatives. Many of those who had returned to the ruins of their homes were in no position to carry out or pay for a survey; others couldn't find workmen to clear their sites, and, if they *could* find them, they couldn't afford to pay the exorbitant rates which were being charged just then. Christ's Hospital distributed the City's order to all its tenants, and blithely notified them that they should immediately go and measure up the sites where their houses had been, taking workmen with them. When the clerk of St Martin Ludgate sat dutifully in his booth each day from eight till twelve and two till four during the last week of September and the first week of October, he saw only 8 or 9 per cent of the potential claims in his ward.

It was partly to counter this spectacular lack of progress that Charles had appointed the Commissioners in the first place. But their scheme for the survey fared no better. In a seller's market where there was an acute shortage of labour, and in which carpenters, bricklayers, masons and other allied tradesmen could ask for and get any price they named, contractors were slow to come forward. Twelve pence a plot was simply not enough. The City issued a rather desperate proclamation on 10 October, pleading with people to clear their ground for the survey. Up till now, it said, this had been almost totally neglected, 'to the great Discouragement of the Magistrates, and retarding of those Proceedings, which otherwise by Gods Blessing, His Majesties, and the Parliaments Favour and Assistance, and the Indeavours of good Citizens, had by this time far prevailed towards a beginning of this Work'.[23] When this failed, the City began to threaten: 'If any Men shall obstinately oppose what is so much for the Generall good of the said Citty, they shall undergoe such punishment & penaltyes as are due to their Refractoriness, over and above his Majesties displeasure.'[24]

At the same time, the Commissioners were grappling with the shape of the new London. Wren's scheme was still being considered as a real option, but his colleagues decided it would be best to establish basic dimensions for different categories of thoroughfares first, and then to look at where they were placed. Wren was presumably pushing hard for support, but Pratt was the natural leader of the group. He had more architectural experience than Hugh May, and much more than either Wren or Hooke. If Peter Mills and Edward Jerman had the edge on him – well, they were artisans. He was a gentleman. Moreover, he was the gentleman who had just designed Clarendon House in Piccadilly, a huge mansion for the Lord Chancellor; and if Pratt's experience at home and abroad weren't enough, the Earl of Clarendon's patronage ensured that he commanded respect. When his cousin, Sir Edward Pratt, heard of his appointment, he wrote to congratulate him on leading the team: 'I am exceeding glad the King hath commissioned you (no question in the first place) with Mr

May & Dr. Renne: they will get more secrets of your art brought from Rome, & so from Athens, then you from them.'[25]

Wren's ideas for the new London were on a grand scale. He proposed that all principal streets should be ninety feet wide; secondary streets should be sixty feet; and lanes thirty feet. Pratt and the others agreed with him that the streets of pre-Fire London had been much too narrow. Everyone did: Dryden echoed a common feeling when he wrote of the Fire in *Annus Mirabilis* that

> Now down the narrow streets it swiftly came,
> And widely opening did on both sides prey:
> This benefit we sadly owe the flame,
> If only ruin must enlarge our way.[26]

But Wren's broad avenues were scaled down. According to Pratt, the main east–west thoroughfare might be seventy feet wide, with three other categories: fifty feet; forty-two feet; and thirty or twenty-five feet. If there were to be any alleys at all, they should be at least sixteen feet wide. He recommended that the breadth of the new quay should be one hundred feet.

The Privy Council asked Pratt, rather than the whole Commission, to come up with a strategy for moving the project forward, so that 'much time might not be lost in disputes about the manner of the procedure of our future business'.[27] He decided that the next step involved two decisions. One was eminently practical: the City needed somewhere to store the necessary building materials, and someone had to make up his mind where they should be kept.

The other was much more difficult. Assuming the respective widths of particular types of street were agreed, should they be laid out on their pre-Fire lines? Or 'in such other as shall bee demonstrated to be more for the beauty and conveniencie of the citty'?[28] The choice was between restoration and renewal, between Christopher Wren's brave new capital and the consolation of the familiar. While the Commission, the Privy Council, the House of Commons and the City authorities all pondered on the possibilities, however, the necessary prerequisites – streets cleared of debris, plots surveyed, evidence of ownership and tenancy agreements provided – were still not forthcoming. The fee for surveys was raised from 12d to 18d; but contractors still showed no enthusiasm for the task. By 17 October Pratt was arguing that the City authorities really must offer 2s 6d per house, and come up with some more effective plan for clearing the streets; otherwise, given that building work must cease over the winter, the whole reconstruction programme would be stalled until the spring.

In the end, everybody just gave up on the survey of interests. That meant giving up on any major remodelling; since without establishing who owned what, it was impossible to negotiate with landlords, to reassign rights or redistribute property, or to calculate how much compensation should be paid. On 18 October there was a joint session of two Rebuilding Committees – that of the Privy Council, which represented the King's interests, and that of the Court of Common Council, which shared the government of the City with the aldermen. The result was a working document setting out street-widening schemes and, by implication, jettisoning all hopes of a radically new capital. The proposal was:

> That the Key on the Waterside be fowrscore foote, and Thames street forty foote wide.
>
> That the Street from Fleet-Street to the Tower be Fifty foote wide.
>
> The Street from Holborn to Al[d]gate fifty five Foot.
>
> The Street from the Bridge to Byshopsgate Street Fifty foot.
>
> From St Paul's Church-yard into Cheapside Forty five Foot.
>
> From Guild-hall into Cheapside Threescore foot with a Piazza.
>
> And the Street opposite to that Street, out of Cheapside to Thames Street Forty foote.
>
> From Aldersgate into Cheapside, & so into Thames-street Forty foote.
>
> From the Exchange to Thames-street & so to Moregate Forty Foote.
>
> Pater-noster Rowe Forty foote.
>
> Lumbard Street Forty foote.
>
> Old Baylie into Smithfield, Thirty five Foote.

And from Old Baylie to Black-Fryers stayres, Thirty five Foote.

From Warwick-Lane to Puddle Dock, Thirty foote.

That the Middle Rowes in the Shambles & Fish-Street be taken with the Stocks and other such like Buildings.

All streighte [i.e., narrow] Entrances into Cheapside to be widened.[29]

This was more flexible than Wren's modular 90 feet–60 feet–30 feet approach, but even more conservative than Pratt's proposal. The King stumped up £100 to pay for clearing away the rubble, and Alderman Backwell lent the City £200 to finance a detailed street survey, so that at least the authorities could establish how much damage had been done and assess the viability of the scheme. On 19 November, Wren, Hooke and two members of the Common Council were authorised to contract for the measuring and staking-out. Just over two weeks later the streets were clear and the survey finally began.

It was a slow process. The winter was hard, and by January the City was noting with regret that the 'Survey and admeasurement of the Streetes by reason of the wheather could not bee soe soone nor is yet perfected'.[30] Discussions about building regulations and street-widening schemes continued, until on 23 January the Secretary of State for the North, Sir William Morice MP, brought in a bill before Parliament for imposing a tax on coal to pay for some of the works. The issue of finance was a crucial one – even before the economic devastation caused by the plague, the City had been in the habit of spending around twice as much as it received in income, a practice rather less common then than now. It was in no position to fund the rebuilding. A nationwide tax would have been turned down flat by Parliament – why should the rest of the country be made to suffer for London's losses? And a direct local tax was hardly likely to raise much money from citizens whose businesses had been destroyed, whose homes were in ruins, whose inclinations were already to leave London for pastures new.

A duty levied on coal coming into the Port of London, on the other hand, seemed fair. Everyone used coal, and those who could afford to use more would pay more. It was a regional tax, and the City itself could administer it without Parliament or the Crown getting involved. It was fixed at a shilling per chaldron (a measure of capacity very roughly equivalent to an Imperial ton in weight), and was to run for ten years. With luck, this would bring in around £15,000 a year, but none of it was to go towards housing. Instead, it was earmarked for compensating the owners of land taken for street-widening schemes; for buying the land needed for the new quay on the Thames, and for 'the building and makeing such Prisons within the . . . Citty as shall be necessary for the safe custody and Imprisonment of Felons and other Malefactors'.[31] Everything else was to be left to private enterprise and corporate endeavour.

Two other pieces of legislation came up in January. One was a bill 'to prevent suits that might arise . . . concerning rents and houses that were consumed in the late fire';[32] the other was the bill which would enshrine the compromise recommendations of Pratt, Wren and the other Commissioners. A Committee which had been considering these recommendations was supposed to report to MPs on 24 January, but the report was postponed until the next day, and then until the next. The Commons was preoccupied that week with more exciting matters – chiefly the plight of the Constable of Windsor Castle, Viscount Mordaunt. Lord Mordaunt was standing trial in the House of Lords for high crimes and misdemeanours: they included the false imprisonment of William Tayleur, a subordinate at Windsor Castle; the sexual harassment of his daughter; and the violent eviction of his family by soldiers, 'the rude carriage of which soldiers then frightened a young child of the said Mr Tayleur out of its wits, whereof it soon after died'.[33]

On the morning of 26 January the Commons heard a brief account of the Committee's findings before trooping off to hear Mordaunt's impeachment. The MPs were anxious about whether he should be allowed counsel to plead for him and whether he could keep his seat and his hat during the trial. At this point the King sent a gentle reminder that they really should turn their minds to the business of the rebuilding; and that afternoon they returned to the Commons and managed to discuss the bill, the proposed width of streets, the height and width of buildings, and the timescale for the reconstruction programme.

At their next sitting, after more discussion about Lord Mordaunt's seating arrangements, MPs found that there were still two issues on which to decide. One was the width of streets and the legality of taking land for widening. The other involved the City's churches. The bill suggested that thirty-nine would be enough to service the spiritual needs of eighty-six dispossessed congregations – nowhere near as paltry as Evelyn's twenty-five or Wren's nineteen, but still quite a radical shake-up. However, although MPs expressed concern over whether or not thirty-nine churchyards would be able to cope with the City's dead, it wasn't really the *number* of churches which worried them, so much as the proposals for those which were scheduled for extinction. What could be salvaged from the lost churches was to be used in rebuilding the new, while their sites were to be sold with the money going to the same purpose. Where churchyards could usefully form part of street-widening schemes, they would; where they couldn't, 'they shall be put to common uses for buildings and cellars'.[34] Members were understandably uneasy about this. It would mean disturbing the dead, never an easy thing to do; and even where it didn't, 'the ground whereon the churchyards and the churches had been built had been dedicated to a pious use and therfoer ought not to be profaned by converting them to a common use'.[35] It went to a vote, and the proviso for the sale of demolished churchyards was eventually carried by a majority of six.

The Rebuilding Act received the royal assent on 8 February. Its most progressive stipulation, which came out of the Commissioners' meetings the previous autumn, was that the rebuilt London should have standardised building-types. These varied depending on status and location. The meanest sort, fronting alleys and small lanes, were to be of two storeys, with cellars and attics; the minimum ceiling height of the two main storeys was nine feet. Then came houses 'fronting streets and lanes of note and the River Thames'.[36] They were allowed to be three storeys high, with the two lower storeys of ten feet and the third of nine feet. Houses which faced onto 'High and Principal Streets' could be of four storeys. The first was ten feet; the second, which would usually contain the main rooms of state, should be ten feet six inches; the third was nine feet; and the fourth eight feet six inches.

The final category was mansion houses 'of the greatest bignes not fronting upon any of the Streets or Lanes'.[37] These were also limited to four storeys, but the Act didn't presume to make any recommendations as to their heights.

Exterior walls were to be built of brick or stone; the thicknesses of walls were prescribed; and the Act established the principle that where two houses shared a party wall, it should be set out equally on both plots. Any plot left vacant after three years could be purchased by the City and resold.

The Act represented quite an achievement; but, even now, there was a host of difficult decisions left to make. Parliament sidestepped rather a lot of the detailed issues, such as which streets should be widened and by how much. They left such things to be decided by the City and approved by the King. But until they *were* settled, reconstruction couldn't go ahead; and it was now five months since the Fire. Spring, and the start of the building season, was approaching fast.

On 6 March a delegation from the City presented their detailed proposals to the King and the Privy Council at Whitehall. The previous day Peter Mills and Edward Jerman had been told to obtain a supply of stakes for setting out the lines of the new streets, on the assumption that Charles would give the go-ahead and work could begin immediately. They assumed too much: he returned the scheme and asked for it to be mapped out on the plan of London which had been drawn up over the winter by the surveyors, so that he could visualise the changes being proposed.

Six days later the survey plan came back to Whitehall. It had been marked up; and in the Council Chamber overlooking Inigo Jones's Banqueting House, Charles sat with 'the Map of the Citty lying before him . . . looking upon the lines drawne out in the said Map'.[38] In general, he liked what he saw, although like anyone in a position of power who is invited to approve someone else's ideas, he couldn't resist suggesting a few changes here and there. For example, recalling one of Wren's ideas for a grand quayside terrace of Company Halls, he thought that if some of the minor Companies could be persuaded to relocate from their cramped backstreet homes to the new quay, their Halls would considerably enhance the prospect of the Thames. And how about an inner ring road running northward from the river between the Fleet and the City, so that the western suburbs could have access to the Thames, and traffic from Westminster would be able to reach north London without having to enter the City at Ludgate? At present, the planned route from Cheapside to Fleet Street was to be forty feet wide – wouldn't it be better if it was ten feet wider? And the markets in Newgate, Cheapside and Leadenhall – might it be a good idea to give them permanent sites away from the street, so the stalls didn't block the traffic?

The City agreed where it could, and stalled where it couldn't. It told the King that it would pass on to the Companies his idea about a quayside development of Halls, and move the markets away from the main traffic routes. It agreed that the main east–west street should be wider. But fifty feet wasn't viable, so perhaps they should split the difference and settle on forty-five feet? The development in the western suburbs was a good idea, but the Rebuilding Act didn't allow the City to engage in compulsory purchase on that kind of scale.

By the end of April all the ideas for the new post-Fire London – the street-widening schemes, the standardised building-types and the rest – had been parcelled up and embodied in an Order of the Common Council. On 8 May the Lord Chancellor offered that Order to the King for confirmation at an august gathering of the great and the good at Whitehall. The Duke of York was there. So were the Duke of Albemarle, Lord Arlington, the Archbishop of Canterbury and the Earl of Craven. The Order went into tremendous detail. Ornaments on the street façades of buildings should be of rubbed brick; the old way of hanging shop signs so that they projected into the street at right angles from a building was forbidden, and instead 'the signs shall be fixed against the balconies, or some other convenient part of the side of the house'.[39]

London had tried to impose building regulations on its citizens in the past – and its citizens had ignored them. This time was going to be different. No one was allowed to begin building until the official surveyors had measured their site and staked out the foundations. There could be no dispute about this:

Each builder, before he lays his foundation, or such survey shall be taken, do repair to the chamber of London, and there enter his name, with the place where his building is to be set out, and to pay to the chamberlain the sum of six shillings and eight pence for every foundation to be rebuilt; for which Mr Chamberlain shall give acquittances; upon receipt of which acquittances the surveyors shall proceed to set out such persons' foundations.[40]

No fee, no receipt; no receipt, no survey; no survey, no new house. If any citizens were tempted to ignore the rules, they could be gaoled and their house demolished. And if they dared to interfere with the survey, say by moving a stake a few feet one way or another, they faced a fine of £10 or a term of three months in prison. Transgressors from the lower levels of society might expect more direct punishment: the Act provided that those of the meaner sort could be taken to the scene of their crime and flogged until they bled.

The King had promised in March that Pratt, May and Wren would be 'ready at all times upon notice to confer with the Committee of the Citty and their Surveyors and to give their best advice and assistance when ever it shall be required.'[41] The City responded by confirming as Surveyors their original trinity of Robert Hooke, Peter Mills and Edward Jerman. They also added a fourth to their list, a professional surveyor named John Oliver.

In the event, these seven men played very different and unequal parts in the rebuilding. Of the three artisans from the building trades, Jerman and Oliver declined to serve; and ironically enough it was the amateurs, Wren and Hooke, who would do most. Between them, these earnest young mathematicians defined the architectural landscape of the new London; and, in Wren's case at least, London in turn defined him as an architect.

But as building finally got under way in the spring of 1667, that really did seem rather unlikely. Sir Roger Pratt was set to make the major contribution. Experienced, progressive and with first-hand knowledge of the latest architectural trends in France, Holland and Italy, he had already set himself up as natural leader of the Rebuilding Commission. Moreover, his patron, the Earl of Clarendon, was Chairman of the Rebuilding Committee of the Privy Council, and thus perfectly placed to advance Pratt's interest.

But events conspired to keep Pratt out of the architectural limelight. In the early part of 1667 he was preoccupied with finishing Clarendon House, Piccadilly, for the Lord Chancellor. In April his cousin Edward died, leaving him a sizeable country estate at Ryston in Norfolk. Then in June a Dutch squadron sailed up the Medway and captured or burned half a dozen ships of the line, including the *Royal Charles*. De Ruijter's men actually came ashore at Gillingham, evoking uneasy memories of Sir Robert Holmes's bonfire at Terschelling and putting the fear of God into the English, although they conducted themselves with exemplary honour throughout the raid.*

The significance of the Dutch raid for Pratt's career was that when the news broke in London, his patron was blamed for failing to manage the war properly. The brand-new windows of Clarendon House were smashed by a mob who cut down trees in front of it and painted a gibbet on the gate. Clarendon was accused of high treason and forced into exile in France; and Pratt retired discreetly to his Norfolk estate, where he spent the rest of his days tidying up the grounds, building himself a modest

---

*The same couldn't be said for the English troops who arrived on the scene after the Dutch had gone, and seized the opportunity to plunder every house in the locality. The watermen who worked that stretch of the Medway reckoned with good reason that 'our own soldiers are far more terrible to those people of the country-towns then the Dutch themselfs' (Pepys, *Diary*, 30 June 1667).

country house and preparing a treatise on architecture which he would never finish. In the summer of 1668 Charles II knighted him for his work on the Rebuilding Commission, but he played no other part in the reconstruction of London, except to comment on one of Wren's early schemes for St Paul's Cathedral, which he described rather grumpily as weak, ungraceful and useless.[42]

In the spring of 1667 Hugh May also faded from view – less dramatically, but no less completely. (It may be significant that May's fortunes were also tied in with those of Clarendon, although perhaps not as tightly as Pratt's: he was currently remodelling the Lord Chancellor's country seat, Cornbury House in Oxfordshire.) Throughout the autumn and winter May, who was still acting up as Surveyor-General of the King's Works in place of Sir John Denham, had been closely involved in the planning of the new city. He told Pepys in November 1666 that everything was progressing well, and the account he gave convinced the latter that 'it will be mighty handsome, and to the satisfaction of the people'.[43] In the first week of March he also asked for – and was given – a deputy to help at the Office of Works, 'on account of extraordinary business'.[44] But May's role in the rebuilding programme from then on is indistinct; he didn't design any of the City's new buildings, and he didn't figure in subsequent discussions.

This may be because by February Sir John Denham had recovered from his bout of insanity and was back in his post at the King's Works. Towards the end of the month he was involved (with five of his officers, one of whom was presumably May) in surveying the site of the old Custom House, designing a new Custom House and deciding whether there might be a more suitable location than the old one, which was halfway between the Tower and London Bridge. If May's original appointment as one of the King's Commissioners had been a consequence of his acting up for Denham, then the latter's recovery may have made things rather awkward, although it has to be said that Denham himself showed no inclination to take over May's role.

But then the Surveyor-General was still in a difficult position at court – more difficult than ever, in fact. After the Fire, the

Duke of York had returned to his affair with Margaret Denham with vigour and a cheerful disdain for discretion. The high-minded Evelyn was shocked at his behaviour, and even the not-so-high-minded Pepys felt uncomfortable at the sight of the Duke trotting after Lady Denham like a puppy, or talking intimately with her in full view of the court.

In November 1666 Lady Denham fell ill with an intestinal complaint, and claimed she was the victim of poisoning. The doctors said it was just colic, and she recovered; but at the beginning of January she was taken ill again, and again she said she had been given poison, this time in a cup of chocolate. On 6 January she died, and the rumours began to fly. For some reason, John Aubrey blamed the Countess of Rochester; but most people were convinced that Sir John had killed her to put a stop to her infidelity. The Duke of York 'was very sad, and kept his chamber'.[45] He swore he would never ever have another mistress, a resolution which lasted for several months.

Denham also kept his chamber. Not out of grief, or even madness – coincidentally, Margaret's death had coincided with his recovering his senses – but because an angry mob had gathered outside his Scotland Yard house and threatened to stone him if he showed his face. Another story also circulated, to the effect that the Duchess of York had been visited by Lady Denham's ghost, and was so frightened – or so overcome with guilt? – that she bit off a piece of her tongue. On her deathbed Lady Denham asked for a post-mortem, which was duly carried out. No trace of poison was found.*

By virtue of his position as Surveyor-General, Sir John Denham should have been well placed to lead the rebuilding programme. But he was not popular with the King's circle; nor was he a

---

*A final unlikely twist to this Gothick tale emerged the evening after the post-mortem: Alderman Sir Richard Ford told Pepys that when her body was opened, the poor woman had been found to be virgo intacta. Even stranger, this was thought to account for all her pain, thus absolving the Duchess of York from poisoning her and the Duke from sleeping with her. History doesn't record Sir John's reaction to the news.

particular favourite with the City. Apart from overseeing the plans for the new Custom House – which he could hardly avoid, since for historical reasons it fell under the aegis of the Office of Works – he kept his head down and concentrated on repairing the apartments he owned in Scotland Yard, which had been dismantled as a precaution to prevent the Fire reaching the Palace of Whitehall. He managed to persuade the Crown to foot the bill, which came to a sizeable £527.

Others showed no such reluctance to play their part in the rebuilding; and the fact that the building trades were in such demand may be why two of the City's nominees as Surveyors, Edward Jerman and John Oliver, turned the offer down flat. Both men had plenty to occupy them. Oliver designed a new Hall on Dowgate Hill for the Skinners' Company which was finished in about 1670, and went on to assist in the rebuilding of the City churches and St Paul's Cathedral, where he was Assistant Surveyor under Christopher Wren for more than twenty-five years. He also stood in for Peter Mills when the latter was ill and unable to carry out his work for the City in the summer of 1667, and the following year was persuaded to change his mind and take up the offer of a post as one of the City's Surveyors. He was sworn in on 27 January 1668.

Jerman decided that he had had more than enough of surveys and committee meetings over the winter of 1666–7, and turned his attention to working directly for the City and the Livery Companies. They kept him busy: between the Fire and his death in November 1668, he designed new Halls for the Weavers, the Drapers, the Fishmongers, the Mercers and the Wax Chandlers. He also repaired Barber-Surgeons' Hall and Goldsmiths' Hall, was consulted by the Apothecaries and may possibly have designed Vintners' Hall on Thames Street, where his brother Roger was master carpenter.[46]

Jerman's greatest single contribution to the rebuilding was the new Royal Exchange, an institution which until the Fire had been one of London's most important buildings, a centre of trade and commerce more vital to the existence of the City than either of the other two major architectural landmarks, St Paul's and the

Guildhall. A few tradesmen tried to set up shop in the ruins of the old Exchange immediately after the Fire, and rubble was carted over from the ruined Guildhall a quarter of a mile away to create a makeshift pavement in the courtyard. When the civic authorities moved into Gresham College, the merchants and shop-keepers followed suit; but everyone recognised that a rebuilt Exchange would be a powerful symbol of London's resurrection and of its citizens' determination to maintain its leading position in the nation's economy.

Sir Thomas Gresham had appointed the City and the Mercers' Company as joint trustees to manage his estates, and in February 1667 the Committee for Gresham Affairs, as the trustees were known, ordered the grounds of the destroyed Exchange to be cleared in preparation. The *Gazette* of 18 March carried an advertisement telling everyone in the building trade that the Committee would be sitting at the end of the long gallery at Gresham College every Monday morning to negotiate contracts for masonry, joinery, glazing and so on; and the next month Jerman was offered the job of designing the new building and over-seeing the work.

As the City Surveyor, Peter Mills was the obvious choice as architect. But although Mills did a little architectural work in the wake of the Fire — he designed five warehouses on one of the wharves off Thames Street, for example, and rebuilt three houses of his own on land which he leased from Pembroke College, Cambridge — he was elderly and in poor health.* He was also frantically busy, since he and Robert Hooke were strug-gling with the massive job of staking out foundations on their own. So when it came to the Royal Exchange, he was passed over.

Jerman was a decent kind of man, and he accepted the job with reluctance, and only after the authorities had reassured him that he wasn't stepping on Mills's toes:

The committee being very sensible of the greate burthen of

*Mills celebrated his sixty-ninth birthday in February 1667.

businesse lying upon [Mills] for the city att this time; and considering that Mr Jerman is the most able known artist (besides him) that the city now hath; therefore the committee unanimously made choice of Mr Jerman to assist the committee in the agreeing for, ordering, and directing of that worke; and haveing declared the same unto him, hee, after much reluctancy and unwillingness (objecting, it might bee thought an intrenchment upon Mr. Mills his right), at length accepted, being assured first, by the lord mayor and the committee, that itt was no intrenchment, and that this wholle committee, at all times, would acquit him from any scandall in that behalfe.[47]

The new Exchange was a quadrangle with side galleries, like the old one. It covered a rather larger area; a decision which caused no end of problems, because the owners of property in Cornhill, where the extension was to be, refused even the most generous terms until the King threatened them with an Act of Parliament. Charles made a personal appearance at the site on 23 October, when he fixed the first pillar and was entertained to a feast by the Gresham trustees in a makeshift shed which had been put up in the ruins. The Duke of York laid a ceremonial stone some time later, as did Prince Rupert.

Jerman died in the late autumn of 1668, with the building still incomplete, and it was left to the contracting mason, Thomas Cartwright, to finish it to Jerman's designs. He also developed Jerman's ideas, to judge from the fact that in March 1670 he presented to the Gresham Committee 'a draft of the frontispiece to Cornhill and the cupilo as he advised to build it'.[48] Cartwright was also the builder (although not the architect) of Weavers' Hall, Haberdashers' Hall, Drapers' Hall, Tallow-Chandlers' Hall and Mercers' Hall, as well as contracting for three of the City churches. Merchants moved into the Exchange on 28 September 1669, 'with much satisfaction beholding that excellent Structure raised with greater luster from the Ashes of the old', according to the *Gazette*;[49] and the shopkeepers came back to their booths on Lady Day 1671, evoking a rash of celebratory verses:

From East to West, from North to Southern side
There's not the like, in all the World so wide.
So that we may, with Confidence declare,
There's none with us can equally Compare.
We have the Phoenix in our English Nation,
All those that view it, stand in admiration.[50]

13

Consider the Common Calamity

St Stephen Walbrook, rebuilt by Wren.

*O*n the first day of 1668 a consignment of stationery was delivered to the Hall at Clifford's Inn, a medieval Inn of Chancery which stood just north of Fleet Street. Twenty-two skins of ready-ruled parchment and three reams of paper arrived, along with a brazilwood ruler, 300 quills, six pints of ink and a bag of sand for blotting.

The Fire Court was in session.

In the seventeenth century, as in the twenty-first, litigation was the Devil's work. Claims heard under civil law routinely involved lots of money, lengthy delays, complications of Dickensian proportions; then, as now, the only sure winners were the lawyers. And the Fire of London promised to unleash a flood of actions the like of which had never been seen before.

Sir Nathaniel Hobart, who as a judge in Chancery knew exactly what he was talking about, was one of the first to realise that a legal quagmire was about to engulf the blackened capital. Writing on 13 September 1666 he predicted that 'the rebuilding of the Citty will not bee soe difficult as the satisfying all interests, there being so many proprietors'.[1]

He was right. Most Londoners were leasehold tenants rather than owner-occupiers. Their leases contained a standard clause which required the lessee 'to well and sufficiently sustain, maintain, uphold, repair and amend the premises and every part thereof (with oak and elme and not with fir or deal), cause the pavements to be repaired and the privies to be cleansed'. When the period of the lease was up, the tenant must 'yield up the premises sufficiently sustained, maintained, upholden, repaired, paved and cleansed together with all fixtures belonging to the landlord'.[2] This meant that it was the tenant's responsibility to rebuild if the property was damaged or destroyed; and the tenant was also legally bound to pay rent for the full term of the lease, even if that property had ceased to exist.

There was no fire insurance. There was no compensation, no recourse to law, no one with any obligation to make things right. Think for a moment what that meant. While you were still reeling from the loss of your home, your business, quite possibly your stock and your personal possessions, you realised that even though you had no means of earning a living, you still owed your quarterly rent; and your landlord could still take you to law and force you to rebuild your house.

That was the situation for the majority of Londoners in September 1666. There was a ray of hope at the end of October, when it seemed that poor mad Robert Hubert had proved the saviour of the common people. His conviction and execution made the Fire an act of war, and this handed responsibility back to the *owner* of a property. But the appearance in January 1667 of Sir Robert Brooke's Parliamentary Report into the causes of the Fire, and its conclusion that there was no evidence 'to prove it to be a general design of wicked agents, Papists or Frenchmen, to burn the city',[3] was greeted with sighs of relief among the property-owning classes. The pre-Fire status quo was restored, and once again it was up to the tenant to make good the damage.

That wasn't fair. It placed the burden of rebuilding London

squarely on one section of the population – the section which had lost most and which, by and large, could least afford the loss. Even more important than the injustice was the threat to the future of the City: if landlords couldn't be persuaded to contribute to the rebuilding, and tenants couldn't afford to do it themselves, then just how was London supposed to rise from the ashes?

The Act 'For Erecting a Judicature for Determination of Differences touching Houses Burned or Demolished by reason of the late Fire which happened in London' was passed on 8 February 1667, the same day as the Rebuilding Act, and the first sitting of the Court took place in the medieval hall of Clifford's Inn, one of the eight Inns of Chancery, nineteen days later. The legislation provided that three or more of the Justices of the Courts of King's Bench, Common Pleas and Exchequer could decide on all differences 'between Landlords Proprietors Tennants Lessees Under Tennants or late Occupiers'. This didn't mean enforcing the existing law: in his proclamation of 13 September 1666 the King had promised 'that no man shall have cause to complain of wrong and oppression', and plainly a blind adherence to the letter of the law would be both wrong and oppressive in the circumstances. The idea was that all concerned should bear their fair share of the loss, and the Fire Court was meant to arbitrate, 'making new rules between owners and tenants for their material encouragement'.[4] But over and above the desire for justice and a fair distribution of responsibility, the judges' primary remit was to speed the rebuilding. In each case that came before them they tried to decide who was best placed to rebuild, and what inducements might move the process along – a reduction in rent and an extension of a lease being the usual method of giving a helping hand to a tenant. Tenant and landlord were encouraged to agree on the exact figures of who should pay what, but if they couldn't, then the Court would impose a decision. If no one was willing or able to rebuild, then the judges could – and did – declare that a lease was void so that the site could be given to someone who *was* prepared to build on it.

The judges worked hard, and accepted no fees. (As a thank-you gesture, the Court of Aldermen commissioned Joseph Michael

Wright to paint their portraits, to be 'kept in some publique place of the citty for a gratefull memoriall of this good office'.[5]) They were active until 31 December 1668, after which their powers lapsed until 1670, when a second Rebuilding Act reconvened the Court for a further two years. It was revived again in 1673 and finally wound up on 25 February 1676. During the first, most hectic period, a pool of fourteen judges heard between them more than 800 petitions. In 1667 alone the Court was in session at Clifford's Inn for 120 days, hearing an average of three or four cases a day. Although some judges scarcely showed their faces at Clifford's Inn, the majority showed a remarkable degree of commitment: Sir Christopher Turnor, a 'quiet and unpretending' man, heard 292 cases in 1667–8; and Sir Thomas Tyrrell, a septuagenarian Justice of the Common Pleas, heard an awe-inspiring 383.*

The case of *Berry* v. *Waterman* shows how hard the Fire Court judges tried to reach a negotiated settlement, rather than imposing their will on the parties. It also illustrates some of the difficulties faced by landlords and tenants.

In 1658 Daniel Berry had acquired the lease to a dye-house in Cousin Lane, a little alley next door to the Steelyard and running from Thames Street down to the river. It was quite a big site, well over 6,000 square feet, with a jettied upper storey which projected out a full twelve feet over Cousin Lane and contained 'six rooms and two butteries'.[6] Berry was a woodmonger – a timber-merchant – and he had used the premises as a wharf and a warehouse. He paid £50 a year in rent, and when he got the lease it had nearly twenty-one years left to run.

In the Fire Berry lost everything, including the warehouse and £500 of stock. He was prepared to rebuild, but he felt that his landlord, Sir George Waterman, ought to help out by reducing

---

*Tyrrell was uncle to Sir Roger Pratt, and executor of Pratt's father's will. Turnor's finest hour came in 1660, when on his first circuit as a judge he refused to try three people indicted for murder on the grounds that there was no body. His successor at the next assize had no such qualms; the men were convicted and hanged, only for their victim to reappear some years later alive and well (Edward Foss, *The Judges of England* VII [1864], 176).

his rent, extending his lease or both. Waterman, a future Lord Mayor who was described as 'a person almost void of understanding' and 'most perverse',[7] refused to make any contribution to rebuilding costs. He owned a lot of property in Cousin Lane – according to Peter Mills's survey the entire lane 'belonged to Sir George Waterman and two others'[8] – and he wanted Berry to vacate the site, so that he could develop it himself. This was fairly common. Although some landlords sought to enforce the terms of their lease, leaving the tenant to bear the entire loss, others hoped that if they could persuade the lessee to relinquish the lease, they could improve the site themselves. Then they would make a tidy profit from negotiating a new lease with a new tenant in a new London which was crying out for houses, shops and warehouses.

Berry petitioned the Fire Court. The case was heard on 6 November 1667 before Sir Thomas Tyrrell and two other Justices of the Common Pleas, Sir Samuel Browne and Sir John Archer. Both the petitioner and the defendant appeared in person. Berry brought counsel and expert witnesses with him; Waterman apparently did not.

The Fire Court's guiding principle was that the purpose of the Rebuilding Act was to return tenants to their places of trade as swiftly as possible. When the tenant wanted to rebuild, the judges favoured him or her over the landlord, and that was their decision here. They declared that 'the petitioner being the party burnt out ought to be preferred as builder'.[9]

If only it had been as straightforward as that. The two sides couldn't agree on the value of the property, which was likely to be reduced, since jettied upper storeys were prohibited under the terms of the Rebuilding Act. They couldn't agree on the cost of rebuilding. Or their respective contributions. Or how those contributions should be made.

Since Waterman was being called on to contribute towards rebuilding costs, it was in his interest to underestimate them, and he suggested a figure of £600. But Berry brought in two builders, Adam Taylor and Richard West, who swore the rebuilding would cost £700. Eventually landlord and tenant got down to terms.

Berry asked for his rent to be halved to £25 p.a. To make his labours worthwhile, he also wanted his lease to run for fifty-one years from Michaelmas 1667, an extension of thirty-nine years on the original.

Waterman countered by offering his tenant £30 to surrender the lease. Clearly the two sides were still far apart. Berry insisted on his right to rebuild; and the judges stepped in to propose a compromise, a 20 per cent reduction in rent to £40 p.a. Both men turned that idea down flat. Berry upped his offer to £30 p.a., but Waterman held out for the original £50. Berry refused to budge, even when Waterman reluctantly came down to £40.

The Court's judgement shows how many variables they had to take into account. They decreed that Berry should be allowed to rebuild the property, and that his lease should be extended to fifty-one years, as he had asked. His new rent would be £36 p.a., but he was to have a rent holiday until Christmas 1668, by which time they expected him to have completed the building work. He was also ordered to pay rent owing up to the time of the Fire.

This wasn't Daniel Berry's only appearance at the Fire Court. He came to Clifford's Inn in April 1668, when he was an expert witness in a particularly complicated case involving two baronets, Alderman Sir Richard Browne and Sir Thomas Draper. They were cross-petitioning over a wharf in Alsatia, between Bridewell and the Temple. Browne was the tenant and wanted to rebuild a mansion house, counting house and stables on the site, with a corresponding extension of his lease and a reduction of rent. Draper's counsel argued there were only two years left to run on the lease and that before the Fire his client had decided not to renew, but to develop the site himself and build twenty-eight houses on it. 'Such an improvement would be to the public advantage and would be some satisfaction to Draper for his great losses by the Fire in other places.'[10]

Because of the Rebuilding Act, neither landlord nor tenant was allowed to build on a mandatory forty-foot buffer strip next to the Thames. Browne argued that his rent should be halved from £120 p.a. to £60 p.a. because anything left on the open wharf was no longer secure. (No doubt he was remembering that before the Fire Alsatia had been home to many of London's most notorious criminal elements.) Berry's role in the proceedings was to swear that the additional cost of employing men to carry coal and timber from the waterside over this strip would amount to exactly £60 p.a. Browne won the case, although he was told to pay Draper an annual rent of £90 – the judges split the difference.

Berry made yet another appearance at the Court, also in 1668. A neighbour in Cousin Lane, James Best, was petitioning because his landlords wouldn't contribute to rebuilding his wharf, and were suing him in the Sheriffs' Court to recover rent and enforce the covenants on the lease that made him solely responsible for rebuilding. His counsel told the Court that the landlord had in fact already agreed a rent-reduction and an extension of the lease, and Berry was one of two witnesses called to swear to this, which he duly did. Interestingly, one of the builders who gave evidence about the rebuilding was the bricklayer Richard West, who had appeared for Berry in his own case against Sir George Waterman. West quoted £700 as the cost of rebuilding in this case, too. Friends and neighbours stood by each other.

One of the more refreshing cases to come before the Fire Court was that of a Dutch merchant, John Vandermarsh, whose house in Lime Street on the north-east edge of the fire zone had been badly damaged but not destroyed. Vandermarsh leased the property from a man named Godschall, and had sub-let a section of it to one Edward Symons.

As the Fire neared Lime Street, Vandermarsh had moved out his goods and then pulled down the sub-let section to save the rest – or rather, he had paid local people the hefty sum of £50 to do it. His house still caught fire on one side; the firefighters managed to beat it out, although they had to pull off the roof and there was severe water damage to the floors and ceilings, which the Dutchman repaired at his own cost. Now he wanted to rebuild the rest of the property and, since the lease was about to expire, he asked Godschall for a new one on terms which would take account of all the money he was spending on the place. Godschall refused to renew the lease and also threatened to sue him on the covenants.

This was rather a nasty trick: the landlord was trying to force his tenant to make good all the fire damage to the property, but would then throw him out at the expiration of the lease, leaving a new house with vacant possession – and all at no cost to himself. But it got worse. When the case came before the Fire Court on 5 July 1667 Godschall did his best to exploit anti-Dutch feeling, claiming that Vandermarsh was 'an alien born in Holland', and thus legally barred from holding a lease.[11]

The merchant countered by producing papers showing he had become a naturalised citizen three years previously. Godschall then claimed that because the Lime Street house hadn't been totally destroyed, the Fire Court had no jurisdiction over the case. Fighting back, Vandermarsh introduced a parade of witnesses. They included neighbours, the parish constable and Sir Thomas Aleyn – the merchant's alderman, a former Sheriff and Lord Mayor. The gist of their evidence was that the house *had* been severely damaged, but subsequently repaired by Vandermarsh. They also stressed the role he had played in preventing the spread of the Fire, saving neighbouring homes 'by his great industry' and laying out large sums of money to urge the firefighters to greater efforts. The Court was convinced, and the three judges declared that 'in gratitude, civility and humanity the petitioner ought to be looked upon as a tenant fit to be encouraged and not to be turned out of his dwelling where he had so long lived, he being the means of saving the house from being consumed'.[12]

The support Vandermarsh received is all the more creditable since anti-Dutch feeling was still running very high indeed at the time of the hearing. The enemy incursion into the Medway had taken place only three weeks before. If that were not enough, seventy-two hours earlier 3,000 Dutch had landed in Suffolk with the object of capturing Harwich Harbour; they had been beaten back by the militia, but only narrowly. Even as the Court was sitting, enemy vessels were terrorising the south coast and blockading the mouth of the Thames. However, the fear and loathing of the Dutch which was currently sweeping through the City obviously did not extend to friends and acquaintances: it was much easier to hate strangers than it was to hate people you knew.

The evidence of firefighting heard during Vandermarsh's case is quite a rarity: the Fire Court's purpose was to speed up the rebuilding by arbitrating between landlord and tenant, not to hold an enquiry into the events of that first week in September 1666. But here and there details of those events came up. Richard Hilliard lost over £200 in wines and goods when the St John's Head Tavern in Chancery Lane was pulled down. Another vintner, Robert Davy, reckoned he had lost about £1,500 in wine and other goods. And there are frequent references to houses being demolished 'by authority to prevent the Fire spreading'* – such houses had the same status as those which burned down – and occasionally to partial demolitions. A clothworker named George Briers, for example, had just built a new timber house on a plot near Fetter Lane: labourers removed 'the roof and upper rooms and pales about the garden'.[13]

Most of the cases which came before the Fire Court involved a tenant trying to extract better terms from his landlord in order to make rebuilding worthwhile. Sometimes, though, the landlord was the petitioner. For instance, a joiner named William Boyfeild was summoned in May 1668 to explain why he hadn't paid any rent to his landlord since the Fire, or made any move towards rebuilding. He duly appeared to say he had lost the greater part of his estate in the Fire – his stock 'consisted of such materials as could not easily be removed' – and now he just wanted to surrender his lease and walk away. The Court allowed him to do so, on condition he paid two months' rent and a fine of £6 13s 4d.

One of the fears expressed when the Fire Court was first established was that the judges would be arbitrary arbitrators. They had considerable powers, and when the bill setting up the Court was first tabled, there was no right of appeal. This was modified on its way through the Lords, but only slightly: an appeal against

*For example, three houses on Tower Wharf were demolished by an order of the Privy Council dated 8 September 1666 'for preventing the fire coming to His Majesty's magazine in the Tower'; part of a house in Fenchurch Street was pulled down 'by Authority and almost all the rest burnt and spoilt'; and a section of a large house in Mark Lane was blown up (Philip Jones, *Fire Court* I [1966], 3, 24).

one of the Court's decrees was possible, but only to a larger gathering – seven judges – of the same Court. There were six appeals in the first two years; they were all dismissed.

The pattern was set early on. One of the Court's first decrees had been in the case of *Boylston* v. *Cressey*, which was heard on 13 March 1667. Thomas Boylston part-owned and part-leased a large building in Fenchurch Street, some of which had been pulled down 'by Authority'. Almost all the rest had been burned. He was happy to rebuild, asking only for a forty-year extension to his lease. His landlord, Thomas Cressey, refused, but was overruled by the Court 'to the intent that such refractoriness by the defendant should not retard rebuilding'.[14] Cressey's appeal was heard a month later. He argued that little or no part of the property had been burned, that only a small part of the roof had been pulled down, that none of the rooms had been damaged and that Boylston's people carried on working there after the Fire as they had before. Moreover, Cressey said, the place was very old and Boylston had been intending to rebuild it even before the Fire, and had offered to buy out his interest for £180.

The Court threw the case out and awarded costs of £3 6s 8d to Boylston because the appeal had been brought without just cause.

Justice was swift and sudden, but by and large it was remarkably fair: any idea that the Fire Court stood for the interests of the landlords was quickly dispelled. In one case the Bishop of Peterborough, who was only prepared to extend a tenant's lease if he could double his rent, was required to appear in person and told 'to consider the common calamity'.[15] He was allowed a 14 per cent rent rise.

There was gold to be found in London's ashes, and everyone with capital to spare was eager to start digging. On 26 September 1666 Pepys and Sir William Penn walked in the Navy Office garden by moonlight and discussed plans to import timber from Scotland; they came to nothing, but others were bringing in timber from Ireland, Norway, Sweden and, of course, the rest of England. The Privy Council noted in December 1666 that 'divers

Timber Merchants are already buying up the Timber in the Country for the building of London'.[16] Sir Thomas Bludworth, who specialised in importing timber, also began to trade in lead; he was paid £574 by the Fishmongers for supplying them with the lead for the new Hall that Jerman designed. John Evelyn lost £500 in a scheme with a Dutch refugee, John Kiviet, to make bricks from Thameside mud. Quick-witted citizens in Moorfields, St Giles and Islington began excavating their fields for brick-earth and setting up their own brick-making works; we can get some notion of the scale of these enterprises from the example of Henry Tindall, who leased some land in Finsbury and in just over three years managed to manufacture well over 5.5 million bricks. An average house required around 30,000 bricks, while a large mansion might take 2 million.[17]

A number of entrepreneurially minded Dutchmen also saw their chance to capitalise on the disaster, war or no war. One such was a Rotterdam sea-captain, Teunis Willemsen. During the Four Days' Fight in June Vice-Admiral Sir William Berkeley's *Swiftsure* had been cut off from the rest of the fleet and surrounded; he refused to surrender, even when the *Swiftsure* was boarded, and fought on until he was shot through the throat. He retreated to his cabin and was found by the Dutch sprawled over a table and dead. They carried his body back to Holland, where he was embalmed and put on show (or laid in state, depending on one's point of view) in the Grote Kerk in the Hague for several months, before being returned to England for burial. Willemsen was the master in charge of bringing Berkeley home and, as soon as he saw the shortage of timber for building, he petitioned the King for a free pass so that he could fetch and deliver deal boards. At least one other Rotterdam vessel followed his example, petitioning for a licence to bring timber over from Norway, 'which is much needed for the rebuilding of the city after the late calamity of fire'.[18]

Not all foreigners were as welcome as Willemsen, perhaps unsurprising in a city in a state of shock. Years after the Fire Londoners were still on edge. The Dutch raid on the Medway in June 1667 gave the English such a fright that on 31 July they concluded the Treaty of Breda, which brought the war to an end.

But in London especially, foreigners continued to be treated with suspicion and hostility. A servant of the Venetian Ambassador provoked a riot in the autumn of 1668 when he met a drunk on the street late one night and pushed him out of the way. The man fell down and began to shout that he was being murdered: within minutes people came pouring out of their houses and laid siege to the Ambassador's house. They would have broken down the doors if the Sheriff hadn't arrived with a contingent of the militia.

The Spanish Ambassador had an even more difficult time. On 5 November 1668 some boys threw fireworks into his coach as he passed by, attracting a mob which followed him right to the steps of his house. The Ambassador had to draw his sword and barricade his household behind the doors of the embassy while they waited to be rescued by soldiers sent by the Duke of Albemarle.

In the meantime, work pressed ahead with rebuilding the City's key institutions. Along with the Royal Exchange, the Guildhall was at the top of the list, and it had the added appeal of still being reasonably intact. In spite of Vincent's haunting picture of it glowing for hours after the Fire had passed, 'in a bright shining coal, as if it had been a palace of gold', much of the fifteenth-century masonry had survived. Repair work was authorised in November 1666, and it was well advanced by the following winter. In May 1669, three weeks before fear of blindness led him to give up his diary for ever, Pepys walked by and commented that it was almost finished. (He also saw a labourer being carried away from the site, 'dead with a fall, as many there are, I hear'.[19]) He was premature: by the end of 1671, when it was fitted out for the Lord Mayor's Banquet, the Guildhall was still being described as almost rebuilt, and work continued for another four years, by which time it had cost a considerable £37,422, all but a fraction of which was drawn from the coal tax.

If the late 1660s promised to be golden years for the building trades and their suppliers, the authorities were keen to ensure that prices and wages didn't spiral out of control. The Rebuilding

Act foresaw that a finite supply of men and materials coupled with unprecedented demand was likely to end in trouble, and set out some pretty draconian measures to limit the damage. If either building workers or the suppliers of brick, tile and lime went beyond what the City considered reasonable in their charges, then two or more Justices of the King's Bench were empowered to arbitrate between customers and tradesmen and, failing that, to fix a price for materials or a wage for labour. If anyone tried to extort more (or indeed, if anyone agreed to give more) they could be gaoled for up to one month or fined £10.

Ironically, the most effective weapon against opportunistic building workers was deregulation. In theory, only freemen were allowed to practise their trades in the City; so artisans in the building trades had to belong to a Company in order to work there.★ The Act put a stop to that, for the moment at least. It decreed that for the next seven years, anyone employed in the rebuilding of London had the same right to work as had the freemen of the building trades, no matter where they came from. If the rebuilding took longer than seven years, then the right of outsiders to work would be extended; and if any artisan exercised that right for a full seven years, he would be rewarded with the privilege of working as a freeman for the rest of his life.

A steady flow of builders began to move into the ruined City from all over the country, drawn by the prospect of work and rates of pay which even in more settled times were generally higher than elsewhere. The quarry-owner Thomas Strong left his native Cotswolds and 'took up masons with him to London to work with him, to serve the City in what they wanted in his way of trade, and continued there in that employment many years till most of the houses and halls were built'.[20] A neighbour and fellow quarry-owner, Christopher Kempster of Burford, began

★They didn't have to belong to their trade's Company, though. Edward Pierce, a prominent mason-contractor who worked on the Guildhall, five Company Halls and four of the City churches, was a member of the Painter-Stainers; and Thomas Lock, the master carpenter who succeeded Edward Jerman as Surveyor to the new Apothecaries' Hall, belonged to the Fishmongers.

by supplying stone for the rebuilding and ended up following Strong to the capital; so did Thomas Wise, who was involved in running the royal quarries on the Isle of Portland.

Slowly, at first, the massive work of clearing and rebuilding began. In the spring of 1667, Londoners noticed that wooden piles were being driven into the ground to mark out the routes of the major streets. Debris was removed from cellars and gardens, and here and there new homes appeared alongside the huts and temporary shelters. There was also a marked increase in building activity in the outlying suburbs, as displaced families made the decision to settle outside the City's walls. Those suburbs were quick to capitalise on London's ruin and to threaten its old commercial supremacy: walking through Moorfields in April, Pepys was unsettled to see how many substantial new houses had sprung up. The neighbourhood 'must become a place of great trade till the City be built,' he wrote, 'and the street is already paved as London streets used to be – which is a strange, and to me an unpleasing sight.'[21]

Needless to say, the relaxation of restrictive practices didn't go down well with the relevant City Companies, who saw their hard-won monopolies disappearing before their eyes. They harassed the incomers, and petitioned the authorities for powers to monitor their work and control their activities. They argued that only freemen of the City should be allowed to operate as contractors, which would have given them all the profits from building jobs and kept outsiders in the role of hired hands. They ignored the Rebuilding Act altogether and took out civil actions against the carpenters and masons and other trades who were taking work which by right should have been theirs. None of it did any good. If London was to rise from the ashes it needed all the skilled workmen it could find, and even the City authorities, traditional and jealous guardians of the Companies' privileges, realised this. The petitions were rejected, the arguments were ignored, and the order was given that actions against incomers must be abandoned.

The Companies were right to fear deregulation, if the example of the Carpenters is anything to go by. In spite of repeated attempts to prosecute 'forrens' for not conforming to City regulations, the

Company was swamped by outside labour. By the early 1670s, when the flood of building work began to subside, many of its members found themselves out of work. Hardest hit were the journeymen carpenters; things got so bad that the Company petitioned the Court of Common Council to let these journeymen gather each morning in front of the Royal Exchange so that contractors looking for freemen could hire them. The Court agreed, and allowed them 'to stand in a peaceable manner during the pleasure of this Court on the Backside of the Royall Exchange in Threadneedle Streete every working morning from 5 of the clocke till seaven, in order to be hired provided at 7 of the Clocke they doe without faile quitt the said place'.[22]

But there was no question that deregulation had a beneficial effect on the reconstruction, if not on the London building trades. After a brisk start there was a delay during the summer of 1667, probably the result of the general sense of insecurity brought about by the Dutch raid in June and the difficulty in transporting materials round the coast while the Dutch were so active. The 1667 building season came to an end that autumn with only a few hundred houses put up; but builders more than made up for this the following year, completing nearly 1,500 houses. By 1670 around 6,000 had been built, and by the middle of the decade most of the burned houses had been replaced.

This was quite an achievement, and since each and every building had to be approved beforehand by the City's Surveyors, it was only made possible by their Herculean efforts. Between them, Robert Hooke, Peter Mills and John Oliver surveyed, staked out and recorded thousands of foundations. On a single day, Saturday 4 April 1668, Mills and Oliver set out nine sites, and in the course of that month they managed a remarkable seventy-five. Each and every survey was carefully copied into a folio volume. A typical entry reads:

Robert Fuller.
Aprill the 23rd 1668

Two Foundacions set out the day above said scituate in Shoe

Lane belonging to Mr Fuller containing upon the front North and South 33 foot from the out of his own wall South to the out of a brick and a halfe Wall North Mr Richardson on the South side Mrs Brown on the North Side.[23]

Nor were they simply staking out foundations; they also noted transgressions and misdemeanours. 'Mr Allinson hath taken from Tanner at the North end ten inches and at the South end eight inches,' runs one note.[24] Another says that an ironmonger named Thomas Garret had built 'an irregular house' in Foster Lane. The back wall was only two bricks thick, when it should have been two-and-a-half; and the upper part rested on a timber partition eighteen feet long and ten feet high, 'and a Pile of Chimneys placed upon the Timber'.[25] History doesn't record if any action was taken against either Allinson or Garret.

In spite of dire warnings of the fines, imprisonment and floggings that faced anyone who tampered with the Surveyors' work, there is no doubt that there was some sharp practice. Stakes were shifted, and buildings were quietly extended beyond the permitted limits. Josiah Child, a powerful merchant who would later rise to become Governor of the East India Company, saw the Surveyors staking out some land in Billingsgate and told them that they might as well mark off as his a plot which formed part of St Botolph, since the church was not going to be rebuilt and he intended to buy the land when it came onto the market. They did as they were told; but although Child built warehouses on the plot, which he rented out for between £500 and £600 a year, he didn't buy it. It took the City nearly twenty-five years of legal action to recover the land.

The story of Anthony Selby offers a particularly good example of the kind of quagmire into which the authorities could fall when the rules were flouted with bravado. Selby was a rich draper who did not take kindly to being told what he could and couldn't do with his own property. He had been one of the first petitioners to appeal against a Fire Court decision (which related to some premises he leased on Fish Street Hill), a move which led the judges not only to confirm their original verdict against him, but also to show their displeasure by making him give £5 to the defendants. At around the same time, Selby found himself in trouble over four houses he owned on Mincing Lane and its southern extension, St Dunstan's Hill. When the street was staked out in May 1667 he lost several feet to the widening scheme, which called for a new width of twenty-four feet. This wasn't good enough; so while his neighbour across the street, a wine merchant named John Hammond, was away, he persuaded Peter Mills to adjust the line. As Hammond said in a complaint to the City and the Privy Council that July, Mills 'did cause the Stake that was in Mr Selby's Ground to be plucked out, and placed without his foundation & drave one new stake four foote into the Petitioner's Ground'.[26] The street was now crooked: and the timber framework which Hammond had commissioned for his houses was useless. Just as bad was the fact that the new line deprived him of his wine vault under Mincing Lane.

Hammond was told that he could go ahead as planned, and that Selby would have to adhere to the lines that had been set out in the original survey. But Selby was one of those men who not only resent outside interference in their affairs, but also ignore it completely. He continued to regard the strip in front of his property as his, and began building accordingly. 'Both hee, & his workmen give out that they will finish it notwithstanding all Opposition,' complained an anguished Hammond, who took his grievance to the Lord Mayor, to Robert Hooke and, yet again, to the Privy Council.[27] Hooke and the Lord Mayor ignored him, but the Council responded by ordering the City to hold an inquiry to establish if there was any truth in Hammond's claim. It did, and there was: Selby had illegally pushed out his Mincing Lane street frontage by an amount which varied from two feet ten inches at the north end to a full five feet at the south. He had done the same on St Dunstan's Hill. And he declined an invitation to appear before the inquiry and explain himself.

There was a full meeting of the Court of Aldermen, and Selby was ordered to take down his buildings. He refused, and petitioned the Privy Council himself. When that failed, he persuaded the House of Commons to refer the matter to a Parliamentary

Committee, a move which bought him three months of breathing space. Then the City ordered him once more to pull down the offending buildings, and demanded he put up a bond of £1,000 to ensure that he complied within two months. Still he was in no mood to compromise: he responded by 'offering his body to Imprisonment rather than to submitt'; and by continuing to build his houses.[28]

On 19 September 1668 the Restoration equivalent of the bull-dozers moved in. Peter Mills and a group of workmen arrived in Mincing Lane, accompanied by constables who were directed to keep the peace. They demolished Selby's four houses. Mills, whose error of judgement had started the whole business, rather sanctimoniously noted with disapproval that 'all the back parts are built with Timber'.[29]

Anthony Selby sounds like a detestable man; however, one can't help but admire his perseverance. With his new houses in ruins, and a string of judgements against him, he reacted by suing Mills, Hooke, Oliver and the workmen who had carried out the demo-lition work. To the dismay of the City, Sir Matthew Hale, the Chief Baron of the Exchequer who heard the case, didn't find against the draper. Instead he recommended a negotiated settle-ment. More than three months later the City finally reached an agreement with Selby, whereby they bought the site from him as it stood for £2,000, plus another £70 in compensation for the strip which the street-widening scheme demanded. It emerged that Selby had actually bought the land *after* the Fire, and had paid only £450 for it.

The whole affair goes to show what happens when consensus breaks down. If enough people had behaved as Anthony Selby did, then the rebuilding of London would have descended into a confusion of anarchy and litigation. Fortunately, Selby's case wasn't typical; but it served to show the City that their grasp of the rebuilding process was fragile, and that they must do every-thing possible to hang on to it.

All things considered, the progress of the rebuilding was quite remarkable. The Exchange was in use by September 1669 and finished in 1671, by which time the Guildhall was also usable, if still far from complete. The Old Bailey Sessions House was one of the first City institutions to be rebuilt, and its next-door neighbour, Newgate Prison, was completed by 1672. Most of the Company Halls were finished by the early 1670s, and Charles II's promise immediately after the Fire to 'use all the expedition we can to re-build our custom-house . . . and enlarge it with the most conveniencies for the merchants that can be devised' was fulfilled in 1671.[30]

It was with the new Custom House, a project which had been dogged with difficulties from the start, that Christopher Wren made his first real impact on the new City. The Custom House was managed by the Farmers of Customs, and not directly by the Crown; the freehold of the site was owned by Sir Anthony Cope, and the building itself was part of a complex of private warehouses leased by their tenants from Cope. Charles's efforts to make the rebuilding of the Custom House a priority were bogged down in a mire of legal wrangles over just who was going to pay for what, and it was only in February 1669 that they were sorted out and the Treasury agreed a grant of £6,000.

As Surveyor-General of the King's Works, Sir John Denham, who had surveyed the site with Hugh May two years earlier, was nominally responsible for the design of the building. But a few weeks after the grant was approved he died and, much to everybody's surprise, King Charles appointed Wren as his successor. Wren kept his chair in astronomy at Oxford (he didn't resign until 1673), but he launched into his new job with enthusiasm, discarding Denham's plans, coming up with his own *and* persuading the Treasury to accept them and increase their grant by 50 per cent – all within weeks of his appointment. Finished in the summer of 1671, his Custom House was a grand two-storeyed affair with pavilions and arcades, set back from the river on a new site immediately in front of the old. It was only his fourth building, and his first in London.

But throughout the late 1660s Wren had maintained his links with the capital. In the immediate aftermath of the Fire, the authorities in charge of St Paul's had opted to repair the old building, and the Dean, William Sancroft, had turned for advice to Wren, whose hopes for the future of the cathedral had been so spectacularly dashed. In November 1666 he suggested that in the short term the west end of the nave could be roofed over and used for services; but he also urged Sancroft to consider launching an appeal to fund an entirely new building. Given the times, it was impractical to hope that the new could be on a similar scale to the old; but 'I believe the reputation of Paules and the compassion men have for its ruines may at least produce some neate fabrick, wch shall recompence in Art and beauty what it wants in bulke.'[31]

It was not until the spring of 1668 that work finally began on the repairs. It soon stopped: part of the surviving section of the nave collapsed, taking the scaffolding with it and causing the workmen to run for their lives. Sancroft wrote again to Wren, who responded by urging 'a new fabrick upon new foundations, artificiall durable and beautifull, but lesse massive, and to use the old but as you would use a quarry'. He realised that, with labour and materials in short supply and commanding premium prices, now was a bad time to begin building, but 'a few years will rid away much of the private worke of the town, and then handes and materialls will be cheaper'.[32]

In May 1668 Wren came up to London to survey the damage caused to the ruins by the fall of masonry. Yet again he pushed Sancroft to begin fund-raising for a new cathedral. His efforts paid off: in July he was formally invited to 'frame a Design, handsome and noble, and suitable to all the Ends of it, and to the Reputation of the City, and the Nation'.[33] He was to take it for granted that money would be forthcoming.

Demolition work began on the old choir and crossing tower in August. This in itself was a massive task; and it caused more deaths than the Fire, as an army of labourers clambered over the dangerously unstable walls and battered away with pickaxes at the stonework. Broken limbs and fatal falls were regular occurrences; and after workmen refused to climb up the great tower, which still stood nearly 200 feet high, a military engineer from the Tower of London was brought in to mine one of the four pillars supporting it. Working with Wren, he placed an eighteen-pound charge of gunpowder in a deep cavity at the foot of the pillar, sealed it in with stone and mortar and laid a long train of powder as a fuse.

The spectacular explosion that followed was described much later by Wren's son. It shifted the masonry, he said, 'somewhat leisurely, cracking the Walls to the Top, lifting visibly the whole Weight about nine Inches, which suddenly jumping down, made a great Heap of Ruin in the Place without scattering, it was half a Minute before the Heap already fallen open'd in two or three Places, and emitted some Smoke'.[34] The ground shook, and citizens in the neighbourhood thought there had been an earthquake.

The experiment was such a success that it was repeated by one of Wren's assistants. However, he overestimated the amount of powder needed and underestimated the depth of the cavity; the result was that when the mine was detonated, a chunk of masonry flew across St Paul's Churchyard and landed in a private house, much to the surprise of the women who were sitting in it at the time. Understandably anxious for the safety of their newly rebuilt homes, local people petitioned the Dean; and Wren was directed to leave off the use of gunpowder.

Nevertheless, more than 45,000 loads of rubble were carted away from the site. The debris in St Faith's was cleared, the coffins and bones that had been disturbed were reinterred, and masons sorted through the stones to find material that could be recycled. The rubbish was washed and sifted for lead, which was melted and cast for use in the new building. And to ensure that it *was* used in the new building, wooden fences were put up, night watchmen were employed and two mastiffs guarded the site.

The progress of St Paul's depended on two things – a design which everyone approved of, and the money to turn that design into a building. Wren, whose pre-Fire interest in the cathedral had blossomed into an obsession, was the de facto architect in charge (although he wasn't officially appointed until November 1673); and he was eager and willing to produce the design. But he was aware that, as he told Sancroft, 'it is silver upon which the foundation of any work must be first layd';[35] and his first proposal, worked up in the winter of 1669–70, reflected the financial constraints. It flouted the conventions for Anglican cathedrals, discarding the traditional components of nave, choir and transepts in favour of a single auditory box; and it was small, only about 180 feet by 70 feet.★

In 1670 Parliament passed the second Rebuilding Act. This made various amendments to the 1667 Act – the Fire Court was revived, for example – but its most significant effect was a dramatic extension of the coal tax. As of May 1670 this was levied on all parishes served by the Port of London, which effectively meant the entire Thames estuary; it was trebled to three shillings per chaldron; and its life was extended for an extra ten years. Half of the money was to go towards rebuilding the City's churches, and a quarter of that sum – 4½d per chaldron – was earmarked specifically for St Paul's.

The prospect of all this money led Sancroft and Wren to rethink their ideas, and over the next five years the latter created at least three different designs for the cathedral.

There was the so-called 'Greek Cross', a huge and very unEnglish centralised space covered by a monumental dome, with four stubby arms projecting out to the cardinal points of the compass. This evolved into the 'Great Model', which extended the western arm of the Greek Cross to house a library and vestibule under a second dome. The Great Model, which derives its name from the fact that Charles II ordered an eighteen-foot-long wooden model of it to be built 'as a perpetual and unchangeable rule and direction for the conduct of the whole work', was Wren's favourite, and throughout his long life – he died in 1723 at the age of ninety-one – he always regretted that he was denied the chance to build it. But England and Holland went to war again in 1672, and this had a serious effect on the coal dues, since the vast majority of English coal was transported by sea and was thus an easy prey for Dutch raiders. As a result, the revenue which Sancroft and Wren had expected simply didn't materialise, and the Dean and Chapter decided they would prefer a more conventional cathedral plan with a choir, transepts and a nave. They wanted something which could be built in easy stages

★The final scheme for St Paul's Cathedral was 550 feet by 320 feet.

as and when funds became available; and they were more than a little anxious about the unconventional, rather Catholic appearance of the Great Model. Wren had set out to provide a Protestant rival to St Peter's Rome, and they were all in favour of that. But did it have to look quite so odd, quite so *foreign*? Couldn't their architect come up with something a little more familiar?

Wren reluctantly obliged. His next design, worked out in the early months of 1675, was an odd mixture, a traditional plan plastered in the kind of classical detail which Inigo Jones had introduced to the old cathedral in the 1630s. It was, as Wren's son later said, an attempt 'to reconcile, as near as possible, the Gothick to a better Manner of Architecture'.[36] A warrant was issued for its construction in May 1675, nearly nine years after the Fire, and on 21 June the foundation stones were laid. Although the Warrant design was accepted as the official scheme, the King told Wren that he might tinker with the details as he went along, making 'variations, rather ornamental, than essential, as from Time to Time he should see proper';[37] and that the management of the whole project was left in his hands. The architect took a liberal view of what was involved in varying the ornaments: he dispensed with the old-fashioned Jonesian trappings, designed a marvellous and innovative triple-skinned dome, and in the process created the familiar London landmark which is still one of Britain's greatest buildings.

Restoration Londoners had been proud of their great cathedral, and looked forward to seeing it rebuilt:

> Now let our *Pauls*, and stately buildings rise,
> And be a terror to our Enemies;
> Surely ambitious States will now despair,
> When they shall hear how brave and rich we are.[38]

Little did they realise that by the time it was finished in 1710, nearly half a century after the Fire, most of them would be dead. But their relationship with their churches was more intimate, more vital. The parish church was where the rituals of baptism, marriage and burial took place, the centre of communal life. It was where congregations gathered on Sundays and holidays to worship a God who intervened in their daily lives in a direct manner which the twenty-first century finds hard to understand; a God who did not wait until after death to mete out punishment and reward.

The whole question of rebuilding the City's burned churches hung in the air for years after the Fire. The Church of England's first post-Fire scheme, to reduce them from eighty-six to thirty-nine, was not popular. The choice of which to resurrect and which to damn to oblivion was fraught with problems. It led to accusations of vested interests and of a disregard for the needs of ordinary people, as the most powerful patrons insisted that *their* churches must be among the chosen. The entire process was calculated 'to add humane Rage against those places where the Divine displeasure hath left us hope of making them agayne fit for his service'.[39] The Church could not make up its mind quite what to do; so for four years it did nothing. In the meantime, a number of individual parishes took matters into their own hands. By 1670, seven churches, mainly those whose walls at least were still standing, were being patched up, with the repairs paid for by public-spirited parishioners.

Under the 1670 Rebuilding Act the figure of thirty-nine churches scheduled for reconstruction rose to a more acceptable fifty-one, and each pre-Fire parish was given guarantees that it would retain its own identity, even where it shared a church with its neighbour. Most importantly, the new Act gave the building programme public funding. From now on the rebuilding of churches would be financed by the extended coal dues – a move which immediately led those parishes which had jumped the gun and gone ahead with repairs to petition for retrospective funding. By and large, they were successful.

The Commissioners appointed under the new Act – the Archbishop of Canterbury, the Bishop of London and the Lord Mayor – named Wren as the man 'to direct and order the dimensions, formes and Modells of the said Churches',[40] to negotiate with contractors and craftsmen, and to control the payment of the considerable sums of money which would be involved in such a huge building scheme. The following month Robert Hooke and Edward Woodroffe (the Surveyor to the Dean and

Chapter of Westminster) were appointed as Wren's assistants. But, as with St Paul's, money from the coal dues was slow to come in. It would have been absurd even to think of beginning work on all of the churches simultaneously, so the Commissioners chose a first wave of fifteen, including five of those which had already been started. The work was slower than anyone could have imagined; it would continue for another forty-seven years. For now, though, Wren, Hooke and Woodroffe were instructed to:

> take an account of the extent of the parishes, the sites of the churches, the state and conditions of the ruins and accordingly prepare fit models and draughts to be presented for his Majesty's approbation and also estimate proper to inform us what share and proportion of the money out of the imposition upon coals may be requisite to allow for the fabric of each church.[41]

As a stopgap measure, twenty-seven wooden huts, each with a communion table and a pulpit, were set up in churchyards around the City. They were pulled down and their materials sold as and when their sites were needed.

Meanwhile, on Thursday and Saturday mornings the three men* met at the Surveyor-General's house in Scotland Yard or the site office in Paul's Churchyard to discuss progress. They were businesslike, and much of their time was spent in the prosaic business of negotiating with contractors, fending off impatient deputations of parish worthies and accepting the occasional 'present' of wine, plate or hard cash given to encourage them to devote their efforts to one particular church or another. Wren and Hooke did most of the creative work, and between them they designed the fifty-one churches, along with four new ones in the western suburbs.† It is all but impossible to disentangle

---

*Woodroffe died in 1675. He was replaced by John Oliver.

†St Anne Soho; St Bride Fleet Street; St Clement Dane; St James Piccadilly. A fifty-sixth church, St Thomas the Apostle, Southwark, is usually included in the list, simply because by 1697 it was falling down — through no fault of the Fire — and funds from the coal tax were voted towards a new building.

their respective roles in what was a very close collaboration, but they clearly revelled in the challenges presented by difficult sites and difficult clients: the sheer variety of buildings which went up bears witness to that. There were simple but beautiful boxes, like St Benet Gracechurch or St James Piccadilly; squares and rectangles and wildly irregular parallelograms; a hexagon (St Olave Old Jewry); even a decagon, St Benet Fink. Seven churches had central domes; three were based on the cross-within-a-square design which derived from Jacob van Campen's Nieuwe Kerk in Haarlem. In three cases – St Alban Wood Street, St Mary Aldermary and St Sepulchre – the parish put its foot down and insisted on a comfortable and familiar pre-Fire Gothic. But, like St Paul's, most were aggressively contemporary and classically inspired – a new architecture for a new London.

14

Malicious Hearts

The phoenix: an early Wren design for the Monument.

*I*n 1681 a commemorative plaque was placed in Pudding Lane. Apart from the Butchers' Hall, put up when the Company abandoned the ruins of their old Hall in Newgate Street, the lane where the 'dreadful conflagration' had begun was filled with modest houses and shops – much as it had been before the Fire, in fact. But the Pudding Lane that had risen from the flames was wider, and the houses were brick-fronted and only two storeys high, without the projecting overhangs which had been barred by the Rebuilding Acts.

The plaque was set into the wall of one of these new buildings, the one which stood on the site of Farriner's bakery. When it was unveiled, presumably to mark the fifteenth anniversary of the disaster, its deeply incised and deeply felt message of hate was revealed for all London to see:

Here by ye Permission of Heaven Hell broke loose upon this Protestant City from the malicious hearts of barbarous Papists,

264

by ye hand of their Agent Hubert, who confessed, and on ye Ruines of this Place declared the Fact, for which he was hanged, (vizt.) that here began that dredfull Fire, which is described and perpetuated on and by the neighbouring Pillar.

Erected Anno 1681 in the Mayoraltie of Sr Patience Ward Kt.

The Fire was not an act of God after all, it seemed, but an act of terrorism. Its commemoration was not a call to reconciliation, but a cry for revenge.

As the inscription implies, the chief instigator of the Pudding Lane plaque was Sir Patience Ward, the current Lord Mayor. Ward was a wealthy merchant with a background typical of any man who achieved mayoral office: he had been an alderman for eleven years; he was an ex-Sheriff; he was a past Master of his Company, the Merchant Taylors. He was also a man of determined views,* chief among which was a hatred of Roman Catholics and everything they represented. In his election speech as Lord Mayor at Michaelmas 1680 he expressed an ardent Protestantism, and one of the themes of his mayoral pageant was the need for unity among Protestants: 'Divide them, and destroy them, is the Pope's / Maxim, and Ready road to all his Hopes'.[1]

But Ward's zeal in blaming the Fire of London on 'the malicious hearts of barbarous Papists' was a product of his time as well as a personal statement. In 1672–3 James, Duke of York had come out as a Roman Catholic. If, as seemed likely, Charles had no legitimate offspring and his brother succeeded him, a Papist would sit on the throne of England. No one dared attack the Duke publicly or in print, but the Fifth of November was celebrated with a new intensity, with bigger bonfires and plenty of Pope-burnings. And some vicious libels circulated in manuscript. One, for example, asked if was not high time to settle the question of the succession 'so as may secure us from those bloody massacres and inhuman Smithfield butcheries, the certain consequences of

*As was his father: Thomas Ward apparently called his son Patience because he was hoping for a daughter and saw no reason to alter his choice of forename when his wife gave birth to a boy.

a Popish government?'[2] Rumours began to grow of a military coup, sponsored by France and led by James, which would bring in Catholicism and arbitrary government.

Then in the late summer of 1678 two anti-Catholic agitators, Titus Oates and Israel Tonge, went before a justice of the peace in Westminster and swore that they had evidence of a Jesuit plot to kill the King and bring about the succession of his brother. London was to be burned, and 20,000 Catholics would rise up and cut the throats of 100,000 Protestants. Oates was a crook and a liar, Tonge a zealous bigot with more than a touch of religious mania; and their story, which they embellished until it implicated even the Duchess of York and the Queen, was full of contradictions and inconsistencies. But as Bishop Gilbert Burnet wrote in his *History of My Own Times*, 'there are seasons of believing as well as of disbelieving, and believing was then so much in season that improbabilities or inconsistencies were little considered'.[3] The season of believing was given a helping hand by the fact that a few weeks after Oates and Tonge made their formal depositions, the Westminster JP who heard them, Sir Edmund Berry Godfrey, was found dead in a ditch with his own sword stuck through him. Godfrey's death has never been satisfactorily explained; at the time it was manna from heaven for the conspiracy theorists, cast-iron evidence of a Popish plot.

It is hard for us to understand the irrational fear and loathing with which English Protestants regarded Catholics during the late 1670s. Paranoia spread through society like fire. A maid was hanged for burning a house in Southwark as part of a Catholic plot; packs of playing cards were distributed showing Jesuits offering money to people to burn down buildings; prints circulated with an image of the Pope spewing flames from his mouth while London burned.[4] The evidence originally presented to Sir Robert Brooke's Parliamentary Committee was reissued, under the title of *London's Flames*: it included more recent accounts 'touching the Insolency of Popish Priests and Jesuits and the Increase of Popery', and left its readers to draw their own conclusions about the Duke of York's conduct in rescuing so many suspicious foreigners during the Fire.[5] When a blaze broke out in the Middle Temple in January 1679 and the Duke turned up to deal with it – in a reprise of his heroic role during the fire-fighting in 1666 – he had to run for his life as the crowds barracked him and yelled that he was a Popish dog.

Anti-Catholic rhetoric plumbed new and frightening depths. Soon after the Middle Temple fire – which was of course blamed on the Papists – an otherwise civilised lawyer named William Lawrence wrote with approval of a Swedish method of deterring Jesuits. When the Swedes caught a Jesuit, he was placed in a shed and had his testicles stapled to a block; then he was given a knife and the shed was set on fire, so that he was faced with a choice between castrating himself and being burned alive. 'Thus the Swedes have secur'd their Nation from this vermine, and now none of them dare be nibbling there for feare of the Trap.'[6]

By the time the madness was over, thirty-five innocent men had been executed for their parts in a non-existent conspiracy, and an epidemic of fanatical Protestantism had infected the entire country. One result was a re-evaluation of the Fire. Titus Oates and his friends had focused everyone's minds on the Catholics' ruthless ability to use fire as a weapon: according to Oates's narrative, part of the plan to destabilise the nation involved burning Westminster, Whitehall and all the shipping at anchor downriver at Wapping. But Oates also claimed that in 1666 eighty Irish and French Jesuits and Dominicans had used seven hundred fire-balls to reduce London to ashes; and that the looting and pilfering that went on was not carried out by ordinary thieves. While the fire merchants were at work, their confederates had ransacked houses and taken anything worth stealing. Some of the plunder was stored in a secret warehouse, but the most valuable goods – fine cloths, quantities of plate, and a box of jewels which had been stolen from a goldsmith – were taken to Somerset House. (Somerset House had long been regarded with suspicion because it harboured the Catholic chaplains of Henrietta Maria and Catherine of Braganza.) Oates said his Jesuit source had admitted that they had intended to kill the King while he was directing the firefighting operations, 'but then they were not secure of the duke, who was then but a well-wisher to them, and besides, they seeing the king so industrious, could not find it in their hearts to do it'.[7]

In January 1681, the hysteria roused by this emetic nonsense led to the House of Commons (of which Patience Ward was a member) passing a series of resolutions. One gave thanks to the City of London for its loyalty to the King and its vigilance in preserving His Majesty's person and the Protestant religion; another put forward the opinion that the prosecution of Protestant Dissenters was an encouragement to Popery and a danger to the peace of the kingdom. A third stated that the Duke of Monmouth had been removed from office by the influence of the Duke of York. The King's bastard son was the darling of the Protestant cause, and a focus for opposition to James; two years earlier he had been dismissed from most of his court appointments after claiming that Charles had secretly married his mother, thus making him the legitimate heir to the throne.

A fourth resolution stated quite unequivocally that 'the City of London was burnt in the Year One Thousand Six hundred Sixty-and-six, by the Papists; designing thereby to introduce arbitrary Power and Popery into this Kingdom'.[8]

The culture of blame spread like a plague; and there were some surprising casualties. The loyal Samuel Pepys was one of the victims. Pepys had had a rough time of it in the years following the Fire. Elizabeth died of typhoid in 1669, when she was only twenty-nine; in 1673, his Seething Lane home was burned to the ground in a fire which destroyed the Navy Office and spread to another thirty houses in the neighbourhood. Then in 1679 he was caught up in the wake of the Popish Plot; he was accused in the Commons of being a clandestine Catholic, forced to resign from the Admiralty (to which he had moved from the Navy Board) and thrown into prison on suspicion of selling naval secrets to the French. John Evelyn, who refused to be caught up in the general paranoia, had dinner with him in the Tower and noted in his diary afterwards that 'I believe he was unjustly charged.'[9] He was released after six weeks and never brought to trial, but it would be years before he regained his position.

Joseph Williamson was another victim of the witch-hunt. From working on the *Gazette* as chief spin doctor to the Crown, Williamson had risen to become Charles II's principal Secretary of State. But in 1679 he dared to speak in Parliament against a motion to exclude the Duke of York from the King's presence and councils, and the Commons had him committed to the Tower. Within hours Charles stepped in to order his release, but he was nevertheless removed from office.

Others who played a part in the Fire had gone. Thomas Farriner died in 1670. So did George Monck; King Charles paid for his state funeral and the Bishop of Salisbury preached his oration in Westminster Abbey, praising Albemarle's 'impregnable Taciturnity'.[10] His wayward admiral Sir Robert Holmes retired to the Isle of Wight, where he held office as Governor-General and ruled over his territory like a feudal warlord. After surviving plague and fire, Thomas Vincent's luck had run out: he died suddenly in 1678, aged only forty-four, after years of 'excellent and unwearied labours in the pulpit, to a numerous congregation' in Hoxton.[11] William Taswell's education at Westminister School had obviously done him some good: he became an academic, and in 1681 was made Greek Professor of Christ Church, Oxford. Sir Robert Vyner, the rich goldsmith-banker who had done so much to finance the government in the 1660s, was no longer rich. He had been ruined in the Stop of the Exchequer of 1672, when the government arbitrarily ceased paying interest on some of its debts; after struggling on for years, he went bankrupt in 1681.

Sir Thomas Bludworth had only a year left to live. Aged and ailing, his days were still dogged by memories of the Fire. In 1672 an anonymous report on the state of government in London judged, quite rightly, that 'his greatest misfortune was that he was Mayor when London was burnt down'.[12] Now, in the anti-Catholic hysteria that was sweeping through every level of society, it was being suggested that he had conspired with the Papists to fire the City, that he was wicked rather than merely incompetent.

A letter to his prospective son-in-law gives one of very few glimpses into Bludworth's personal life. Writing in May 1679 from his country house at Leatherhead in Surrey, he laments that his delicate physical condition may not allow him to bring his daughter up to London:

> If my health doth compel me to stay my company and keep your mistress from you till Monday (as I believe it must), I pray put it upon my score who will promise to redeem it for time to come to your better advantage and satisfaction; and if in the meantime your joys be not so full as people give you, make it up with thinking that the time will come.[13]

Curiously enough, the ardent bridegroom-to-be was Hanging Judge Jeffreys, who was already well known for his cruelty in the trials following the Popish Plot, and who would achieve lasting notoriety at the 'Bloody Assizes' in the wake of the Monmouth Rebellion of 1685. And, even more curiously, Bludworth's daughter Ann seems to have been a match for him: described as a 'dragon' in a contemporary lampoon, she gave birth exactly eight months after their marriage, 'much too early for a common calculator to say otherwise than that there had been a mistake somewhere'. The author of the 'mistake' was popularly supposed to be Jeffreys' cousin.

Throughout the sound and fury of the Popish Plot, petitions expressing loyalty to the King and the Protestant religion were all the rage. London inns were provided with tables, forms and pen and ink specifically so that drinkers could be persuaded to sign – one petition given to the King in 1680 was three hundred feet long. On 2 September 1681, the fifteenth anniversary of the outbreak of the Fire, a deputation called at the Guildhall to present Sir Patient Ward with a petition which, they claimed, was from over 20,000 loyal Protestant apprentices. Expressing their abhorrence of Catholicism 'and all its Bloody Traiterous Practices', the petitioners said that they had chosen to visit him that day because it commemorated 'the Burning that Famous Protestant City by Papists, Jesuits, and Tories'.[14]

Declarations of faith and hate were everywhere. Ward and the City authorities were responsible for the memorial in Pudding

Lane; but as the inscription on that tablet implied, there was a second, more prominent monument to the Fire. The first Rebuilding Act had stipulated that 'the better to preserve the memory of this dreadful visitation', a pillar of brass or stone should be put up on or near the site of Farriner's bakery.[15] Early in 1671 the City approved a model, but the pillar, which was put up on the site of St Margaret Fish Street at the northern end of London Bridge, took another six years to complete; and its long commemorative inscriptions took another two years after that. Costing a grand total of £13,450 11s 9d, the 'Fish Street Piller' is in the form of a fluted Doric column on a square pedestal, with a square viewing platform at the top; it is crowned by a drum, a little dome and finally a flaming urn of gilt bronze. The column is hollow, with 311 steps leading up to the observation deck, and the whole thing is 202 feet high, which was said to be the exact distance from the base to Farriner's bakery in Pudding Lane.

The Monument (and the fact that it is always referred to simply as 'the Monument' speaks volumes for the Fire's place in the capital's consciousness) was designed by Christopher Wren and Robert Hooke. Together and separately they worked on several schemes, including a plain obelisk and a column garnished with tongues of fire. They also toyed with a number of different ornaments for the crown. Wren's first idea was a phoenix rising from the flames, but at quite a late stage he changed his mind, arguing that no one would be able to recognise it from the ground, and it would in any case be a danger to the public 'by reason of the sayle, [since] the spread winges will carry in the winde'.[16] In the end, he favoured a fifteen-foot statue of King Charles, or perhaps a sword-wielding female personification of London triumphant. The King himself wanted a gilded copper ball with flames sprouting from its top, which would be simple, and cheap — around a third of the price of the statue. It was Hooke who came up with the idea of the flaming gilt-bronze urn; and, perhaps because he was the City's man, the City agreed with him.

There are four panels around the base of the column. Three of them are filled with Latin inscriptions which were devised by

Dr Thomas Gale, who was the high master of St Paul's School and, like Wren and Hooke, a Fellow of the Royal Society. Gale did a good job, although one wonders how many passers-by, even in the more classical climate of the late seventeenth century, were able to appreciate his eloquence.

The panel on the north side records the story of the City's destruction – the extent of the damage, the houses, churches and public buildings that were burned. 'Merciless to the wealth and estates of the citizens, it was harmless to their lives, so as throughout to remind us of the final destruction of the world by fire.'[17] On the south panel Gale focused on the rebuilding. King and Parliament were praised for remitting taxes, for setting up the Fire Court, for building the Monument and establishing an annual service of intercession.★ And the objectives of the Rebuilding Acts were described in surprising detail:

> That churches, and the cathedral of St Paul's should be rebuilt from their foundations, with all magnificence; that the bridges, gates and prisons should be new made, the sewers cleansed, the streets, made straight and regular; such as were steep levelled and those too narrow made wider, markets and shambles removed to separate places. They also enacted, that every house should be built with party-walls, and all raised of an equal height in front, and that no man should delay building beyond the space of seven years.

Gale went on to announce that 'three short years complete that which was considered the work of an age'; and historians have taken him to task for his optimistic approach to the truth. Even in 1681, two years after his inscription was cut, the landmark that was St Paul's Cathedral was nowhere near complete. The walls of the choir had only reached a height of about thirty feet, and there

★The 1667 Rebuilding Act set aside 2 September to be 'yearely for ever hereafter observed as a day of Publique fasting and humiliation'. The annual ritual in St Paul's, which was attended by the Lord Mayor, the Sheriffs, the aldermen and the Court of Common Council, was only allowed to lapse in the nineteenth century.

were no floors – just a vast open pit sixteen feet deep down to the bare foundations. 'There is an appearance of a church below as well as above the ground', wrote one visitor that November.[18] Seventeen of the City churches hadn't been started yet; eighteen were in the process of being built; and of the twenty-one which could be considered finished, most had neither tower nor steeple, and three would need a lot more work when the long-term effects of fire damage and hasty repairs started to show in the 1690s.

But that should not blind us to an incredible achievement. Most of London's homes, businesses and corporate institutions had indeed been resurrected, like Wren's phoenix, from the flames which destroyed them. The Monument celebrated the fact that replacement housing had been finished, the arguments over compensation and landlord–tenant relations had been settled, the Fire Court had done its work and been disbanded. The streets were wider and the houses more solid; the burnt-out City Companies had new halls and the Guildhall was repaired. Thomas Gresham's Royal Exchange had been rebuilt, hence the inscription's reference to 'three short years' – the Exchange was in use by September 1669, and, for a community which revolved around commerce, a restored Exchange was a renewed City.

The Monument's east panel, a necessary civic namecheck listing the seven Lord Mayors under whose auspices it was built, is less interesting than the other two. But in any case, in late 1680 or early 1681 Sir Patience Ward and the City authorities decided that the whole thing needed a little more edge to it. In Gale's Latin original the inscription on the north side ended by announcing that on the third day, at the bidding of heaven, the flames stayed their course and died out. Now, a new sentence was added: 'But Popish frenzy, which wrought such horrors, is not yet quenched'. And, round the pedestal, Ward and the Court of Common Council introduced an extra inscription, echoing the sentiments of the Pudding Lane plaque:

This Pillar was set up in perpetual remembrance of the most dreadful Burning of this City; begun and carried on by the treachery and malice of the Popish Faction, in the beginning of September, in the year of our Lord 1666, in order to the effecting this horrid Plot, for the extirpating the Protestant Religion, and English Liberties, and to introduce Popery and Slavery.[19]

The Fire was reinvented as a Popish plot. Its Monument was not a glorious commemoration of a city which had been triumphantly resurrected from the ashes of a hideous accident, but a constant reminder of perfidy and sedition. Charles Blount, the author of *An Appeal from the Country to the City, for the Preservation of His Majesties Person, Liberty, Property, and the Protestant Religion*, urged those of his readers who had the strength to climb to the top of the column, where they could imagine 'the whole Town in a flame, occasioned this second time, by the same Popish malice which set it on fire before'.[20]

Tablet, addition and pedestal inscription were all removed when the Duke of York came to the throne as James II in 1685, only for them to be recut and returned to their places in the reign of his Protestant daughter Mary and her husband William of Orange. For another 140 years the words provoked anger and bitterness among English Catholics and their friends. Alexander Pope's couplet in the *Moral Essays* is the most well-known comment on its message of bigotry and hate – 'Where London's column pointing at the skies, / Like a tall bully, lifts the head, and lies'[21] – but Thomas Ward, in *England's Reformation* (1710), is more bitter still. Discussing Titus Oates and his accusation that Catholics had burned the City in 1666, he writes of how

> That sniffling Whig-mayor Patience Ward,
> To this damn'd lie had such regard,
> That he his godly masons sent
> T' engrave it round the Monument.
> They did so; but let such things pass,
> His men were fools, and he an ass.[22]

It was not until 1830, the year after the passing of the Catholic Emancipation Act, that the Court of Common Council ordered the offending words to be removed. The Pudding Lane tablet ended up in two pieces in a cellar, where it was found in 1876 and presented to the Guildhall Museum.

Luckily, Sir Patience Ward did nothing to interfere with the sentiments expressed in the Monument's fourth panel. Carved by the Danish artist Caius Gabriel Cibber, the panel on the west side of the column is one of London's most moving pieces of allegory, and perhaps the finest single work of art to be spawned by the Fire.★

Cibber portrays London as a distraught woman, an image which also occurs in Fire literature.† She half sits, half lies on a pile of broken masonry – exhausted, damaged, her head dropping down and her long hair loose about her shoulders. Winged Time is supporting her and helping her rise to her feet, while a female figure, perhaps the personification of Good Government, points with her sceptre to the goddesses of Peace and Plenty who hover, full of promise, in the clouds. Houses are burning in the background, while a beehive, a symbol of Industry, lies at London's feet.

To the right of this group stand the King and the Duke of York, both in Roman dress. Charles is commanding Science and Architecture to go to the aid of stricken London, and Liberty is following them. James clutches a garland of bays and waits, ready to offer it to the rising city, while Justice and Fortitude look on and a new urban landscape takes shape in the background.

★Cibber's other work includes the altarpiece in the chapel at Chatsworth in Derbyshire, the poignant figures of Melancholy and Raving Madness which were carved for Bethlehem Hospital, and the remarkable monument to Thomas Sackville in St Michael's Church at Withyham in Sussex, described by Rupert Gunnis as 'undoubtedly one of the finest in England'. The £600 Cibber was paid for his Fire allegory must have been particularly welcome, since he was in prison for debt at the time; he was allowed out each day to work on the relief, but had to return to his cell at night.

†As for instance, in 'Vox Civitatis: or, Londons Call to her Natural and Adopted Children' (1666), ll. 19–20 – 'And now, methinks I see the aged Head/Of *London* Town move from her too warm Bed'.

The sentiment, like the figures, is a little stiff, perhaps a little too mannered for modern taste. But the allegory still has the power to move us, and to remind us that London would eventually emerge from the ruins not twisted by hate, but braver and better-equipped to face the future. It is reassuring to see that Cibber's image of hope and confidence has survived into the twenty-first century, while the words of intolerance smeared over its stones by Ward and his kind have long gone.

At St Paul's, that other, greater icon of London's renewal, Cibber created an equally potent symbol of optimism for the future. Over the south transept of the cathedral the sculptor carved a phoenix, nine feet high and with a wingspan of eighteen feet – the creature which Christopher Wren had first proposed and then discarded as the crowning feature of the Monument. The mythical bird hovers over a single word taken from Matthew 27:63 – *Resurgam*. 'I will rise again.'

The idea for the design was Wren's. One day in the early 1670s, when he was laying out the site of the new St Paul's, the architect asked a labourer to bring him a flat stone to use as a marker. The man sorted through a pile of rubble and came back with a fragment from a gravestone, with nothing left of the inscription except that one word, *Resurgam*.

But the anecdote had a significance which went beyond the personal. This resonance with Christ's promise to his disciples was a happy omen to those who heard the story at the time, and a source of reassurance to those who saw it cut in stone when the new cathedral was unveiled decades later. London had survived its trial by fire. If it really *was* by permission of heaven that hell broke loose on that Sunday morning in September 1666, then perhaps heaven was ready to make amends.

Notes

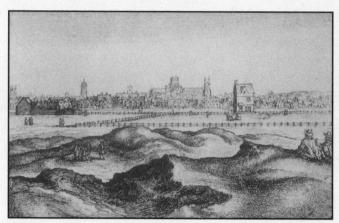

Fields and open country to the north of pre-Fire London.

Chapter 1

1   *The Journals of Sir Thomas Allin 1660–1678*, ed. R. C. Anderson, (Navy Records Society, 1939), 286.

2   John Evelyn, *A Character of England* (1659), 4.

3   John Stow, *The Survey of London* (1603; Everyman edn., 1912), 243.

4   Anne Crawford, *A History of the Vintners' Company* (Constable, 1977), 160.

5   Roger L'Estrange, *Newes*, quoted in Walter G. Bell, *The Great Plague in London in 1665* (Bodley Head, 1924), 277.

6   Quoted in Ben Weinreb and Christopher Hibbert, *The London Encyclopaedia* (Macmillan, 1995), 498.

7   *The Diary of John Evelyn*, ed. William Bray (Simpkin, Marshall, Hamilton, Kent & Co., N.D.), 29 October 1664.

8   'The Plague of London Anno Domini 1665', anonymous MS poem quoted in Bell, *Great Plague*, 346.

9   *The Diary of Samuel Pepys*, eds. Robert Latham and William Matthews (HarperCollins, 1983), 29 June 1665.

10   Thomas Vincent, *God's Terrible Voice in the City* (1722 edn.), 42.

11   *ibid.*, 43.

12 M. A. E. Green (ed.), *C[alendar] of S[tate] P[apers], D[omestic] series of the reign of Charles II, 1666–7* (1864), 17.

13 Ralph Hope to Joseph Williamson, *CSPD 1666–7*, 53.

14 Robert Scrivener to James Hickes, *CSPD 1666–7*, 75.

15 Richard Watts to Joseph Williamson, *CSPD 1666–7*, 70.

16 Evelyn, *Character of England*, 7.

17 John Evelyn, *Fumifugium, or The Inconveniencie of the Aer and Smoak of London Dissipated* (1661), 6.

18 Pepys, *Diary*, 25 June 1665.

19 *ibid.*

20 J. R. Powell and E. K. Timings (eds.), *The Rupert and Monck Letter Book, 1666* (Navy Records Society, 1969), 122.

21 R. C. Anderson (ed.), [An anonymous contemporary account of] 'Naval operations in the latter part of the year 1666', *The Naval Miscellany* III (Navy Records Society, 1927–8), 20–1.

22 *ibid.*, 23.

23 Powell and Timings (eds.), *Rupert and Monck Letter Book, 1666*, 126.

24 Anderson (ed.), *The Naval Miscellany* III, 24.

25 Marc Antonio Giustinian, Venetian Ambassador in France, to the Doge and Senate, 31 August 1666 (N.S.); *C[alendar] of S[tate] P[apers] Venetian* XXXV (HMSO, 1935), 60.

26 The attack on Terschelling inspired several anonymous street poets, of whom the best is the author of 'Sir Robert Holmes his Bonfire, or the Dutch Doomsday' (1666).

Chapter 2

1 George Wharton, *Calendarium Carolinum* (1666).

2 William Lilly, *Monarchy or No Monarchy* (1651).

3 Anon., 'Mourne London Mourne', Bodleian MS Ashmole 47, 140 v.

4 Walter Gostelo, *The coming of God in Mercy, in Vengeance; Beginning with fire, to Convert, or Consume, at this so sinful City London* (1658).

5 Christopher Wren (ed.), *Parentalia: or, Memoirs of the Family of the Wrens* (1750), 146.

6 Francis Potter, *Interpretation of the number 666* (1642), 11, 77.

7 Pepys, *Diary*, 10 November 1666.

8 Quoted in Derek Parker, *Familiar to All: William Lilly and Astrology in the Seventeenth Century* (Jonathan Cape, 1975), 227.

9 Richard Saunders, *Apollo Anglicanus* (1666).

10 Roger L'Estrange, *The Newes*, 5 January 1665.

11 William Lilly, *Merlini Anglici Ephemeris* (1666).

12 Saunders, *Apollo Anglicanus*.

13 William Andrews, *Newes from the Starres* (1666).

14   Evelyn, *Diary*, 29 May 1660.

15   *Gazette*, 30 April 1666.

16   *ibid.*

17   Peter Crabb to Lord Arlington, *CSPD 1666–7*, 31.

18   C[orporation] of L[ondon] R[ecords] O[ffice], Sessions File, July 1663; quoted in Tim Harris, *London Crowds in the Reign of Charles II* (CUP, 1987), 61.

19   'The Rump Carbanado'd', in *A Collection of Loyal Songs Written Against the Rump Parliament, Between the Years 1639 and 1661* (1731), II, 124.

20   Richard Watts to Joseph Williamson, *CSPD 1666–7*, 81.

21   *Gazette*, 30 August 1666.

22   *CSPD 1666–7*, 37.

23   *Gazette*, 30 August 1666.

24   Samuel Sorbière, *A Voyage to England, Containing Many Things Relating to the State of Learning, Religion, and other Curiosities of that Kingdom* (1709), 16.

25   *Les Voyages de M. de Monconys en Angleterre* III (1695), 38.

26   Quoted in Peter Earle, *The Life and Times of James II* (Weidenfeld & Nicolson, 1972), 59.

27   Powell and Timings (eds.), *Rupert and Monck Letter Book, 1666*, 143.

28   *ibid.*, 138.

29   Pepys, *Diary*, 27 August 1666.

30   *ibid.*, 1 September 1666.

31   *ibid.*

32   *Journals of Sir Thomas Allin 1660–1678*, ed. Anderson, 287.

33   Anderson (ed.), *The Naval Miscellany* III, 33.

34   *ibid.*

Chapter 3

1   Stow, *Survey of London*, 189.

2   *ibid.*, 195.

3   Samuel Wiseman, 'A Short and Serious Narrative of London's Fatal Fire' (1667), ll. 29–34.

4   'Rege Sincera', *Observations both Historical and Moral upon the Burning of London, Harleian Miscellany* III (1809), 292.

5   Pepys, *Diary*, 2 September 1666.

6   *ibid.*, 17 March 1663.

7   Unknown correspondent to Lord Conway, September 1666, in Marjorie Hope Nicolson (ed.), *The Conway Letters: the Correspondence of Anne, Viscountess Conway, Henry More, and their Friends, 1642–1684* (OUP, 1930), 278.

8   James Peller Malcolm, *Londinium Redivivum* (1802–7); quoted in Gordon

Huelin, *Vanished Churches of the City of London* (Guildhall Library, 1996), 12.

9   See E. L. Jones, S. Porter and M. Turner, *A Gazetteer of English Urban Fire Disasters, 1500–1900* (Historical Geography Research Series XIII, 1984), *passim.*

10   John Hilliard, *Fire From Heaven* (1613); quoted in David Underdown, *Fire From Heaven: Life in an English Town in the Seventeenth Century* (HarperCollins, 1992), 4.

11   Pepys, *Diary*, 29 December 1662.

12   1643 broadside, reprinted in *Harleian Miscellany* VI (1810), 400.

13   Gottfried von Bülow (trans.), 'Journey through England and Scotland made by Lupold von Wedel in the years 1584 and 1585', *Transactions of the Royal Historical Society* New Series IX (1895), 255. The translation uses the phrase 'fire engines', an anachronism which is not justified by the original text.

14   1643 broadside, *Harleian Miscellany* VI (1810), 400.

15   Abstract from the Patent Roll No. 2329, 22 James I, pt. 6, No. 12; quoted in Rhys Jenkins, 'Fire-extinguishing Engines in England, 1625–1725', *Transactions of the Newcomen Society* 11–12 (1932–33), 23.

16   Thomas Fuller, *History of the Worthies of England* (1662); quoted in *ibid.*

17   Lords of the Council to the Lord Mayor and Court of Aldermen, 1637; quoted in J. B. P. Karslake, 'Early London Fire-Appliances', *Antiquaries' Journal* IX (1929), 232.

18   Sir Edward Atkyns to Sir Robert Atkyns, 8 September 1666, in *Archaeologia* XIX (1821), 105.

19   William Taswell, 'Autobiography and Anecdotes by William Taswell D.D.', ed. George Percy Elliott, *Camden Miscellany* II (1853), 11.

20   Quoted in Karslake, *Antiquaries' Journal* IX, 231.

21   Vincent, *God's Terrible Voice*, 66.

22   Pepys, *Diary*, 2 September 1666.

23   *ibid.*

24   *ibid.*

25   Sir Edward Atkyns to Sir Robert Atkyns, 8 September 1666, in *Archaeologia* XIX (1821), 105.

26   Taswell, 'Autobiography', 11.

27   *Gazette*, 3 September 1666.

28   Vincent, *God's Terrible Voice*, 69.

29   Pepys, *Diary*, 2 September 1666.

30   Vincent, *God's Terrible Voice*, 68.

Chapter 4

1   Edward Hyde, Earl of Clarendon, *The Life of Edward, Earl of Clarendon* II (OUP, 1857), 281.

2   William Cobbett (ed.), *Cobbett's Complete Collection of State Trials and Proceedings* VI (1810), 848.

3   Vincent, *God's Terrible Voice*, 67.

4   Taswell, 'Autobiography', 11.

5   Petition, 1612, in *H[istorical] M[anuscripts] C[ommission]* 9 (Salisbury MSS XXII), 5–6; quoted in Tim Harris, *London Crowds in the Reign of Charles II* (CUP, 1987), 199. I am indebted to Dr Harris's illuminating study for much of the following discussion of foreigners in Restoration London.

6   W. H. Overall and H. C. Overall, *Analytical Index to the Series of Records known as the Remembrancia* (1878), 305.

7   Evelyn, *Character of England*, 4.

8   Frances Parthenope Verney and Margaret M. Verney, *Memoirs of the Verney Family During the Seventeenth Century* II (Longmans, Green & Co., 1907), 255.

9   *CSPD 1666–7*, 95.

10 *Cobbett's State Trials* VI, 849.

11 Vincent, *God's Terrible Voice*, 71.

12 Evelyn, *Diary*, 3 September 1666.

13 John Rushworth to an unknown correspondent, 8 September 1666, in *Notes and Queries* 5th Series V (15 April 1876), 306.

14 Windham Sandys to Viscount Scudamore; quoted in W. G. Bell, *The Great Fire of London* (John Lane, 1923), 316.

15 James Hickes to Joseph Williamson, 3 September 1666, *CSPD 1666–7*, 95.

16 *HMC* 25 (Le Fleming MSS), 41.

17 *Gazette*, 3 September 1666.

18 Pepys, *Diary*, 3 September 1666.

19 *ibid*.

20 Undated letter to Lord Conway in Nicolson (ed.), *Conway Letters*, 277.

21 Anon., 'London Undone; or, A Reflection upon the Late disasterous fire' (1666), ll. 37–42. 'Corydon' was a generic proper name in pastoral poetry for a shepherd, or a rustic of any kind.

22 Vincent, *God's Terrible Voice*, 72.

23 *ibid*., 71.

24 Simon Ford, 'London's Remains', *Three Poems Relating to the Late Dreadful Destruction of the City of London by Fire* (1667), ll. 207–10.

25 Wiseman, 'London's Fatal Fire', ll. 171–4.

26 Joseph Guillim, 'The Dreadful Burning of London: Described in a Poem' (1667), ll. 199–208.

27 Taswell, 'Autobiography', 12.

28 Stow, *Survey of London*, 122.

29 Wiseman, 'London's Fatal Fire', ll. 141–2.

30 Vincent, *God's Terrible Voice*, 72.

31   Evelyn, *Diary*, 3 September 1666.
32   *CSPD 1666–7*, 95–6.
33   Powell and Timings (eds.), *Rupert and Monck Letter Book*, 148.
34   Coventry in conversation with Pepys, *Diary*, 4 June 1664.
35   Pepys, *Diary*, 3 September 1666.
36   Sir William Coventry to Lord Arlington, *CSPD 1666–7*, 95.

Chapter 5

1   *CSPD 1666–7*, 99.
2   Guillim, 'Dreadful Burning of London', ll. 227–32.
3   Quoted in Tom Girtin, *The Triple Crowns – A Narrative History of the Drapers' Company 1364–1964* (Hutchinson, 1964), 258.
4   Vincent, *God's Terrible Voice*, 75.
5   John Rushworth to an unknown correspondent, 8 September 1666, in *Notes and Queries*, 5th Series V, 306.
6   *Gazette*, 10 September 1666.
7   Unknown correspondent to Lord Conway, September 1666, in Nicolson (ed.), *Conway Letters*, 277.
8   Simon Ford, 'Conflagration of London', *Three Poems . . .* , 211–12.
9   John Rushworth to an unknown correspondent, 8 September 1666, in *Notes and Queries*, 5th Series V, 306.
10   Clarendon, *Life* II, 292.
11   *ibid.*, 295.
12   *CSPD 1666–7*, 99.
13   *ibid.*
14   *HMC* 29 (Portland MSS III), 298.
15   P. D. A. Harvey (ed.), 'A Foreign Visitor's Account of the Great Fire, 1666', *London & Middlesex Archaeological Society* New Series 20 (1961), 84.
16   *ibid.*
17   Cobbett's *State Trials* VI, 846.
18   Harvey (ed.), *London & Middlesex Archaeological Society* New Series 20, 84.
19   Guillim, 'Dreadful Burning of London', ll. 237–44.
20   Sorbière, *Voyage to England*, 16.
21   Vincent, *God's Terrible Voice*, 76.
22   John Crouch, '*Londinenses Lacrymae*: London's Second Tears mingled with her Ashes' (1666), ll. 201–2.
23   Pepys, *Diary*, 4 September 1666.
24   'The True Report of the Burning of the Steeple and Church of St Paul's in London', in A. F. Pollard (ed.), *Tudor Tracts 1532–1588* (Archibald Constable & Co., 1903), 405.
25   Sir John Denham, *Cooper's Hill* (1642), ll. 15–18, in Brendan O. Hehir, *Expans'd Hieroglyphicks – A Critical Edition of Sir John Denham's Cooper's*

Hill (University of California Press, 1969), 139; Evelyn, *Diary*, 19 October 1661.

26   *The Wren Society* XIII (OUP, 1923–43), 14.

27   Evelyn, *Character of England*, 4.

28   *Wren Society* XIII, 13.

29   Roger Pratt's first report on the fabric of the cathedral, Bodleian Tanner MS 145, No. 109, in *ibid.*, 15.

30   R. T. Gunther (ed.), *The Architecture of Sir Roger Pratt* (OUP, 1928), 290.

31   Abraham Hill to John Brookes, 19 May 1663, quoted in Charles Saumarez Smith, 'Wren and Sheldon', *Oxford Art Journal* 6 (1, 1983), 46.

32   Christopher Wren, 'Proposals to the Right Honourable the Commissioners for the Reparation of St Paul's Cathedral', Bodleian Tanner MS 145, 110–12; reprinted in *Wren Society* XIII, 16, 17.

33   Bodleian Tanner MS 145, 112–13; reprinted in *ibid.*, 18.

34   Bodleian Tanner MS 145, 115; reprinted in *ibid.*, 44.

35   Evelyn, *Diary*, 27 August 1666.

36   *ibid.*

37   Taswell, 'Autobiography', 12.

38   Vincent, *God's Terrible Voice*, 74.

39   Evelyn, *Diary*, 4 September 1666.

40   Crouch, 'Londinenses Lacrymae', ll. 179–84.

41   Evelyn, *Diary*, 5 September 1666.

42   Windham Sandys to Lord Scudamore; quoted in Bell, *Great Plague*, 316.

Chapter 6

1   Wiseman, 'London's Fatal Fire', ll. 285–8.

2   Crouch, 'Londinenses Lacrymae', ll. 223–4.

3   Verney and Verney, *Memoirs of the Verney Family* II, 257.

4   Windham Sandys to Viscount Scudamore, quoted in Bell, *Great Fire*, 317.

5   *ibid.*

6   Pepys, *Diary*, 5 September 1666.

7   *ibid.*

8   Evelyn, *Diary*, 7 June 1659.

9   Evelyn, *Fumifugium*, 17.

10   *CSPD 1666–7*, 100.

11   John Dryden, *Annus Mirabilis*, ll. 1129–30; in *The Poems of John Dryden* I, ed. Paul Hammond (Longman, 1995).

12   Andrew Clark (ed.), *The Life and Times of Anthony Wood, Antiquary, of Oxford, 1632–1695* II (1892), 86.

13   Richard Johnson, *Pleasant Walks of Moorfields* (1607); quoted in N. Brett-James, *The Growth of Stuart London* (George Allen & Unwin, 1935), 455.

14   Evelyn, *Diary*, 5 September 1666.

15   Clarendon, *Life* II, 294.
16   Proclamation of 19 September 1666, *CSPD 1666–7*, 140.
17   Proclamation of 5 September 1666, *ibid.*, 100.
18   Clarendon, *Life*, 287.
19   Quoted in Bell, *Great Fire*, 173.
20   Evelyn, *Diary*, 7 September 1666.
21   Stow, *Survey of London*, 242.
22   Pepys, *Diary*, 5 September 1666.
23   John Tabor, 'Seasonable Thoughts in Sad Times' (1667), ll. 181–6.
24   Clarendon, *Life* II, 287.
25   'Theophilus Philalethes', 'Great Britains Glory' (1672), ll. 55–8.
26   Vincent, *God's Terrible Voice*, 77.
27   Harvey (ed.), *London & Middlesex Archaeological Society* New Series 20, 85.
28   Evelyn, *Diary*, 7 September 1666.
29   Windham Sandys to Viscount Scudamore, quoted in Bell, *Great Fire*, 317.
30   *ibid.*
31   Crouch, *'Londinenses Lacrymae'*, ll. 209–18.

Chapter 7

1   Tabor, 'Seasonable Thoughts', ll. 225–6.
2   In Philip E. Jones (ed.), *The Fire Court* I (William Clowes & Sons, 1966), 3 (G. A–8; B.M. 5063–7).
3   'Theophilus Philalethes', 'Great Britains Glory', ll. 83–6.
4   *CSPD 1667–7*, 104.
5   *ibid.*
6   Taswell, 'Autobiography', 13.
7   Crouch, *'Londinenses Lacrymae'*, ll. 167–70.
8   James Wright, 'An Essay on the Present Ruins of St Paul's Cathedral' (1668), ll. 53–6.
9   *ibid.*, ll. 59–60.
10   John Aubrey, *Aubrey's Brief Lives*, ed. Oliver Lawson-Dick (Mandarin, 1992), 70. One of the tasters was Edmund Wylde, a Fellow of the Royal Society; his companion was the scientific instrument maker Ralph Greatorex.
11   Taswell, 'Autobiography', 13.
12   *ibid.*
13   *ibid.*
14   Pepys, *Diary*, 6 September 1666.
15   Silas Taylor to Joseph Williamson, *CSPD 1666–7*, 99.
16   Clark (ed.), *Wood's Life and Times* II, 86–7.
17   Richard Watts to Joseph Williamson, *CSPD 1666–7*, 102.
18   John Knight to Joseph Williamson, *ibid.*, 103.

19   Col. Thomas Middleton to Samuel Pepys, *ibid.*, 96.
20   Lord Arlington to Sir Thomas Clifford, *ibid.*, 99.

Chapter 8

1   Pepys, *Diary*, 7 September 1666.
2   Verney and Verney (eds.), *Memoirs of the Verney Family* II, 142.
3   Gilbert Burnet, *The History of My Own Times* I (1833 edn.), 397.
4   Evelyn, *Diary*, 7 September 1666.
5   *HMC* 25 (Le Fleming MSS), 42.
6   Sir Edward Atkyns to Sir Robert Atkyns, 8 September 1666, in *Archaeologia* XIX, 106.
7   Hollar's 'before' view of London was actually a reworking of his 1647 panorama, the famous *Long View of London From Bankside*; the artist adapted it as a companion piece for the new 'after' view of the City in ruins. Hollar's vantage point of St Mary Overie still stands, although much altered: it became the Cathedral Church of St Saviour and St Mary Overie in the late nineteenth century.
8   Clarendon, *Life* II, 293.
9   John Evelyn to Sir Samuel Tuke, 27 September 1666; reprinted in Evelyn, *Diary*, 398n.
10   Clarendon, *Life* II, 292.
11   Quoted in Girtin, *The Triple Crowns*, 259.
12   Quoted in F. T. Phillips, *A Second History of the Worshipful Company of Cooks* (Worshipful Company of Cooks, 1966), 43.
13   Sir Edward Atkyns to Sir Robert Atkyns, 8 September 1666, in *Archaeologia* XIX, 107.
14   *Gazette*, 13 September 1666.
15   Verney and Verney (eds.), *Memoirs of the Verney Family* II, 258.
16   Nicolson (ed.), *Conway Letters*, 277.
17   *Gazette*, 10 September 1666.
18   Burnet, *History* I, 426.
19   Pepys, *Diary*, 14 January 1668.
20   'Rege Sincera', *Harleian Miscellany* III, 287.
21   Tabor, 'Seasonable Thoughts', ll. 195–6, 199–200, 203–6.
22   Dryden, *Annus Mirabilis*, ll. 903–4; Evelyn, *Diary*, 7 September 1666.
23   Clarendon, *Life* II, 289.
24   Vincent, *God's Terrible Voice*, 88, 89.
25   'Diary of William Whiteway', *Proceedings of the Dorset Natural History and Antiquarian Field Club* XIII (1892), 62.
26   'Rege Sincera', *Harleian Miscellany* III, 292.
27   Pepys, *Diary*, 2 September 1666.
28   Clarendon, *Life* II, 286.

29   Pepys, *Diary*, 8 September 1666.

30   Vyner's bill for the coronation regalia alone came to a colossal £31,978 – Dorothy K. Clark, 'A Restoration Goldsmith-Banking House: The Vine on Lombard Street', *Essays in Modern English History in Honor of Wilbur Cortez Abbott* (Kennikat Press, 1971), 12–13. I am indebted to Ms Clark's article for what follows on Vyner's career.

31   R. P. Mahaffy (ed.), *Calendar of the State Papers relating to Ireland 1666–9* (Stationery Office, 1911), 259.

32   Pepys, *Diary*, 7 September 1665.

33   *Gazette*, 10 September 1666.

34   *ibid.*

35   *ibid.*

36   *ibid.*, 20 September 1666.

37   James Hickes to Joseph Williamson, *CSPD 1666–7*, 340.

38   Pepys, *Diary*, 23 April 1668.

39   *ibid.*, 7 September 1666.

40   *ibid.*, 3 June 1667.

41   John Evelyn to Sir Samuel Tuke, 27 September 1666; reprinted in Evelyn, *Diary*, 399*n*.

42   A. Rupert Hall and Marie Boas Hall (eds.), *The Correspondence of Henry Oldenburg* III (University of Wisconsin Press, 1966), 226.

43   Clark (ed.), *Wood's Life and Times* II, 86.

44   Verney and Verney, *Memoirs of the Verney Family* II, 259.

45   Pepys, *Diary*, 11 September 1666.

46   *ibid.*, 12 September 1666.

47   *ibid.*, 15 September 1666.

48   *ibid.*, 27 September 1666.

49   *CPSD 1666–7*, 246.

50   Pepys, *Diary*, 9 November 1666.

51   *ibid.*

52   *ibid.*, 28 February 1667.

53   *ibid.*, 23 March 1667.

54   *ibid.*, 24 March 1667.

Chapter 9

1   Anon., *A Poem on the Burning of London* (1667), ll. 7–8.

2   Marc Antonio Giustinian, Venetian Ambassador to France, to the Doge and Senate, 5 October 1666 [N.S.]; *CSP Venetian* XXXV, 80.

3   *ibid.*

4   *Extraordinarie Gazette*, 15 October 1666. Was this a jibe at Sir Robert Holmes's behaviour in August?

5   *Kurtze jedoch warhafftiger Relation von dem erschrechkichen Feuer-Brunst welcher den 12, 13, 14, 15 und 16 Septembris die Stadt Londen getroffen;* translated in Bell, *Great Fire*, 331.

6   *Relatione esattissima del' Incendio Calamitoso della citta di Londra* (1666); translated in *ibid.*, 323.

7   *Relacion Nueva y Verdadera del formidable incendio que ha sucedido en la cidad de Londres* (1666); translated in *ibid.*, 327, 328.

8   *ibid.*, 325.

9   Marin Zorzi, Venetian Ambassador to Spain, to the Doge and Senate, 20 October 1666 [N.S.]; *CSP Venetian* XXXV, 92–3.

10 Burnet, *History* I, 421.

11 *Gazette*, 13 September 1666.

12 Thomas Waade to Joseph Williamson, *CSPD 1666–7*, 114.

13 Ralph Hope to Joseph Williamson, *ibid.*, 168.

14 Francis Bellott to Joseph Williamson, *ibid.*, 113.

15 Deposition of Thomas Field and Anthony Mills, of Haseler, and Richard Kempston, of Binton, Warwickshire; *ibid.*, 117.

16 Ralph Hope to Joseph Williamson, *ibid.*, 127.

17 *ibid.*

18 Hope to Williamson, *ibid.*, 168.

19 Hope to Williamson, *ibid.*, 188.

20 William Cobbett (ed.), *Cobbett's Parliamentary History of England* IV (1808), 332. Cobbett gives the proceedings in full.

21 Caroline Robbins (ed.), *The Diary of John Milward* (CUP, 1938), 7.

22 John Rushworth to an unknown correspondent, 8 September 1666, in *Notes and Queries*, 5th Series V, 306.

23 *Cobbett's State Trials* VI, 811.

24 *ibid.*, 814.

25 *ibid.*, 841.

26 *ibid.*, 820–1.

27 *ibid.*, 847.

28 *ibid.*, 847–8. The exchanges which follow come from the same source.

29 Denis de Repas to Sir Robert Harley, *HMC* 29 (Portland MSS III), 298.

30 William, Lord Maynard to Joseph Williamson, *CSPD 1666–7*, 110.

31 *Cobbett's State Trials* VI, 846–7.

32 James Janeway, *Heaven upon Earth* (1667). The quotation comes from Janeway's preface, which is dated 24 September 1666.

33 Burnet, *History* I, 424

34 *Cobbett's State Trials* VI, 842.

35 *ibid.*, 844.

36 *ibid.*, 850.

37 Estimates vary wildly. The figure of *c.*60,000 is convincingly argued in John Miller, *Popery and Politics in England 1660–1688* (CUP, 1973), 9–12. I have drawn on Miller's excellent study for the account of anti-Catholicism which follows.

38 Bodleian MS Add c.307, fo. 68; quoted in Miller, *Popery and Politics*, 59.

39 Henry Care, *The Weekly Pacquet of Advice from Rome, or the History of Popery* III (4 vols., 1678–82), 160; quoted in Miller, *Popery and Politics*, 75.

Chapter 10

1   *Cobbett's State Trials* VI, 827.

2   *ibid.*, 829.

3   Clarendon, *Life* II, 291.

4   *Cobbett's State Trials* VI, 840.

5   *ibid.*

6   Old Bailey Sessions Papers, 1666; quoted in Bell, *Great Fire*, 354.

7   HMC (Portland MSS III), 301.

8   Pepys, *Diary*, 24 February 1667.

9   Clarendon, *Life* II, 291.

10 *ibid.*

11 *Cobbett's State Trials* VI, 826n.

12 *CSPD 1666–7*, 171.

13 C. J. Kitching, 'Fire Disasters and Fire Relief in Sixteenth-century England: the Nantwich Fire of 1583', *Bulletin of the Institute of Historical Research* 54 (1981), 174. I have drawn on this article for a number of details of the mechanics of fire relief in the discussion which follows.

14 Michael Farr (ed.), 'The Great Fire of Warwick 1694', *Dugdale Society* XXXVI (1992), 117.

15 Commissioners' Order Book, September 1694; reprinted in *ibid.*, 8.

16 *CSPD 1666–7*, 119.

17 Evelyn, *Diary*, 10 October 1666.

18 *CSPD 1666–7*, 200.

19 Court minutes; quoted in Bell, *Great Fire*, 218.

20 *ibid.*, 201.

21 *Cobbett's Parliamentary History* IV, 337.

22 Clarendon, *Life* II, 333.

23 Milward, *Diary*, 54.

24 *ibid.*, 47.

25 Viscount Conway to Sir George Rawdon, HMC 78 (Hastings MSS II), 373–4.

26 Milward, *Diary*, 55.

27 Burnet, *History* I, 423.

28 Margaret Blundell, *Cavalier: Letters of William Blundell to his Friends* (Longmans, Green & Co., 1933), 115.

29 Pepys, *Diary*, 5 November 1666.

30 *CSPD 1666–7*, 175.

31 Andrew Browning, *Thomas Osborne, Earl of Danby and Duke of Leeds* II (Jackson, Son & Co., 1951), 15.

32 Milward, *Diary*, 69.

33 Pepys, *Diary*, 5 November 1666.

34 John Ward, *Diary . . . extending from 1648 to 1679*, ed. C. Severn (1839), 94.

35 Richard Saunders, *Apollo Anglicanus* (1667).

36 John Tanner, *Angelus Britannicus* (1667).

37 William Lilly, *Merlini Anglici Ephemeris* (1667).

38 John Gadbury, *Ephemeris* (1667).

39 John Booker, *Telescopium Uranicum repurgatum . . .* (1667).

40 Richard Edlyn, *Prae-Nuncius Sydereus: An Astrological Treatise of the Effects of the Great Conjunction of the two Superiour Planets, Saturn and Jupiter, October the Xth 1663* (1664).

41 Pepys, *Diary*, 23 April 1665.

42 *ibid.*, 20 January 1667.

43 *ibid.*, 10 October 1666.

44 *Observations* was published in 1667; but in the preface its author mentions that the treatise had 'lain dormant in a Corner of my Desk ever since its Birth (which was three Weeks after the Fire)' ('Rege Sincera', *Harleian Miscellany* III, 287).

45 *ibid.*, 291.

46 *ibid.*, 292.

47 Janeway, *Heaven upon Earth*, preface.

48 *Journals of the House of Lords* XI (1660), 8.

49 Richard Baxter, *Reliquiae Baxterianae*, Part III, 2; quoted in Michael R. Watts, *The Dissenters* I (Clarendon Press, 1978), 226.

50 John Oldmixon, *The History of England, during the reigns of the royal House of Stuart* (1730); quoted in *Cobbett's State Trials* VI, 832n.

51 Vincent, *God's Terrible Voice*, 63.

52 Anon., *Pyrotechnica Loyolana, Ignatian fireworks; or the fiery Jesuits' temper and behaviour exposed to publick view* (1667), 124.

53 *ibid.*, 123.

54 Janeway, *Heaven upon Earth*, preface.

55 Vincent, *God's Terrible Voice* (1722 edn.), 153.

56 Vincent, *God's Terrible Voice* (5th edn., corrected, 1667), 74, 88, 99, 118, 146.

57 Vincent, *God's Terrible Voice* (1722 edn.), 183.

58 *ibid.*, 80.

59   *Gazette*, 10 September 1666.
60   Pepys, *Diary*, 7 September 1666.
61   *CSPD 1666–7*, 167–8.
62   Pepys, *Diary*, 29 October 1666.
63   MS poem; quoted in Bell, *Great Fire*, 347.
64   Quoted in Stephen Porter, *The Great Fire of London* (Bramley, 1998), 84.

Chapter 11

1   Henry Oldenburg to Robert Boyle, 10 September 1666; in Hall and Hall (eds.), *Correspondence of Henry Oldenburg* III, 226.
2   John Evelyn to Sir Samuel Tuke, 27 September 1666; reprinted in Evelyn, *Diary*, 399n.
3   Clarendon, *Life* II, 288.
4   *Gazette*, 17 September 1666.
5   *ibid.*
6   *ibid.*
7   This analysis of streets, lanes, alleys and courts is taken from M. J. Power, 'The Social Topography of Restoration London', in A. L. Beier & Roger Finlay (eds.), *London, 1500–1700: the Making of the Metropolis* (Longman, 1986), 199–223.
8   T. F. Reddaway, *The Rebuilding of London After the Great Fire* (Arnold, 1951), 50.
9   *Gazette*, 17 September 1666.
10 *ibid.*
11 Walter de Gray Birch (ed.), *The Historical Charters and Constitutional Documents of the City of London* (1887), 227–8.
12 *ibid.*, 228.
13 Evelyn, *Fumifugium*, 13.
14 Quoted in John Evelyn, *London Revived*, ed. E. S. de Beer (Clarendon, 1938), 12.
15 Evelyn, *Diary*, 13 September 1666.
16 Thomas More, *Utopia* (1516), Book II, 'Their Cities, Especially Amaurot'.
17 John Evelyn to Sir Samuel Tuke, 27 September 1666; reprinted in Evelyn, *Diary*, 398–9n.
18 Henry Oldenburg to Robert Boyle, 18 September 1666; in Hall and Hall (eds.), *Correspondence of Henry Oldenburg* III, 231.
19 CLRO, Journal of the Court of Common Council, 46, fo. 121.
20 Clarendon, *Life* II, 295–6.
21 John Evelyn to Sir Samuel Tuke, 27 September 1666, reprinted in Evelyn, *Diary*, 398n; Henry Oldenburg to John Evelyn, 25 February 1668, in Hall and Hall (eds.), *Correspondence of Henry Oldenburg* IV, 206.
22 Anthony Wood, *The History and Antiquities of the University of Oxford*,

ed. John Gutch (1792–6); quoted by Robert G. Frank jr, 'Medicine', in Nicholas Tyacke (ed.), *The History of the University of Oxford* IV: *Seventeenth-Century Oxford* (Clarendon Press, 1997), 543.

23 Sir William Petty, *The Petty Papers* I (Constable, 1927), 27.

24 Quoted in A. E. J. Morris, *History of Urban Form Before the Industrial Revolution* (Longman, 1994), 43.

25 'Proposals of a new model for rebuilding the city of London . . .', *CSPD 1666–7*, 170.

26 Richard Waller (ed.), *The Posthumous Works of Robert Hooke* (1705), xiii.

27 Anon., 'The Citizens Joy', ll. 62–4.

28 Evelyn, *London Revived*, 38.

29 *ibid.*, 39, 40.

30 *See* John Evelyn to Henry Oldenburg, 22 December 1666; in Hall and Hall (eds.), *Correspondence of Henry Oldenburg* III, 299–300; and Oldenburg to Evelyn, 25 February 1668; in *Correspondence* IV, 203–4.

31 Evelyn, *London Revived*, 42.

32 *ibid.*, 45.

33 *ibid.*, 37.

34 *ibid.*, 41.

35 Much of the following account of Wren's scheme has appeared in a slightly different form in my *His Invention So Fertile: A Life of Christopher Wren* (Jonathan Cape, 2001), 152–4, 158–9.

36 J. Ralph, in *A critical review of the publick buildings . . . in, and about London and Westminster* (1734), 2.

37 Wren, *Parentalia*, 263, 269.

38 Reddaway, *Rebuilding of London*, 311–12.

39 Morris, *History of Urban Form*, 258–9.

40 Evelyn, *London Revived*, 45–6.

41 *ibid.*, 42.

42 *ibid.*, 34.

43 Henry Oldenburg to Robert Boyle, 18 September 1666; in Hall and Hall (eds.), *Correspondence of Henry Oldenburg* III, 230.

44 Milward, *Diary*, 8.

45 *ibid.*, 9.

46 Henry Oldenburg to Robert Boyle, 2 October 1666; in Hall and Hall (eds.), *Correspondence of Henry Oldenburg* III, 238.

47 Quoted in Howard Colvin, *Biographical Dictionary of Architects 1600–1840* (John Murray, 1978), 459.

Chapter 12

1 Anon., 'The Plague of London Anno Domini 1665'; reprinted in Bell, *Great Plague*, 343.

2   Anon., 'London Mourning in Ashes'; reprinted in *The Pepys Ballads* III, ed. Hyder E. Rollins (Harvard University Press, 1930), 5. This was in Samuel Pepys's own collection, and according to Rollins it was one of the first ballads Pepys acquired.

3   Anon., 'London Undone; or, A Reflection upon the Late disasterous fire' (1666), l. 50.

4   *Poems of John Dryden* I, ed. Hammond, 196 and *n.*

5   Anon., 'London Undone', ll. 17–20.

6   Anon., 'London's Fatal-Fall: Being an Acrostick, &c. Written (as a Second Poetical Diversion) the 8th of September, 1666', *Rome Rhym'd to Death* (1683), 24. If the date of composition mentioned in the title is correct, this is one of the very first Fire poems.

7   Simon Ford, *A Discourse concerning Gods judgments, preached at Old Swinford . . . and now published to accompany the narrative concerning the man whose hands and legs lately rotted off in the parish of Kings-Swinford in Staffordshire, penned by another author* (1678).

8   Tabor, 'Seasonable Thoughts'.

9   *ibid.*, ll. 53–6.

10   Wiseman, 'London's Fatal Fire', ll. 109–10.

11   Guillim, 'Dreadful Burning of London', ll. 370, 371.

12   Thomas Gilbert, 'England's Passing-Bell' (1679), ll. 183–8.

13   Ford, 'Conflagration of London', *Three Poems . . .* , l. 329; Anon., 'The Londoners' Lamentation' (1666), ll. 113–14.

14   Ford, 'Conflagration of London', ll. 344–7.

15   Anon., 'Londoners' Lamentation', l. 96.

16   Crouch, *'Londinenses Lacrymae'*, ll. 227–30.

17   Guillim, 'Dreadful Burning of London', ll. 387–8.

18   Crouch, *'Londinenses Lacrymae'*, l. 234; Anon., 'London Undone' l. 100.

19   Anon., 'The Citizens Joy For the Rebuilding of London' (1667), ll. 57–60.

20   Jeremiah Wells, 'On the Rebuilding of London', ll. 141–4, in *Poems upon Divers Occasions* (1667).

21   Royal proclamation of 13 September 1666; in Birch (ed.), *Historical Charters*, 229.

22   *Gazette*, 24 September 1666.

23   Guildhall Library Broadsides, 13, 85; quoted in Reddaway, *Rebuilding of London*, 66.

24   Quoted in *ibid.*, 65.

25   Sir Edward Pratt to Sir Roger Pratt, 29 October 1666; in Gunther (ed.), *Architecture of Sir Roger Pratt*, 11.

26   Dryden, *Annus Mirabilis*, ll. 105–8.

27   Gunther (ed.), *Architecture of Sir Roger Pratt*, 13.

28   *ibid.*

29   P[ublic] R[ecord] O[ffice], Privy Council Register 2/59, 196–7.

30   CLRO, Journal of the Court of Common Council, 46, 47.

31   First Rebuilding Act, s. 37.

32   Milward, *Diary*, 51.

33   *Cobbett's State Trials* VI, 790. Mordaunt eventually got off, although he was ruined and forced to resign his post as Governor of Windsor Castle.

34   Milward, *Diary*, 73.

35   *ibid.*, 74.

36   First Rebuilding Act; quoted in Reddaway, *Rebuilding of London*, pl. 6.

37   *ibid.*

38   CLRO, Journal of the Court of Common Council, 46, 147.

39   Confirmation of the Order of Common Council, 8 May 1667; in Birch (ed.), *Historical Charters*, 232.

40   *ibid.*, 233.

41   Journal of the Court of Common Council 46, fos. 147–8.

42   'Objections against the Model of St Pauls standing in the Convocation House there as its now designed by Dr Renne', 12 July 1673; in Gunther (ed.), *Architecture of Sir Roger Pratt*, 213.

43   Pepys, *Diary*, 25 November 1666. Pepys's only worry was that in spite of May's reassuring words, the scheme for rebuilding was moving too slowly. 'I pray God it come not out too late', he wrote.

44   *CSPD 1666–7*, 548.

45   Edward Berwick (ed.), *The Rawdon Papers* (1819), 227.

46   For Jerman's career (and for those of Oliver and Mills) I have drawn ruthlessly on Sir Howard Colvin's indispensable *Biographical Dictionary of British Architects 1600–1840* (John Murray, 1978).

47   Quoted in Colvin, *Biographical Dictionary*, 459.

48   Quoted in *ibid.*, 201.

49   *Gazette*, 30 September 1669.

50   'Theophilus Philalethes', 'Great Britains Glory', ll. 483–8.

Chapter 13

1   Verney and Verney, *Memoirs of the Verney Family* II, 258.

2   Philip E. Jones (ed.), *The Fire Court* I, (William Clowes & Sons, 1966), vi.

3   Milward, *Diary*, 68.

4   *Journal of the House of Lords* XII, 87.

5   CLRO, Repertory of the Court of Aldermen, 75 (Starling), 160 v.

6   G. A–483; B.M. 5065–39, *Daniell Berry* v. *Sir George Waterman kt.*; in Jones, *Fire Court* I, 134.

7   'Anonymous report on the Aldermen and Common Council' (1672), in *Gentleman's Magazine* XXXIX (November 1769), 516.

8   Peter Mills and John Oliver, *The Survey of Building Sites in the City of London* I (London Topographical Society, 1946), 45.

9   Jones, *Fire Court* I, 134.

10   Philip E. Jones, *The Fire Court* II (William Clowes & Sons, 1970), 114.

11   G. A–141; B. M. 5064–160; in Jones, *Fire Court* I, 44. It wasn't only Vandermarsh's Dutch origins that were at issue here: technically, *all* foreigners were barred from holding leases.

12   *ibid.* Godschall was still reluctant to admit defeat, but he grudgingly agreed to a ten-year lease at the same rent, and to let another burnt-out property to Vandermarsh for fifty-one years.

   Sir Thomas Aleyn is not to be muddled with Admiral of the White Sir Thomas Allin. There was also a Sir Thomas Allen, who was MP for Finchley in the early 1660s. Although the three usually spelled their names slightly differently – Aleyn, Allin, Allen – their contemporaries did not, which can be very confusing.

13   G. A–421; B. M. 5066–57; in Jones, *Fire Court* I, 118.

14   G. A–5; B. M. 5063–5; in Jones, *Fire Court* I, 3.

15   G. C–198 v; B. M. 5070–51; in Jones, *Fire Court* II, 108.

16   PRO, Privy Council Register 2/59, 229; quoted in Reddaway, *Rebuilding of London*, 121.

17   City Cash Books, 1/12 200 v; 1/13 51 v, 125 and 211 v.

18   *CSPD 1666–7*, 156, 170.

19   Pepys, *Diary*, 7 May 1669.

20   R. Clutterbuck, *History and Antiquities of the County of Hertford* I (1815), 167.

21   Pepys, *Diary*, 7 April 1667.

22   CLRO, Repertory of the Court of Aldermen, 80, 40b–41.

23   Peter Mills and John Oliver, *The Survey of Building Sites in the City of London after the Great Fire of 1666* II (London Topographical Society, 1956), 16.

24   Mills and Oliver, *Survey* II, 17.

25   Mills and Oliver, *Survey* I, 123.

26   CLRO, Repertory of the Court of Aldermen, 72, fo. 142; PRO, Privy Council Register 2/59, 509. There is a good account of the Selby case in Reddaway, *Rebuilding of London*, 145–50.

27   PRO, Privy Council Register 2/60, 149–50.

28   CLRO, Repertory of the Court of Aldermen, 72, fo. 240.

29   Mills and Oliver, *Survey* II 125.

30   Proclamation of 13 September 1666; in Birch, *Historical Charters*, 230.

31   Bodleian, Tanner MS 145, 127; reprinted in *Wren Society*, XIII, 45.

32   Christopher Wren to William Sancroft, 28 April 1668, Bodleian Tanner MS 145, 144.

33   William Sancroft to Christopher Wren, 2 July 1668; *Parentalia*, 279.

34   *ibid.*, 284.

35   Christopher Wren to William Sancroft, 24 May 1668, Bodleian Tanner MS 145, 145; reprinted in *Wren Society* XIII, 48.

36 Wren, *Parentalia*, 282.
37 *ibid.*, 283.
38 Anon., '*Troia Rediviva*, or, the Glories of London' (1674), ll. 439–42.
39 Bodleian Tanner MS 142, fo. 118.
40 Guildhall Library MS 25540/1, 1, 17 May 1670.
41 Guildhall Library MS 25540, 3, 13 June 1670.

Chapter 14

1   We can blame Ward for a lot of things, but not the bad verse. This is the work of the City poet Thomas Jordan in *London's Glory; Or, the Lord Mayor's Show* (1680); quoted in Harris, *London Crowds*, 123.
2   Quoted in Miller, *Popery and Politics*, 133.
3   Burnet, *History* II, 190.
4   Harris, *London Crowds*, 111.
5   *Cobbett's State Trials* VI, 850.
6   G. E. Aylmer (ed.), *The Diary of William Lawrence* (Toucan Press, 1961), 37.
7   *Cobbett's State Trials* VI, 1449.
8   *Journals of the House of Commons* IX, 703.
9   Evelyn, *Diary*, 4 June 1679.
10 Seth Ward, 'The Christian's Victory over Death' [Albemarle's funeral sermon] (1670); quoted in Maurice Ashley, *General Monck* (Jonathan Cape, 1977), 247.
11 Obituary by John Evans in the preface to the 1722 edn. of Vincent's *God's Terrible Voice*.
12 H. M. Hyde, *Judge Jeffreys* (Butterworth, 1948), 88.
13 *ibid.*, 89.
14 Quoted in Harris, *London Crowds*, 175.
15 19 Charles II, Chap 3, Sec 29.
16 Report to City Lands Committee, 28 July 1675; reprinted (from a transcript) in *Wren Society* V, 47.
17 This and subsequent translations from Gale's inscriptions are taken from *The Official Guide to the Monument* (Corporation of London, 1994), 13–15.
18 Blundell (ed.), *Cavalier*, 233.
19 *Cobbett's State Trials* VI, 866.
20 Charles Blount, *An Appeal from the Country to the City, for the Preservation of His Majesties Person, Liberty, Property, and the Protestant Religion* (1679), 2.
21 Alexander Pope, *Moral Essays* (1732), Epistle III, 'To Allen Lord Bathurst', ll. 339–40.
22 Thomas Ward, *England's Reformation* (1710), Canto IV, 100.

Chronology

1649   Trial and execution of Charles I. The monarchy and the House of Lords are abolished, and England is proclaimed a 'Commonwealth or Free-State'.

1651   Charles II is crowned King in Scotland, and invades England. His army is routed at the Battle of Worcester by Parliamentarian forces led by Oliver Cromwell, and he escapes to France.

1652   Commercial rivalry with Holland leads to the first Anglo-Dutch war, which ends in 1654.

1653   Cromwell is declared Lord Protector.

1655   A failed royalist rebellion is met with military rule. The country is divided into eleven districts, each under the command of a major-general.

1657   In an effort to curb the powers of the major-generals, Parliament offers Cromwell the crown; he refuses, but agrees to certain measures that increase his control over the military, including the right to nominate his successor.

1658   Cromwell dies, and is succeeded as Lord Protector by his son Richard.

1659   Richard Cromwell is ousted by a military junta led by John Lambert. Troops take over public buildings in London; Parliament is expelled from Westminster, and a royalist rising in Cheshire, though abortive, leads to fears of another civil war.

1660   The moderate Parliamentarian general George Monck marches on London and declares for a free parliament; Lambert is persuaded not to oppose him. Charles II is recalled from exile on the Continent and restored to the throne. His chief adviser is the Earl of Clarendon, the Lord Chancellor, whose daughter

Anne is married to James, Duke of York, the King's brother. Samuel Pepys begins writing his diary.

1662 Charles II marries the Portuguese princess Catherine of Braganza. The marriage delivers Bombay and Tangier to England.

1664 Tension between England and Holland. English ships capture Dutch possessions on the West African coast, and an English squadron seizes the Dutch colony of New Netherland on the east coast of America; it is renamed New York in honour of the Duke of York.

1665 England and Holland are at war once again. An outbreak of bubonic plague devastates the population of London, and spreads to many other parts of the country.

1666 The Great Fire of London.

1667 After a daring Dutch raid on the Thames, England makes peace with Holland. Blamed for the mis-handling of the war, Clarendon is deprived of office and goes into exile in France.

1669 Worried about his failing eyesight, Pepys abandons his diary.

1671 Death of Anne, Duchess of York.

1672 The third and last Anglo-Dutch war begins; it ends in 1674.

1673 Parliament passes the first Test Act, which requires all holders of public office to swear allegiance to the King as head of the Church of England, to receive Anglican communion and to repudiate the Catholic doctrine of transubstantiation. James, Duke of York, who has converted to Catholicism in the 1660s, resigns all his offices. He also remarries; his wife is Mary of Modena.

1675 The foundation stones of the new St Paul's Cathedral are laid.

1678 Widespread anti-Catholic feeling is whipped up by the alleged discovery of a Jesuit plot to assassinate the King and replace him with the Duke of York.

A number of prominent Catholics are executed, and a second Test Act excludes Catholics from Parliament. (The Duke of York is exempted.)

1679 A bill designed to exclude the Duke of York from the succession to the throne is introduced into Parliament. It fails, as will two further exclusion bills in 1680 and 1681.

1683–4 The Thames freezes over, in one of the coldest winters of the century.

1685 Death of Charles II; accession of his brother, the Duke of York, as James II. An uprising led by Charles' illegitimate son, the Duke of Monmouth, is suppressed at the Battle of Sedgemoor; Monmouth is executed, and his supporters are savagely punished at the 'Bloody Assizes' by the notorious Lord Chief Justice, Judge George Jeffreys.

1688 Alarmed at measures to increase the power of the monarch and relax anti-Catholic legislation, a group of noblemen ask for help from the Dutch-born, Protestant William of Orange, who is married to James II's daughter Mary. William lands with an army at Torbay on the south coast; James is allowed to flee the country; and when William and Mary accept the Declaration of Rights, which condemns James' autocratic acts as unconstitutional, they are offered the throne. They are crowned the following year.

Dramatis Personae

Henry Bennet, Lord Arlington (1618–85). A professional politician, and Secretary of State from 1662 to 1674.

Sir Thomas Bludworth (1620–82). A successful Levant merchant, and Lord Mayor of London in 1665–6. Bludworth's reputation never recovered from his mishandling of the disaster.

Gilbert Burnet (1643–1715). An Anglican churchman, an historian and an astute commentator on contemporary events, as his *History of My Own Times* demonstrates.

Catherine of Braganza (1638–1705). Queen of England and daughter of João IV, King of Portugal. A Roman Catholic, Catherine married Charles II in 1662 and remained a rather private person, forced to endure her husband's many infidelities as well as sporadic public attacks because of her religion.

Charles II (1630–85). King of England, 1660–85. His reputation as the indolent, pleasure-loving 'Merry Monarch' is accurate, but gives only half the story. Charles possessed considerable political skills, and it was his refusal to be panicked by the Great Fire that held the nation together during the crisis.

Sir William Coventry (1627–86). Secretary to the Lord High Admiral the Duke of York, and a Navy Commissioner.

Sir William Craven, Earl of Craven (1608–97). An experienced professional soldier, a colonel in the Coldstream Guards and, as Lieutenant-General of the Kingdom, a deputy to the Duke of Albemarle.

Sir John Denham (1615–69). A poet and politician. Denham served the royalist cause well during the 1650s, and was rewarded at the Restoration by being made Surveyor-General of the King's Works. He had a mental breakdown in the summer of 1666, apparently brought on by his young wife's affair with the Duke of York.

John Evelyn (1620–1706). A virtuoso, public servant and diarist. Evelyn was a God-fearing Anglican, a staunch royalist and, as his diary account of the Fire shows, a man who felt great compassion for the suffering of his fellows.

Thomas Farriner (?–1670). The baker in whose Pudding Lane premises the Great Fire started. Farriner always swore that his oven was properly damped down, and that the fire must have been started deliberately by outsiders.

Sir Robert Holmes (1622–92). The naval commander whose attacks on Dutch trading stations in West Africa did much to provoke the Anglo-Dutch conflict. His destruction of the Dutch merchant fleet and burning of the town of West-Terschelling in August 1666 was celebrated in England as 'Sir Robert Holmes' Bonfire.'

Robert Hooke (1635–1703). A brilliant experimental scientist and an amateur architect. Hooke's post-Fire plan for London was praised by the City authorities, and he was appointed to the Commission for Rebuilding London. He designed a number of the City churches.

Robert Hubert (c. 1640–66). Little is known of Hubert, except that he was hanged at Tyburn after confessing that he started the Great Fire. The son of a Rouen watchmaker, he drifted around Europe during the early 1660s and was variously described as a watchmaker, like his father, and a common labourer.

Edward Hyde, Earl of Clarendon (1608–74). A trusted adviser to Charles II during the latter's exile in the 1650s, and Lord High Chancellor of England after the Restoration.

Peter Mills (1598–1670). A bricklayer, surveyor and architect who produced a plan (now lost) for rebuilding London and who, together with John Oliver, surveyed the ruined city and staked out its new streets.

George Monck, Duke of Albemarle (1608–70). A moderate during the Commonwealth, General Monck was largely responsible for restoring Charles II to the throne in 1660. As a result he was made Duke of Albemarle and appointed Captain-General of the Kingdom. In the summer of 1666 he was fighting the Dutch as joint commander of the fleet, along with Prince Rupert.

John Oliver (c. 1616–1701). A surveyor who took over the detailed survey of London after Peter Mills became ill in 1667, and who eventually (in 1686) was made Master Mason to the Crown.

Sir William Penn (1621–70). A Navy Commissioner and an experienced seaman. His son, also William, was the Quaker leader and founder of Pennsylvania (the colony was actually named after the elder Penn).

Elizabeth Pepys (1640–69). The wife of Samuel Pepys and the daughter of a Huguenot, Alexander de St Michel. Elizabeth and Samuel wed when she was fifteen, and although they got on reasonably well, her husband was both pathologically jealous and pathologically unfaithful for much of their married life.

Samuel Pepys (1633–1703). A senior official in the Navy Office, and a gifted administrator. From 1660 to 1669, a dedicated diarist with a prodigious appetite for detail. Pepys' descriptions of the Fire and its aftermath are among the most dramatic and poignant that we have.

Prince Rupert of the Rhine (1619–82). A cousin of Charles II and James, Duke of York. Prince Rupert was a glamorous but impetuous military leader, who was given joint command of the English fleet (along with George Monck) in 1666.

William Taswell (1652–1731). A merchant's son and a pupil at Westminster School during the Fire. Although written in later life, Taswell's 'Autobiography' contains a vivid and detailed account of the disaster as seen through the eyes of a fourteen-year-old.

Thomas Vincent (1634–78). A Puritan preacher and a writer, and an eye-witness to the Great Plague and the Fire. His rousing and popular 1667 tract, *God's Terrible Voice in the City*, blames both disasters on the profane and debauched ways of Londoners.

Sir Robert Vyner (1631–88). A goldsmith and banker in Lombard Street, and one of the most powerful financiers in the kingdom.

Joseph Williamson (1633–1701). Under-Secretary of State from 1660 to 1674 and, as publisher of the twice-weekly London *Gazette,* Charles II's most able propagandist. Williamson kept a tight control over the English press and ran an effective intelligence-gathering network.

Christopher Wren (1632–1723). In 1666, a professor of astronomy at Oxford University, with an international reputation in the mathematical sciences and an interest in architecture. He was quick to see the opportunities the disaster offered, and the Fire made him as an architect.

Anne, Duchess of York (1637–71). The daughter of the Lord High Chancellor, the Earl of Clarendon. Much to her father's distress, she was secretly married to James, Duke of York, in September 1660. Anne was a clever and politically astute woman, and it was said that she ruled her husband in everything but his love affairs.

James, Duke of York (1633–1701). Lord High Admiral and brother of Charles II. James had made a name for himself as a soldier in the Low Countries in the 1650s, and he was most comfortable when he was in action, as his heroic deeds during the Fire showed so well.

Bibliography

Abbott, W. C. 'English Conspiracy and Dissent, 1660–74', *American Historical Review* 14 (1908–9), 503–28, 696–722

Anderson, R. C. (ed.) *The Journals of Sir Thomas Allin 1660–1678* (Navy Records Society, 1939–40)

Anderson, R. C. (ed.) [An anonymous contemporary account of] 'Naval operations in the latter part of the year 1666', *The Naval Miscellany* III (Navy Records Society, 1927–8)

Andrews, W. *Newes from the Starres* (1666)

Anon. 'London Undone; or, A Reflection upon the Late disasterous fire' (1666)

Anon. 'London's Fatal-Fall: Being an Acrostick, &c. Written (as a Second Poetical Diversion) the 8th of September, 1666', *Rome Rhym'd to Death* (1683)

Anon. 'Mourne London Mourne', Bodleian MS Ashmole 47, 140 v

Anon. *Pyrotechnica Loyolana, Ignatian fireworks; or the fiery Jesuits' temper and behaviour exposed to publick view* (1667)

Anon. 'Troia Rediviva, or, the Glories of London' (1674)

Anon. 'The True Report of the Burning of the Steeple and Church of St Paul's in London', in Pollard, A. F. (ed.) *Tudor Tracts 1532–1588* (Constable & Co., 1903), 401–8

Ashley, M. *General Monck* (Jonathan Cape, 1977)

Atkyns, E. 'Copy of a Letter to Sir Robert Atkyns . . . Written from London during the Fire 1666', *Archaeologia* XIX (1821), 105–8

Aubin, R. A. (ed.) *London in Flames, London in Glory* (Rutgers University Press, 1943)

Aubrey, J. *Aubrey's Brief Lives*, ed. O. Lawson-Dick (Mandarin, 1992)

Barnes, W. M. (ed.) 'The Diary of William Whiteway, 1618–24', *Proceedings of the Dorset Natural History and Antiquarian Field Club* XIII (1892), 57–81

Beier, A. L. and Finlay, R. (eds.) *London, 1500–1700: the Making of the Metropolis* (Longman, 1986)

Bell, W. G. *The Great Fire of London in 1666* (John Lane, 1923)

Bell, W. G. *The Great Plague in London in 1665* (Bodley Head, 1924)

Beloff, M. *Public Order and Popular Disturbances 1660–1714* (OUP, 1938)

Berwick, E. (ed.) *The Rawdon Papers, consisting of letters on various subjects . . . to and from Dr. John Bramhall, Primate of Ireland* (1819)

Besant, W. *London in the Time of the Stuarts* (A. & C. Black, 1903)

Birch, W. de G. (ed.) *The Historical Charters and Constitutional Documents of the City of London* (1887)

Blount, C. *An Appeal from the Country to the City, for the Preservation of His Majesties Person, Liberty, Property, and the Protestant Religion* (1679)

Blundell, M. *Cavalier: Letters of William Blundell to his Friends* (Longmans, Green & Co., 1933)

Bolton, A. T. and Hendry, H. D. (eds.) *The Wren Society* (OUP, 1923–43)

Booker, J. *A New Almanack and Prognostication* (1666, 1667)

Brett-James, N. G. *The Growth of Stuart London* (George Allen & Unwin, 1935)

Browning, A. *Thomas Osborne, Earl of Danby and Duke of Leeds* (Jackson, Son & Co., 1951)

Bülow, G. von (trans.) 'Journey through England and Scotland made by Lupold von Wedel in the years 1584 and 1585', *Transactions of the Royal Historical Society* New Series IX (1895), 223–70

Burnet, G. *The History of My Own Times* (2nd edn., enlarged, 1833)

Burrage, C. 'The Fifth Monarchist Insurrections', *English Historical Review* 25 (1910), 722–47

Calendar of State Papers Venetian XXXV (HMSO, 1935)

Capp, B. S. *Astrology and the Popular Press: English Almanacs 1500–1800* (Faber, 1979)

Capp, B. S. *The Fifth Monarchy Men: a Study in Seventeenth-century English Millenarianism* (Faber, 1972)

Clark, D. K. 'A Restoration Goldsmith–Banking House: The Vine on Lombard Street', *Essays in Modern English History in Honor of Wilbur Cortez Abbott* (Kennikat Press, 1971)

Clutterbuck, R. *History and Antiquities of the County of Hertford* (1815–27)

Cobbett, W. (ed.) *Cobbett's Complete Collection of State Trials and Proceedings* (1809–26)

Cobbett, W. and Wright, J. (eds.) *Cobbett's Parliamentary History of England* (1806–20)

Colvin, H. *Biographical Dictionary of British Architects 1600–1840* (John Murray, 1978)

Crawford, A. *A History of the Vintners' Company* (Constable, 1977)

Crouch, J. '*Londinenses Lacrymae*: London's Second Tears mingled with her Ashes' (1666)

Delaune, T. *The Present State of London* (1681)

Denham, J. *Expans'd Hieroglyphicks – A Critical Edition of Sir John Denham's Coopers Hill*, ed. B. O. Hehir (University of California Press, 1969)

Dryden, J. *The Poems of John Dryden*, ed. P. Hammond (Longman, 1995)

Edlyn, R. *Prae-Nuncius Sydereus: An Astrological Treatise Of the Effects of the Great Conjunction of the two Superiour Planets, Saturn and Jupiter, October the Xth 1663* (1664)

Evelyn, J. *A Character of England* (1659)

Evelyn, J. *The Diary of John Evelyn*, ed. W. Bray (Simpkin, Marshall, Hamilton, Kent & Co., N.D.)

Evelyn, J. *Fumifugium: or The Inconveniencie of the Air and Smoak of London Dissipated* (1661)

Evelyn, J. *London Revived: Consideration for its Rebuilding in 1666*, ed. E. S. De Beer (Clarendon Press, 1938)

Evelyn, J. *A Parallel of the Antient Architecture with the Modern* (1707 edn.)

Farr, M. (ed.) 'The Great Fire of Warwick 1694', *Dugdale Society* XXXVI (1992)

Ford, S. *Three Poems Relating to the Late Dreadful Destruction of the City of London by Fire* (1667)

Gadbury, J. *Ephemeris* (1667)

Gilbert, T. 'England's Passing-Bell' (1679)

Girtin, T. *The Triple Crowns – A Narrative History of the Drapers' Company 1364–1964* (Hutchinson, 1964)

Gostelo, W. *The coming of God in Mercy, in Vengeance; Beginning with fire, to Convert, or Consume, at this so sinful City London* (1658)

Green, M. A. E. *et al.* (eds.) *Calendar of State Papers, Domestic series of the reign of Charles II* (Longman & Co., 1860–1947)

Guillim, J. 'The Dreadful Burning of London' (1667)

Gunther, R. T. (ed.) *The Architecture of Sir Roger Pratt* (OUP, 1928)

Hall, A. R. and Hall, M. B. (eds.) *The Correspondence of Henry Oldenburg* (University of Wisconsin Press, 1965–86)

Harris, T. *London Crowds in the Reign of Charles II* (CUP, 1987)

Harvey, P. D. A. (ed.) 'A Foreign Visitor's Account of the Great Fire, 1666', *London & Middlesex Archaeological Society* New Series 20 (1961), 76–87

Hill, C. *The Experience of Defeat: Milton and Some Contemporaries* (Bookmarks, 1994)

Historical Manuscripts Commission 25, Le Fleming MSS

Historical Manuscripts Commission 29, Portland MSS III

Historical Manuscripts Commission 78, Hastings MSS II

Hooke, R. *The Posthumous Works of Robert Hooke*, ed. R. Waller (1705)

Howgego, J. 'The Guildhall Fire Judges', *Guildhall Miscellany* 2 (February 1953), 20–30

Huelin, G. *Vanished Churches of the City of London* (Guildhall Library, 1996)

Hyde, E. *The Life of Edward, Earl of Clarendon . . . Written by himself* (1857)

Hyde, H. M. *Judge Jeffreys* (Butterworth, 1948)

Janeway, J. *Heaven upon Earth* (1667)

Jeffery, P. *The City Churches of Sir Christopher Wren* (Hambledon, 1996)

Jenkins, R. 'Fire-extinguishing Engines in England 1625–1725', *Transactions of the Newcomen Society* 11–12 (1932–3), 15–25

Jones, E. L., Porter, S. and Turner, M. *A Gazetteer of English Urban Fire Disasters, 1500–1900* (Historical Geography Research Series XIII, 1984)

Jones, P. E. (ed.) *The Fire Court* (William Clowes & Sons, 1966–70)

Journals of the House of Commons

Journals of the House of Lords

Karslake, J. B. P. 'Early London Fire-Appliances', *Antiquaries' Journal* IX (1929), 229–38

Kitching, C. J. 'Fire Disasters and Fire Relief in Sixteenth-century England: the Nantwich Fire of 1583', *Bulletin of the Institute of Historical Research* 54 (1981), 171–87

Lacey, D. R. *Dissent and Parliamentary Politics in England, 1661–1689* (Rutgers University Press, 1969)

Lang, J. *Rebuilding St Paul's* (OUP, 1956)

Lawrence, W. *The Diary of William Lawrence*, ed. G. E. Aylmer (Toucan Press, 1961)

Lilly, W. *Merlini Anglici Ephemeris* (1666, 1667)

Lilly, W. *Monarchy or No Monarchy* (1651)

London Gazette

Mahaffy, R. P. (ed.) *Calendar of the State Papers relating to Ireland 1666–9* (Stationery Office, 1911)

Malcolm, J. P. *Londinium Redivivum; or An Antient History and Modern Description of London* (1802–7)

Miller, J. *Popery and Politics in England 1660–1688* (CUP, 1973)

Mills, P. and Oliver, J. *The Survey of Building Sites in the City of London* (London Topographical Society, 1946–56)

Milward, J. *The Diary of John Milward*, ed. C. Robbins (CUP, 1938)

Morris, A. E. J. *History of Urban Form Before the Industrial Revolution*, (3rd edn., Longman, 1994)

Nicolson, M. H. (ed.) *The Conway Letters: the Correspondence of Anne, Viscountess Conway, Henry More, and their Friends, 1642–1684* (OUP, 1930)

The Official Guide to the Monument (Corporation of London, 1994)

Overall, W. H. and Overall, H. C. *Analytical Index to the Series of Records known as the Remembrancia* (1878)

Parker, D. *Familiar to All: William Lilly and Astrology in the Seventeenth Century* (Jonathan Cape, 1975)

Pepys, S. *The Diary of Samuel Pepys*, eds. R. Latham and W. Matthews (HarperCollins, 1983)

Petty, W. *The Petty Papers: Some Unpublished Writings of Sir William Petty*, ed. Marquis of Lansdowne (Constable, 1927)

Phillips, F. T. *A Second History of the Worshipful Company of Cooks* (Worshipful Company of Cooks, 1966)

Picard, L. *Restoration London* (Weidenfeld & Nicolson, 1997)

Pope, A. 'Epistle To Allen Lord Bathurst', *Moral Essays* (1732)

Porter, S. *The Great Fire of London* (Bramley, 1998)

Porter, S. 'The Oxford Fire Regulations of 1671', *Bulletin of the Institute of Historical Research* 58 (1985), 251–5

Potter, F. *Interpretation of the number 666* (1642)

Powell, J. R. and Timings, E. K. (eds.) *The Rupert and Monck Letter Book, 1666* (Navy Records Society, 1969)

Ralph, J. *A critical review of the publick buildings . . . in, and about London and Westminster* (1734)

Reddaway, T. F. 'The London Custom House 1666–1740', *London Topographical Record* XXI (1958), 1–25

Reddaway, T. F. *The Rebuilding of London After the Great Fire* (Arnold, 1951)

'Rege Sincera' *Observations both Historical and Moral upon the Burning of London, Harleian Miscellany* III (1809), 282–94

Rollins, H. E. (ed.) *The Pepys Ballads* III (Harvard University Press, 1930)

Rushworth, J. 'Fire of London – Letter of 8 September 1666', *Notes and Queries* 5th Series V (15 April 1876), 306

Saunders, R. *Apollo Anglicanus* (1666, 1667)

Smith, C. S. 'Wren and Sheldon', *Oxford Art Journal* 6 (1, 1983), 45–50

Sorbière, S. *A Voyage to England, Containing Many Things Relating to the State of Learning, Religion, and other Curiosities of that Kingdom* (1709)

Stow, J. *Survey of London* (Everyman edn., 1912)

Tabor, J. 'Seasonable Thoughts in Sad Times' (1667)

Tanner, J. *Angelus Britannicus* (1666, 1667)

Taswell, W. 'Autobiography and Anecdotes by William Taswell D.D.', ed. G. P. Elliott, *Camden Miscellany* II (1853), 1–37

'Theophilus Philalethes' 'Great Britains Glory' (1672)

Tinniswood, A. *His Invention So Fertile: A Life of Christopher Wren* (Jonathan Cape, 2001)

Tyacke, N. (ed.) *The History of the University of Oxford: Seventeenth-Century Oxford* (Clarendon Press, 1997)

Underdown, D. *Fire From Heaven: Life in an English Town in the Seventeenth Century* (HarperCollins, 1992)

Verney, F. P. and Verney, M. M. *Memoirs of the Verney Family During the Seventeenth Century* (Longmans, Green & Co., 1907)

Vincent, T. *God's Terrible Voice in the City* (5th edn., corrected, 1667)

Vincent, T. *God's Terrible Voice in the City* (1722 edn.)

Ward, J. *Diary … extending from 1648 to 1679*, ed. C. Severn (1839)

Ward, T. *England's Reformation* (1710)

Watts, M. R. *The Dissenters* (Clarendon Press, 1978)

Weinreb, B. and Hibbert, C. *The London Encyclopaedia* (Macmillan, 1995)

Wells, J. *Poems upon Divers Occasions* (1667)

Wharton, G. *Calendarium Carolinum* (1666)

Wiseman, S. 'A Short and Serious Narrative of London's Fatal Fire' (1667)

Wood, A. *The Life and Times of Anthony Wood, Antiquary, of Oxford, 1632–1695*, ed. A. Clark (1891–1900)

Wren, C. (ed.) *Parentalia: or, Memoirs of the Family of the Wrens* (1750)

Wright, J. 'An Essay on the Present Ruins of St Paul's Cathedral' (1668)

Index

and Hubert's confession, 166, 168
maid killed, 43, 132
Farriner, Thomas, Jr, 168
fast (national): proclaimed, 172
Feltmakers' Company, 130
Felton, John, 167n
Fetter Lane
command post at, 74, 76
Fire checked at, 98
Fifth Monarchy men, 25, 55, 161, 179
Filarete, Antonio: *Trattato d'Architettura*, 196
Finch, Sir Heneage, 153
Finch, Sir John, 147
Finsbury Fields
Fire refugees in, 103
stolen goods ordered to be returned to, 106
temporary market set up, 107
Fire Court
cases and judgements, 242–7, 253
revived under 1670 Rebuilding Act, 259
set up, 238, 240–1
fire engines (carriage-mounted pumps), 50–2
fire posts *see* command posts
fire precautions, 48–51
fireballs: manufacture, 164
Fish Street Hill, 45, 47, 53–4, 55, 135
Fishmongers' Company, 5, 248
Hall, 56, 234, 248
Fitz Ailwyn, Henry, 56
Fitzgerald, Colonel John, 75
Five Mile Act (1666), 27, 183
Fleet Bridge, 75–6
Fleet River
Fire crosses, 77, 87
as firebreak, 75
Fleet Street
burned, 102
rebuilding, 191
as route into City, 33
Fleming, Alexander, 126
Fleming, Count Jöran, 83
food supply, 106–7, 168–9
prices, 136, 172

Ford, Sir Richard, 120, 233n
Ford, Simon: *Three Poems Relating to the Late Dreadful Destruction of the City of London by Fire*, 70, 216, 218
foreigners
attacked and persecuted, 59–62, 73, 83–4, 110, 133, 146, 148, 249
evacuate and hide, 156
residents in London, 59–60
sheltered by royal court, 157–8
suspected of causing Fire, 59, 66
see also France (and French); Netherlands (and Dutch)
Foster Lane, 79, 93
Four Days' Fight (1666), 14, 248
Fox, Sir Stephen, 34
Foxe's Book of Martyrs, 161
Frampton, Revd Dr Robert (*later* Bishop of Gloucester), 181
France (and French)
contacts and trade with, 31
fears and rumours of attack by, 29
London residents, 59–60
rumoured Catholic coup against England, 266
rumoured further incendiarism, 142
suspected of causing Fire, 51, 59, 62, 66, 109, 120, 145
war with England, 14, 31
Frazier, Sir Alexander, 34
Fréart de Chambray, Roland: *Parallèle de l'architecture antique et de la moderne*, 195
Friday Street, 78
Frowde, Sir Philip, 64
Fruiterers' Company, 129
Fuller, Robert, 252–3

Gadbury, John, 22, 179
Brief (yet full) Account of the III late Comets, 24
Gale, Thomas, 272
Gamble, John, 169
Garret, Thomas, 253
Gauden, Alderman Denis, 119, 168
Gazette (London)
announces Committee for Gresham Affairs, 235

ADRIAN TINNISWOOD is the author of *His Invention So Fertile: A Life of Christopher Wren* and *Visions of Power: Ambition and Architecture from Ancient Times to the Present.* A respected author, lecturer, and broadcaster in Britain and the United States, Tinniswood lives in Bath, England.